FOOL HEN

The Spruce Grouse on the
Yellow Dog Plains

FOOL HEN

The Spruce Grouse on the Yellow Dog Plains

William L. Robinson

with illustrations by Deann De La Ronde Wilde

The University of Wisconsin Press

Published 1980

THE UNIVERSITY OF WISCONSIN PRESS
114 North Murray Street
Madison, Wisconsin 53715

The University of Wisconsin Press, Ltd.
1 Gower Street
London WC1E 6HA, England

First printing

Printed in the United States of America

For LC CIP information see the colophon

ISBN 0-299-07960-0

Contents

List of Figures   vii
List of Tables   ix
List of Illustrations   xi
Acknowledgments   xiii
Introduction   xv

1   What Is a Spruce Grouse?   3
2   The Yellow Dog Plains   19
3   Stalking the Wild Spruce Grouse   25
4   Through the Seasons with the Spruce Grouse   35
5   Habitat Requirements—A Place in the Pines   45
6   General Behavior   59
7   Behavior of Male Spruce Grouse   63
8   Behavior of Female Spruce Grouse and Broods   81
9   Growth and Plumages   113
10 Physiology   125
11 Diseases of the Spruce Grouse   137
12 Predators of the Spruce Grouse—Friend or Foe?   147
13 Population Ecology   153
14 The Hunter and the Spruce Grouse   179
15 Some Thoughts about Spruce Grouse, Man,
    and Nature   189

    Appendix. Where and How to See a Spruce Grouse
    in Upper Michigan   195
    References Cited   197
    Index   209

List of Figures

Figure 1. The range of the spruce grouse, modified from Aldrich (1963) and Johnsgard (1973) by information supplied by state and provincial wildlife agencies. 6

Figure 2. A hybrid spruce grouse × willow ptarmigan has a broad dark tail, brown, black, and white mottled back, and a necklace of black feathers across the white throat and breast (drawn from Lumsden, 1969). 13

Figure 3. A hybrid spruce grouse × blue grouse is intermediate in size and plumage between its parent species (drawn from Jollie, 1955). 14

Figure 4. A family tree of the grouse of the world, according to Short (1967). The spruce grouse has developed along the main stem of grouse evolution. 17

Figure 5. Map of the Yellow Dog Plains study area. 26

Figure 6. A ruffed grouse wintering on the Yellow Dog Plains must travel a considerable distance to obtain buds of deciduous shrubs. 58

Figure 7. Spruce grouse on the Yellow Dog Plains sometimes tunnel beneath the snow. 62

Figure 8. Spruce grouse chicks grow rapidly, as this graph shows. "Known-age" chicks are those from nests which we saw hatch, while "known-interval" chicks are those from broods captured and weighed more than once and whose age at first capture was estimated by comparison with known-age chicks. 114

Figure 9. Appearance of growing young spruce grouse at 1 day, 5 days, and 17 days. Chicks can fly at 6 days of age. 115

Figure 10. The progress of molting of wing primaries in spruce grouse chicks. The numbers in parentheses indicate the number of chicks examined at each stage of molt. 118

Figure 11. The length of juvenal primary 7, because it grows rapidly and at a steady rate for 30 days, can be used as a good indicator of age of young spruce grouse chicks. 119

Figure 12. Juvenal primary 9 grows less predictably than number 7, but its length can be used to approximate the age of spruce grouse chicks after juvenal primary 7 reaches 85 mm. 120

Figure 13. Male spruce grouse undergo the molt three to four weeks before females with broods. This chart shows the averages and ranges of dates when the wing primary feathers are dropped. Females without broods molt at dates intermediate between males and brood females. Numbers in parentheses indicate the number of birds examined at each state of molt. 122

Figure 14. Male spruce grouse on the Yellow Dog Plains outweigh females at all times of the year except in May, when the females are laden with developing eggs. Numbers in parentheses indicate the number of birds weighed. 129

Figure 15. It appeared that there was a close relationship between early survival of spruce grouse chicks on the Yellow Dog Plains and June temperatures, but direct cause and effect was not conclusively shown. 166

List of Tables

Table 1. Races of the spruce grouse recognized by various authors since 1930   9

Table 2. Estimated size of territories of male spruce grouse on the Yellow Dog Plains (only birds with six or more sightings are included)   69

Table 3. Responses of male spruce grouse to recorded sounds   79

Table 4. Responses of female spruce grouse to recorded sounds   82

Table 5. Sociability of female spruce grouse   87

Table 6. Observations of orphan spruce grouse chicks   108

Table 7. Movements in miles of female spruce grouse banded as chicks   110

Table 8. Movements in miles of male spruce grouse banded as chicks   111

Table 9. Cloacal temperatures, breathing rates, and heart rates of captured spruce grouse   127

Table 10. Comparison of average weights, cloacal temperatures, breathing rates, and heart rates of spruce grouse and ruffed grouse   128

Table 11. Comparison of average weights in grams of female spruce grouse with broods and without broods   131

Table 12. Blood parasites found in spruce grouse   142

Table 13. Blood parasites found singly or in combination in 80 adults and 55 chicks of spruce grouse, summer, 1968   143

Table 14. Comparison of survival rates of spruce grouse carrying *Haemoproteus* and/or *Leucocytozoon* blood parasites with those not carrying them   145

Table 15. Predators of spruce grouse on the Yellow Dog Plains, 1965–70   149

Table 16. Minimum breeding populations of spruce grouse on the Yellow Dog Plains study area   156

Table 17. Age structure of breeding populations of spruce grouse on the Yellow Dog Plains study area   158

Table 18. Recovery of banded chicks after their first winter   159

Table 19. Production of spruce grouse chicks on the Yellow Dog Plains study area, based upon brood sizes when first seen away from the nest   162

Table 20. Average spruce grouse brood sizes on the Yellow Dog Plains study area   164

Table 21. Values used to correlate survival of spruce grouse chicks in the second month with weather conditions   167

Table 22. Minimum survival rates of banded spruce grouse over 1 year old on the Yellow Dog Plains   172

Table 23. Survival rates of spruce grouse chicks inferred from adult and yearling survival rates   176

Table 24. Estimated annual harvest of spruce grouse in the United States, based upon information from state wildlife agencies   182

Table 25. Estimated annual harvest of spruce grouse in Canada, based upon information from provincial and territorial wildlife agencies   183

List of Illustrations

A grouse can carry a small radio transmitter on its back.   31

A displaying male cocks his head to identify a suitable branch to land upon, flies with spread tail to the branch, then continues to strut from his perch.   37

A strutting male spreads his neck feathers, presenting a cobra-like effect.   66

A territorial male spruce grouse climaxes a display sequence by spreading his tail fully for a brief moment and uttering a high-pitched "shik-sheek."   71

A female spruce grouse strolls in spots of June sunshine among blooming dwarf dogwood.   83

Incubating females are well camouflaged and seldom fly unless they are touched by an intruder.   95

A male spruce grouse displays in May in a small clearing.   *follows* 118

The beauty of the female spruce grouse lies in her subtly mingled patterns of brown, gray, black, and white.   *follows* 118

A twelve-day-old chick pauses while feeding among the blueberries in early July.   *follows* 118

This spruce grouse nest was situated beneath a fallen jack pine top. The site, clutch size, and scarcity of insulating materials are typical of a spruce grouse nest.   *follows* 118

When jack pines are clear cut spruce grouse habitat may be rejuvenated, but it is barren for many years.   *follows* 118

Spruce grouse from the northern edge of their range are larger than those from the southern edge following Bergmann's Rule.   130

Acknowledgments

Many people in various ways helped me to learn about the spruce grouse and to prepare this book.

The following former students subjected themselves to irregular hours, inclement weather, bloodthirsty insects, and a gruff supervisor, in order to further the cause of knowledge: Mike Brundage, Bob Delonchamp, Rudy Emerick, Steve Gurchinoff, Harry Harju, Tom Jones, Mark Leider, Don Maxwell, John Randall, Jon Springer, Bob Sullivan, Craig Sunne, Dick Verch, Calvin Waisanen, Al Westover, and Roger Zettle.

I received encouragement and inspiration directly and indirectly from Dr. Durward Allen of Purdue University, Dr. David Boag of the University of Alberta, Dr. Larry Ellison of Office National de la Chasse, France, and Dr. William Marshall of the University of Minnesota.

My family, Glenda, Tommy, and Becky, provided encouragement and tolerance of my strange behavior.

Financial support was provided by the National Science Foundation in the form of research grants GB 4705 and GB 6202 and by Northern Michigan University in the form of a Summer Faculty Grant and a one-semester Sabbatical Leave to prepare the manuscript.

I am very grateful for all of this help.

W. L. R.

Introduction

In the coniferous forests that stretch wide and ever green across northern North America there lives a strange and gentle bird. On January afternoons it feeds among the branches of spruces or jack pines, filling its crop with needles. Then, as evening approaches, it may burrow beneath the snow to spend the night insulated from the cold. In springtime, when patches of bare ground show through the melting snow, the male struts and stamps like a flamenco dancer in black, white, and red to impress a passing female or to warn a competing male. In July the female stands sentinel duty on a stump while her growing offspring catch ants and black flies in spots of summer sunshine.

Because a hungry woodsman can sometimes walk up to one of these birds and knock it dead with a stick, it is widely known as the "fool hen." But its real name is spruce grouse.

Although its extraordinary tameness has earned for the spruce grouse the reputation of being a fool, this very show of trust and curiosity establishes a point of contact between man and bird that can not be readily matched. For here is a bird which, if it is not immediately threatened, permits humans to approach and to observe it closely while it goes about its business. And occasionally a spruce grouse may approach a human—not for a free handout as some birds might (the food of humans and spruce grouse is vastly different)—but perhaps only to study and learn something about humans.

When I began to work as Assistant Professor of Biology at Northern Michigan University in Marquette in the fall of 1964, I knew that there were spruce grouse on the Yellow Dog Plains about 30 miles northwest of Marquette. I had heard stories about novices shooting "limits" of grouse in the jack pines there, only to learn to their dismay that what they thought were legal ruffed grouse were actually illegal spruce grouse. I felt that this population of spruce grouse, despite the occasional shotgun depredations on their numbers, would be interesting to study.

From my readings about the spruce grouse I had been struck by two things: the shortage of good biological information, and the scarcity of these birds in places where they had once been abundant, particularly in Michigan. The Hamerstroms (1963) had recently pointed out that although the spruce grouse has the second largest geographic range of the ten species of North American grouse, the least literature had been published on it. Andy Ammann, in an article entitled *Status of Spruce Grouse in Michigan* (1963), observed that spruce grouse had been common or abundant in the northern two-thirds of the state before declining around 1912, and that despite being protected from hunting since 1914, they had never regained their former levels of abundance. Since 1940, however, they had been at least maintaining their numbers, and some observers had reported slight increases of spruce grouse in the Upper Peninsula.

Why was the spruce grouse not more abundant? This general question suggested other questions. Is the habitat suitable? How many eggs do spruce grouse lay? How many hatch? What are their predators? Their diseases? How long do they live? How important is man in regulating spruce grouse numbers? I felt that information we might gather on the spruce grouse could contribute not only to our understanding of the spruce grouse but also to our general knowledge of the ecology of birds.

In 1965 I received a grant from Northern Michigan University to begin a study of the habitat and population dynamics of the spruce grouse on the Yellow Dog Plains. From 1966 through 1968 the National Science Foundation sponsored our research, and in 1969 when federal money became very hard to get for small projects at small universities, Northern Michigan University again paid my summer salary to continue the grouse study. By 1970 our sources of financial support had given out, despite the fact that much remained to be learned about the spruce grouse.

But several students and I had spent the summers and parts of the autumns, winters, and springs of the years 1965 through 1969 on the Yellow Dog Plains accumulating, in a more or less systematic way, information about the spruce grouse and enjoying ourselves while doing so. This book is primarily a compilation of information about this bird, gathered by us and by a few other researchers across North America. But it is also meant to describe some of the events that contributed to our successes and failures during several years of studying the spruce grouse and its domain, and to convey some of the feelings we developed. The book presents data that revealed to us some of the secrets about this unusual member of the grouse family. I have tried to interpret the facts and figures in a way that will satisfy the scientific reader, but will not tempt the interested layman to doze. I hope that this volume will further our understanding of the spruce grouse and help us to appreciate more fully one of the other creatures that share the earth with us.

FOOL HEN

*The Spruce Grouse on the
Yellow Dog Plains*

Chapter *1*

What Is a Spruce Grouse?

Appearance

I saw my first spruce grouse the morning of May 11, 1965, on the Yellow Dog Plains. She stood quietly in a patch of spring sunshine on the gray reindeer moss watching me as I walked almost past before spotting her. When I turned and approached her for a closer look, she showed no objection. Her glistening brown eyes sized me up carefully, but she did not run or fly away. Occasionally she would cluck quietly, twitching her tail with each cluck, and take a step or two away from me.

She was a brown and patterned bird, a little bigger, a little plumper, and a lot prettier than a pigeon. Her brown feathers were barred with black. Above each eye was a slender comb of bare reddish skin, and I noticed especially how far out her beak was feathered. Along her flanks there were white bands on the tips of her feathers. The amount of white on each feather increased toward her breast and belly, making her appear light below and darker above. Shadows cast by the bird fell upon the lighter colored underparts, making shadow and bird blend together. This effect, coupled with the mixing of brown, black, and gray, helped to blend her into the dead pine needles and lichens beneath. I understood now how I had almost passed this bird without spotting her, and I won-

3

dered how many spruce grouse I had passed on previous days of fruitless searching.

Her fan-shaped tail was tipped with a buffy band, and ahead of that the mottled brown and black barring of her tail feathers disappeared beneath soft, gray-tipped tail coverts. Her legs were feathered to her toes. I had been used to seeing ruffed grouse, and I could not help but think of how compact and ptarmigan-like a spruce grouse appeared in comparison.

Dick Verch, a graduate student, was with me that day. Our mission was to capture and band spruce grouse, but for a while we had to just stand there and admire this lovely bird. After a few minutes we heard, from behind us, a rustling sound, like that of a deck of cards being riffled. We turned to see a male spruce grouse strutting stiff-legged toward us.

He planted each foot with exaggerated pomp and carried his exquisite tail erect, closing and spreading it, alternating first to one side then the other with each step, apparently challenging our right to approach a female on his territory. While the beauty of the hen's plumage lay in subtleties of mingling patterns of brown, black, gray, and white, there was nothing subtle about the plumage of the male. He was a bright resplendent bird full of contrasts—white against black and crimson against gray.

His head was dark and the brilliant papillate red combs above his eyes were distended so that they almost touched each other at the top of his head. A thin white line curved beside each cheek; the lines met beneath his throat. The short feathers of his chin were erect, giving him a bearded appearance. The black feathers of the sides and front of the neck were spread and flat, like the neck of a cobra, and the white tips of the black lower neck feathers formed a bold white horizontal line across his chest. Beneath that an oval shield of black covered the center of his breast.

The pattern of each feather of his back was visible; gray with two curved black bars. His tail glistened nearly pure black and ended in a half-inch-wide band of orange. As he turned slightly away from us we could see the long under-tail feathers standing out individually, their tips forming soft white spots against the blackness of his tail. All birds are things of beauty, but this proud male spruce grouse was one of the most magnificent birds I had ever seen.

After a while his resentment of us diminished. He rested a few yards away and watched us curiously while we nervously and excitedly draped a mist net to the ground between two trees, hoping he would not go away before we could catch and band him. We had never tried this before, but it turned out to be easy. We simply shooed the male spruce grouse and his female companion ahead of us into the net, banded and released them.

I was glad to find those birds that day. This was our third trip to the Yellow Dog Plains, and on the previous two we had not seen hide, feather, tracks, or droppings of a spruce grouse. I was beginning to think that perhaps I had swindled Northern Michigan University out of a $2,000 grant to do research on a nonexistent bird. I had written the proposal on faith that rumors were true that there were such birds on the Yellow Dog Plains. If we had not found spruce grouse, my final report to the Faculty Grants Committee could have been embarrassing for all concerned, especially me.

Later that day Dick and I found another pair of birds and banded the male. We drove home excited and elated. There indeed were spruce grouse on the Yellow Dog Plains, and three of them were now wearing our colored bands. Our field research had begun.

Geographic Range of the Spruce Grouse

Spruce grouse can be found in coniferous forests across the northern part of the North American continent. They seem to need short-needled conifers, and their range is generally congruent with that of the northern coniferous forest (Fig. 1). The northern border is defined by the shores of Hudson Bay and the southern edge of the vast treeless tundras. The Pacific Ocean forms the western border of the range and the Atlantic its eastern edge. At its southern boundary the spruce grouse encounters and is probably turned back by the arid sage brush deserts in valleys of Washington, Oregon, and

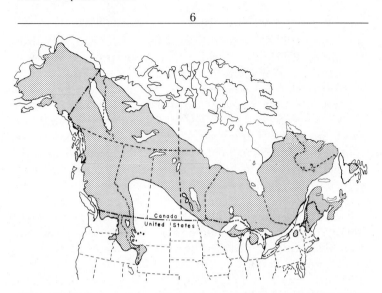

Figure 1. The range of the spruce grouse, modified from Aldrich (1963) and Johnsgard (1973) by information supplied by state and provincial wildlife agencies.

Idaho, the great grasslands and wheat fields of western Canada, and the deciduous forests in the Great Lakes area and northeastern United States.

The Name of the Spruce Grouse

Johnsgard (1973) compiled a list of names for the spruce grouse. They include black partridge, Canada grouse, cedar partridge, fool hen, Franklin's grouse, heath hen, mountain grouse, spotted grouse, spruce partridge, swamp partridge, Tyee grouse, and wood grouse. In Michigan both sexes are commonly called "spruce hen," but everywhere woodsmen know what bird you are referring to when you say "fool hen."

The Latin name of the spruce grouse is *Canachites canadensis*. According to Edward Gruson's (1972) book on bird names, *Canachites* means "maker of noise," and *canadensis*, of course, means "of Canada." Thus the name translates into "Canadian noise-maker," which sounds more like something you might encounter at a New Year's Eve party in Toronto than like a bird that probably spends New Year's Eve peacefully asleep in a snowdrift a few hundred miles to the north, oblivious to the curious celebrations of its intellectual superior, Man. Why noise was associated with the spruce grouse in its naming is not known, but it is possible that the noise made by the drumming ruffed grouse was mistakenly attributed to a spruce grouse, and the name stuck. The spruce grouse is a quiet bird.

Races of the Spruce Grouse

Aldrich (1963) remarked upon how uniform in appearance the spruce grouse is throughout its range, but some investigators have reported racial differences among birds from different areas.

Descriptions of the races of spruce grouse have been largely based upon subtle plumage differences among samples of museum skins. I have not examined enough specimens from different areas to make an original assessment of the various races of spruce grouse if they do exist, but will review and interpret the literature I have seen.

The Fifth Edition of the *Checklist of North American Birds*, published in 1957 by the American Ornithologists' Union (A.O.U.), recognizes five races of the spruce grouse. Supplements to the checklist published subsequently contain no pertinent revisions. The race of spruce grouse that we studied on the Yellow Dog Plains, and which occurs in the southeastern parts of the range of the species, is designated as the Canada spruce grouse (*Canachites canadensis canace*).

The neighboring race to the north is the Hudsonian spruce grouse (*Canachites canadensis canadensis*), which according to Bent (1932) differs from the Canada spruce grouse in the more rusty or rufous coloration among the females of the Hudsonian race. Rand (1948), however, upon examining many specimens, found that *C. c. canadensis* differs from *C. c. canace* in that the females of *canadensis* have less reddish brown and more grayish brown, but that there is considerable overlap. If one author says the females are more reddish and another says they are less reddish, and both say the males are alike, it seems that the differences are not very definable, and the existence of separate races must be questionable.

A third race, recognized in the 1957 A.O.U. checklist and by Rand (1948), but not by Uttal (1938), Ridgway and Friedmann (1946), or Aldrich (1963), is *C. c. osgoodi* from far northwestern Canada and eastern and northern Alaska. According to Rand, the females of this race differ from those of *canadensis* in that they are grayer with less brown and tawny in the plumage, although considerable overlap occurred between 15 specimens from this range and 70 specimens he examined from the described range of *canadensis*. It is undoubtedly because of the uncertain basis of recognition that some authors have failed to give *osgoodi* its credentials as a race or subspecies.

Such was the case with the short-lived recognition of a race designated as *torridus*, found in Nova Scotia, Gaspe, and New Brunswick, where the females supposedly have more brownish coloration than those of *canace*. This subspecies was erected in 1939 by Uttal, was recognized but questioned by Ridgway and Friedmann (1946), and fell into oblivion after Rand (1948) failed to find differences between birds from the supposed range of *torridus* and those from the range of *canace*.

A fourth race is the Valdez spruce grouse (*Canachites canadensis atratus*). This race is isolated from others of its species, occupying the coastal region of southern Alaska and Kodiak Island. Its markings, according to Grinnel (1910) as cited by Ridgway and Friedmann (1946), vary from the other spruce grouse in that its coloration is generally darker, with fewer white markings, more black areas, and more olivaceous than ashy gray.

The fifth and most distinctive race is Franklin's spruce grouse (*Canachites canadensis franklinii*). Members of this race are found from southern Alaska down the Pacific Coast to Washington and inland to the eastern edge of the Rocky Mountains. The rectrices (large tail feathers) of the males are black to the tip, lacking the buffy terminal band of the other races. The 12 upper tail covert feathers have conspicuous white tips which, when the tail is spread, form an attractive symmetrical pattern of white spots against the black tail. In addition, the courtship ritual of the male Franklin's grouse includes a unique quirk. His wings meet violently above his back in flight to produce a loud double clap (MacDonald, 1968). In southwestern Alberta and northern British Columbia, Franklin's spruce grouse interbreed with the Hudsonian spruce grouse.

For a long time Franklin's grouse was regarded as a separate species from the spruce grouse because of plumage differences in the males, including the white-tipped upper tail coverts and lack of the terminal band on the tail. However, the discovery that they commonly interbreed with other spruce grouse where their ranges meet in Alberta and British Columbia convinced ornithologists that Franklin's grouse was not a distinct species, but merely a subspecies of the spruce grouse. It is so listed in the 1957 A.O.U. checklist, after being considered a separate species in the 1931 version. It is unlikely that the 1957 version of the A.O.U. checklist will be the last word in describing races of spruce grouse.

A summary of the past views of different authors as to racial designation is given in Table 1. My own preference, at least until more convincing data are presented, would be to consider only three races; *canadensis, franklinii,* and

Table 1. Races of the spruce grouse recognized by various authors since 1930

	A.O.U. 1931	Uttal 1939	Ridgway & Friedmann 1946	Rand 1948	A.O.U. 1957	Aldrich 1963
			Reference			
canace	X	X	X	X	X	X
torridus		X	X			
canadensis	X	X	X	X	X	X
osgoodi	X			X	X	
atratus	X	X	X	X	X	X
franklinii						
separate species	X	X	X	X		
race					X	X

atratus. The latter, from Alaska, appears to be a larger bird and have larger clutch sizes than the other birds, as will be indicated later. *Franklinii* is well defined by plumage and courtship behavior. I think the remaining spruce grouse should all be considered *canadensis.*

A Close Relative and Recent Reclassification of the Spruce Grouse

In eastern Siberia there is a bird which looks and acts much like the North American spruce grouse. Officially the Siberian spruce grouse is regarded as belonging to a separate genus and species, *Falcipennis falcipennis.* The Latin name refers to its narrow, somewhat sickle-shaped, outer wing primary feathers. A Japanese biologist, Yamashina (1939), studying birds in the deceptively quiet days before World War II, published an article in the French Review of Ornithology about his three visits to the habitat of this bird on the island of Sakhalin.

I found his article recently, and 12 years after taking the exam, I finally discovered why I had to take French to obtain a Ph.D. At last I had found an article I wanted to read in French. To my surprise, I could read it well enough (the pictures also helped) to determine that *Falcipennis falcipennis* seems very closely related to *Canachites canadensis* in almost every respect, including size, general coloration, courtship behavior, egg color and size, and plumage of young. The only notable differences are in the narrow outer primaries, and white tips on the tail feathers of the Siberian bird. Yamashina suggested quite properly that the two species are closely related and should be in the same genus.

But which genus should they be in, *Canachites* or *Falcipennis?* Neither one, according to Lester Short (1967) of the American Museum of Natural History. Short has probably done more extensive work than anyone else on taxonomy of the grouse family. He has compared egg color, studied plumages of the young, counted tail feathers, examined color patterns and shapes of wing and breast feathers, and considered courtship behavior of all the grouse. He agrees with Yamashina that the Siberian spruce grouse should be placed in the same genus as the North American spruce grouse. He further suggests that additional study may reveal that they might be considered the same species. Hjorth (1970), while agreeing that the relationship of the Asian bird is close to the American species, objects to the name "Siberian spruce grouse" because it may not always be associated with spruces. He suggests "spiny-winged" or "Okhotsian grouse."

The genus that Short suggests is *Dendragapus*. This is the genus of the blue grouse of the western United States and Canada. The blue grouse shares the following similarities with the spruce grouse; sexual dimorphism, general body proportions, bill shape, relative size and shape of wings, shape and coloration of the tail, long toes and short tarsi (the tarsus is that part of the foot between the toes and the heel—which many people think of as a knee bent backward), white lines on the neck of the males, color of eggs, juvenal plumage, and courtship flight behavior of the males. Short (1967, p. 20) says, "Merging *Falcipennis* and *Canachites* into *Dendragapus* gives proper emphasis to similarities and relationships among these grouse besides eliminating poorly based monotypic genera." Johnsgard (1973) supports Short's conclusions, and I must also concur.

Geographic Origins

Short suggests that the genus *Dendragapus* originated in North America, as did the whole subfamily of grouse. He believes that the Siberian spruce grouse population probably represents the descendants of some westward pioneering birds that may have crossed the land bridge which, at various times in the distant past, linked what is now Alaska with eastern Siberia.

Johnsgard (1973) believes, however, that the spruce grouse originated in eastern Asia and spread eastward and southward in North America. The only fossil spruce grouse available has been one specimen from relatively recent times (late Pleistocene) from Virginia, which proves very little about the evolutionary history of the spruce grouse.

Hybridization

Hybrid grouse are rare in the wild, except for prairie chicken × sharp-tail crosses. Species are defined as species because their members in nature breed only among themselves. There are two biological factors responsible for this "reproductive isolation"—physiology and behavior. Physiologically, the egg and sperm must carry compatible genetic material. Some hybrids are impossible because the sperm of one species may carry a number of chromosomes different from that of the egg of the other species; or, if the chromosome number is the same, conflicting and incompatible genetic information may be carried on equivalent locations on the chromosomes; or, the chemistry of sperm and egg may prevent their union. If a union occurs, and the genetic material is totally incompatible, the "fertilized" egg never develops. The further apart species have evolved from one another, the less likely it is that they are genetically compatible.

Behavioral isolation arises from the courtship behavior of birds, which consists of a series of rather specific signals and responses between male and female, culminating in copulation. These signs and responses are largely learned or genetically programmed into a bird so that the male of one species will not respond to the appearance and body language of the female of another species and vice versa. This saves a lot of time and reproductive energy by assuring that the male does not go around copulating with every bird which he sets eyes on, wasting his sperm and energy on incompatible mates.

But under certain environmental conditions, inappropriate matings may occur. Often the circumstances of captivity result in the break-down of the behavioral barrier, and physiologically compatible species can produce hybrids.

Lumsden (1969) noted that captive ruffed grouse and blue grouse females at a receptive stage in their breeding cycle have squatted in precopulatory display for humans approaching their eggs. Closely related species may carry the mating act through, and, if the physiological requirements are met, hybrids are produced.

Three cases of hybridization between wild spruce grouse and willow ptarmigan have been documented (Hachisuka, 1928; Taverner, 1931; Lumsden, 1969). Two specimens were collected several years apart in northern Ontario near Hudson Bay. The birds, both males, were splendid birds, each with a back of brown and black boldly mottled with white, a broad dark tail, and a necklace of black feathers separating the pure white of the throat from that of the breast and belly (Fig. 2). Taverner mentioned that the specimen he examined could have passed for a partially albino male spruce grouse except that its feet were fully

Figure 2. A hybrid spruce grouse × willow ptarmigan has a broad dark tail, brown, black, and white mottled back, and a necklace of black feathers across the white throat and breast (drawn from Lumsden, 1969).

feathered like those of a ptarmigan. Lumsden found some indication of hybrid vigor. The specimen he examined showed many body features, such as weight, wing length, and lengths of many skeletal elements, to be larger than those of the willow ptarmigan, the larger of its presumptive parents.

These two hybrids came from an area where spruce forests meet the tundra and the ranges of the ptarmigan and the spruce grouse meet. Lumsden speculated that hybridization probably occurred when members of opposite sexes of both species met at a period in the reproductive cycle when neither was in a mood to be fussy. The result was the rare and beautiful "sprucemigan."

One other hybrid involving a wayward spruce grouse has been reported. Jollie (1955) described a male hybrid spruce grouse × blue grouse (a bluce grouse?) from the mountains of Idaho. In contrast with the "sprucemigan," where the hybrid tended toward large size, Jollie's "bluce grouse" was quite intermediate between its presumptive parents in both size and plumage characters (Fig. 3).

Figure 3. A hybrid spruce grouse × blue grouse is intermediate in size and plumage between its parent species (drawn from Jollie, 1955).

The fact that spruce grouse are in nature both physiologically and behaviorally able to mate successfully, however rarely, with willow ptarmigan and blue grouse suggests close relationships between the spruce grouse and these other members of the family. This seems to further Short's contention that the blue grouse and spruce grouse are closely related. The ptarmigans, according to Short, have likewise not evolved a great distance from spruce grouse.

Who's Who in the Grouse Family

Varying distances from common ancestors separate the spruce grouse from the other members of its family. Because of the scarcity of grouse fossils and other imperfections in determining relationships, there remains ground for interpretation and argument among biologists. The American Ornithologists' Union (1957) and Aldrich (1963) recognized ten species of North American Grouse, belonging to seven genera. Short (1967) proposed only nine species (considering the greater and lesser prairie chickens as subspecies of the same species) and only five genera, lumping the spruce grouse and blue grouse into the same genus and placing the sharp-tailed grouse in the same genus as the prairie chicken.

The species of North American grouse are listed below, with two sets of Latin names, one from the A.O.U. checklist, and one from the revision proposed by Lester Short:

COMMON NAME	A.O.U. (1957)	SHORT (1967)
Blue grouse	*Dendragapus obscurus*	*Dendragapus obscurus*
Spruce grouse	*Canachites canadensis*	*Dendragapus canadensis*
Greater prairie chicken	*Tympanuchus cupido*	*Tympanuchus cupido*
Lesser prairie chicken	*Tympanuchus pallidicinctus*	*Tympanuchus cupido*
Sharp-tailed grouse	*Pedioecetes phasianellus*	*Tympanuchus phasianellus*
Ruffed grouse	*Bonasa umbellus*	*Bonasa umbellus*
Sage grouse	*Centrocercus urophasianus*	*Centrocercus urophasianus*
Willow ptarmigan	*Lagopus lagopus*	*Lagopus lagopus*
Rock ptarmigan	*Lagopus mutus*	*Lagopus mutus*
White-tailed ptarmigan	*Lagopus leucurus*	*Lagopus leucurus*

The willow and rock ptarmigans are also found in the Old World, as are the following other species of grouse:

COMMON NAME	GRZIMEK (1972)	SHORT (1967)
Capercaillie	*Tetrao urogallus*	*Tetrao urogallus*
Black-billed capercaillie	[Not mentioned in Grzimek]	*Tetrao parvirostris*
Black grouse	*Lyrurus tetrix*	*Tetrao tetrix*
Caucasian black grouse	*Lyrurus mlokosiewiczi*	*Tetrao mlokosiewiczi*
Siberian spruce grouse	*Falcipennis falcipennis*	*Dendragapus falcipennis*
Hazel grouse	*Tetrastes bonasia*	*Bonasa bonasia*
Black-breasted hazel grouse	*Tetrastes severtzowi*	*Bonasa sewerzowi*

Short proposed a family tree for gróuse to show the relative distances between members of the family (Fig. 4). In addition, Short believes that the grouse family(*Tetraonidae*) is not sufficiently distinct from the pheasants (*Phasianidae*) to warrant recognition as a separate family. The only difference between the two is that grouse have feathers on their tarsi, while pheasants have only scales on their tarsi.

Most grouse biologists I have talked with have been impressed by the thoroughness and logic of Short's research and recommend that his revision of the family be taken seriously. I agree.

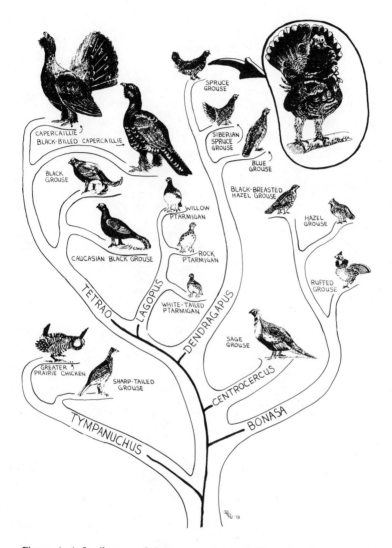

Figure 4. A family tree of the grouse of the world, as they have evolved from ancestral grouse, according to Short (1967). The spruce grouse has developed along the main stem of grouse evolution.

Chapter **2**

The Yellow Dog Plains

From an airplane on a winter day the Yellow Dog Plains appear as a large flat island of green, stretching 10 miles from east to west and 2 to 3 miles from north to south. They are not a grassland, as the term "plains" suggests, nor were they named for a yellow dog, as will be explained later. To the north the land drops off into valleys dissected deeply by tributaries of the Salmon Trout River. Ice-covered beaver ponds spread through the tag alders, and on the hillsides the bare branches and trunks of aspens, maples, and birches cast shadows striping the snow beneath. Lake Superior, a mixture of ice floes and blue water, extends from its shore 9 miles away to the northern horizon.

South of the plains, across the Yellow Dog River and into the white and hazy sunshine, the terrain rises. Granite knobs, lakes, and forests extend to the limit of vision. Dark green patches appear here and there—cedar and spruce swamps, or balsam firs and hemlocks along the stream valleys. But the Yellow Dog Plains are different from these other green patches. They are high, flat, and broad, 900 feet above the level of Lake Superior, and the friendly green trees are jack pines.

As the last glacier wasted away, about 10,000 years ago,

19

its southern edge paused here for several centuries. Gravel, sand, and boulders carried southward from the Canadian shield by the slowly creeping ice were dropped at the margin of the enormous ice sheet, accumulating in a great mass smoothing over the knobby granite and sandstone bedrock surface. The gradually sloping plains were formed as sand and gravel, which were washed into a lake at the edge of the glacier by streams of melting water coursing off the glacier, gradually filled the lake along its north side until only a shallow pond was left. A remnant of that last glacial pond remains today in the form of a large, sparsely vegetated, shallow bog that covers several square miles along the southern edge of the plains.

Patterns on the plains are obvious from the air. Squares and rectangles loosely striped by lines of slashing reveal man's division of the land into 40- and 80-acre parcels and the recent cutting of jack pines. In some areas slender conical black spruces mingle with the assymmetrical jack pines. The bog occupies about 6 square miles along the south edge of the plains where geese stop to feed and rest in the fall. Scattered islands of jack pines, spruces, and tamaracks dot the tundra-like sweep of the sphagnum bog. In the midst of this the Yellow Dog River winds eastward through a tangled jungle of tag alders that in summer turns back all but the toughest-shinned fishermen who come to court the temperamental brook trout hiding beneath its banks.

When white men first came to this north country for timber in the 1890s they found pines growing on the Yellow Dog Plains. Red and white pines 150 feet high and 5 feet in diameter were cut. But even then these pines were not dense on the plains and the smaller and less economically valuable jack pines grew among them. By 1910 the good pine had been cut from the plains and the lumbermen moved on, leaving behind them crumbling cabins, rusting bedsprings, broken axe handles, and piles of dead tops and limbs of trees.

In 1913 a fire swept the whole eastern half of the plains. Jack pines, their cones opened but not destroyed by the heat, spread their seeds among the ashes and by the 1930s the jack pines were again big enough to be harvested, and they were. And yet another generation of jack pines grew back.

An early Danish settler, Christen Andersen, began a homestead at the western edge of the plains in 1906 and became its only permanent resident. The homestead lasted a few decades. Bill Bushy, a "land-looker" or timber cruiser, homesteaded for a few years in the early 30s. In 1956 he returned at the age of 85, and, looking about him, shook his head and said "Who would ever have thought that I would have lived long enough to see two harvests of trees on the Yellow Dog Plains? Now they're ready to be cut again." And the woodcutters did come again in the 1960s.

The vegetation of the Yellow Dog Plains is monotonous in terms of the kind of trees growing there. Ninety percent of the trees are jack pines, a species often scorned by the public for its undignified shape and color. Jack pines lack the towering wind-swept beauty of white pines and the staunch classic look of red pines. But jack pines are easy to walk among, and blueberries do well with them. Special kinds of flowers grow beneath jack pines in springtime—trailing arbutus, pink lady slippers, dwarf dogwood, and, for a few glorious purple days in June, fringed polygala blanketing the ground; reindeer moss moistened by a summer rain is as soft underfoot as a Persian rug; and jack pine needles are food for the spruce grouse.

If you look closely enough there is variety even among the jack pine forests. In places on the western part of the plains the trees stand singly or in small clumps 50 to 100 feet apart, with live branches dragging on the ground. Shrubs such as chokecherry and serviceberry, and short grasses grow among the trees. It was there in 1965 that I watched two courting sandhill cranes compete for the atten.ion of a female. On the same day, Calvin Waisanen and I flushed a sharp-tailed grouse there, the only one we've seen on the plains.

In other places the trees grow dense and straight, their

black trunks rising 20 or 30 feet without a branch. These are the pulp cutters' bread and butter, and when the trunks of trees in such a stand of jack pines reach a diameter of 7 to 10 inches the voice of the chain saw soon will be heard.

A fire in 1949 burned a crooked ribbon along the northern edge of the bog. Modern control methods were applied and the fire was kept from spreading very far upland. By the 1960s a very dense stand of jack pines 15 to 25 feet tall occupied the burn, extending from the edge of the bog in a wavy pattern about 50 to 300 feet inland. Along with the young spruces at the bog edge, these young pines made ideal spruce grouse cover. In 1967-68 pulp cutters removed the adjacent mature jack pines, leaving a curved ribbon of spruce grouse habitat, about a mile long and 50 to 300 feet wide, bounded on one side by a wide open cutting and by the bog on the other.

We found this strip of cover to be useful in our studies because it was only wide enough to accommodate the territory of one male spruce grouse, but long enough to serve several. And so the birds parceled it up, drawing quite specific lines between territories, allowing us to measure the size of their domain.

The climate of the Yellow Dog Plains is harsh for the north-central United States. In winter, northerly winds carry moisture in from Lake Superior and it falls as snow on the high ground. Subzero temperatures are the rule at night during January and February.

Spring always comes late in Lake Superior country, but especially so on the Yellow Dog Plains. On May 1, 1965, we tried to drive to the plains on our first research trip, but were stopped 7 miles short by snow. We walked the rest of the way but found the snow on the plains to be 2 feet deep. On April 11, 1966, I measured 37 inches of snow in several places. That year some snow remained until May 25. In the spring trailing arbutus and pink lady slippers bloom later there than anywhere else in the county.

In the summer a killing frost may occur during any month. In 1966 a severe frost on July 10 killed most of the bracken ferns growing in open areas. We tried to figure out whether that was the last frost of the winter of 1965-66 or the first frost of the winter of 1966-67.

The first snows usually come in late September, but they stay on the ground only a few days. By early or mid-November the ground is blanketed and the snow gets deeper and deeper until late March or April.

The kinds of birds living on the Yellow Dog Plains have a boreal flavor. The gray jay and the boreal chickadee, both northern species, outnumber their Carolinian counterparts, the blue jay and black-capped chickadee; in most of the rest of the Upper Peninsula the opposite occurs. Flocks of red and white-winged crossbills can sometimes be found on the plains during the summer.

I have seen only a few gray squirrels on the Yellow Dog Plains and only once saw a skunk. We never encountered a raccoon, a recent arrival from more southern climes which has become quite common in surrounding deciduous forests. In the winter of 1968 a moose, rare in Upper Michigan, spent a few days on the plains, then ambled off to the north.

In places black spruces and Labrador tea grow on upland sites. Usually these northern species are found only in cool bogs and swamps at this latitude. All in all, the Yellow Dog Plains show a number of climatic, floral, and faunal features typical of areas located two or three hundred miles to the north. They are a sort of ecological island, surrounded by deciduous forests. The climate, the soils, and the plants growing upon them all have helped to make spruce grouse feel at home. The Yellow Dog Plains are not the only place in Michigan these birds are found, but they are one of the best places for them.

On very old maps of the Lake Superior country, a river called the St. John drains the highlands of what is now northern Marquette County. Today there is no St. John River, but a river called the Yellow Dog flows where the St. John once did. How did the name "Yellow Dog" come to replace "St. John"? Images of an early settler with a yellow dog or perhaps the name of a local Indian chief come to mind, but neither seems to be the case. Instead, the name is a strange example of bilingual confusion.

Some Frenchmen apparently thought that the Americans, instead of saying St. John, the original name of the river, were trying to pronounce *"Chien Jaune"* which later was translated literally back into English as "Yellow Dog."

An imaginative cartographer was inspired to name two of the tributaries of the Yellow Dog, the Big Pup and the Little Pup. I have somehow felt that there was something more exciting and colorful about studying spruce grouse on the Yellow Dog Plains than there would have been in working on the St. John's Plains. The spruce grouse probably don't care.

Chapter 3

Stalking the Wild Spruce Grouse

Defining the Study Area

At first we just drove to the Yellow Dog Plains, got out of the car, and looked for spruce grouse. We really didn't know what we would find, if anything. In 1965 Calvin Waisanen, who was my summer student assistant, and I explored much of the Yellow Dog Plains and began to learn what areas were likely to harbor spruce grouse. We identified some accessible study units where we found spruce grouse and where we could effectively concentrate our efforts.

The study units were bounded by roads or identifiable vegetational boundaries such as cuttings, a marsh, or a stand of mature forest. The units included, from east to west (Fig. 5); Pinnacle Falls (200 acres), the Flask Cover (80 acres), Porcupine Camp (80 acres), Dead End Strip—Black Duck Marsh (160 acres), Four Corners—Sand Hill (400 acres), Doughnut Cover (80 acres), and Dinosaur Point (240 acres). All except the Pinnacle Falls are names we invented for various good and not-so-good reasons. (There are no dinosaur bones on Dinosaur Point—only a rusting old iron silhouette of a *Brontosaurus*. Both it and its sponsor, Sinclair

25

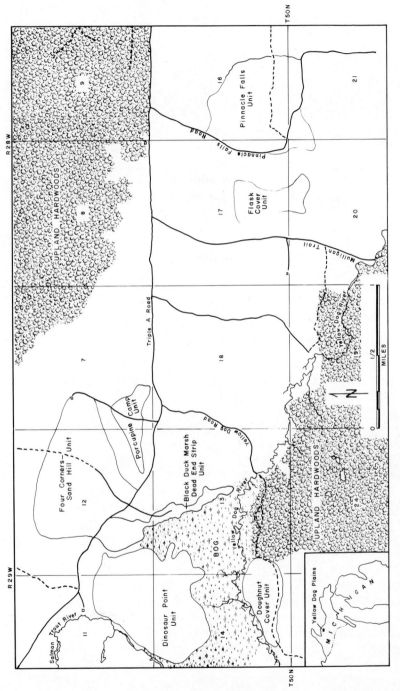

Figure 5. Map of the Yellow Dog Plains study area.

26

Oil, are now extinct.) Some of the units bordered upon one another and spruce grouse (especially dispersing young birds) would move from one unit to another.

The total area of the study units was about 1240 acres. These acreages were sometimes reduced as pulp cutters and their chain saws mowed swaths into them, but on the other hand we would occasionally extend our searches outside the study unit borders. By adding about 300 acres to allow for our wanderings, we get a total of 1540 acres or about 2.5 square miles constituting our study area. This is about one-tenth of the total acreage of the Yellow Dog Plains. It included some of the best spruce grouse habitat on the plains but not all of it. Some of the unstudied areas also had good numbers of spruce grouse.

Once having defined our study units, we would search them systematically, walking at a slow pace parallel with one another about 10 to 30 yards apart, depending on the density of the cover, and sweeping back and forth from one edge to the other. When we found a bird we would record its location by estimating its distance and direction from some recognizable landmark and by reference to aerial photographs and vegetation maps made from them. In the first few years we would sample vegetation around the spot where each bird was seen. This method will be described in detail later. If a bird was a female with a brood, we would record the number of chicks and estimate their age.

Capturing and Banding Spruce Grouse

If the bird we found was not banded, we would attempt to capture it. One method, if the bird was in a tree, involved suspending a mist net between two poles, positioning the net at an appropriate height, and attempting to flush the bird so that it flew into the net. A mist net resembles a volleyball net with very fine black nylon strands. It entangles any bird which attempts to fly through it. If the bird was on the ground, we would tie the net to a convenient tree trunk or limbs, let it drape onto the ground, and walk the bird into the net. About 80 percent of the adults we encountered we could catch in mist nets. Often we would have to flush a bird more than once, however, before it would fly into the net.

In 1967 we began to capture birds with a noose on the end of a pole, a method used by Zwickel and Bendell (1967a) to catch blue grouse and by old woodsmen to catch spruce grouse. I was leery of this method, which involved passing a loop over a bird's head and pulling the bird out of a tree or holding it on the ground while the noose tightened around its neck. But we captured 84 birds with the noose during 3 years and killed only one, as good a record as the mist net, in which we accidentally killed two birds. Naturally we would attempt to loosen the noose as quickly as possible. On a few occasions, before the noose could be slackened the birds appeared to be strangling, with eyes closing and neck getting limp. They were given artificial respiration by gently squeezing the sides of the breast. (Mouth-to-mouth resuscitation seemed somehow inappropriate.) For a noose pole we usually cut a slender jack pine or spruce 12 to 15 feet long. We also used a telescopic fiberglass fishing pole that extended to 16 feet, but we felt that its whipping action tended to tighten the noose and give us less control in bringing a struggling bird down through branches. We left poles leaning against trees here and there throughout the area, so we would not have to cut one each time we needed to capture a bird, since we could always find a used pole within a minute or two. A pulpwood cutter once told us he had spent a lot of thought trying to figure out what these poles he kept finding in the woods had been used for.

We caught chicks either in a fish landing net or by hand. We found that in their first 5 or 6 weeks chicks lack the stamina to sustain more than three or four flights. One of our most effective techniques was to pursue a chick, getting it to fly repeatedly by climbing the tree and shaking the limb it was on, or by throwing sticks near it. After two or three flights it would often flutter down where we could catch it by hand or in the landing net. Recovery of their strength was rapid, as the chicks would fly away after the 10- to 15-minute rest they got while we banded them. The loss of banded chicks so captured was no higher than that of unbanded chicks, judging from subsequent sightings of broods.

Chicks were harder to catch than adults. While we could catch 80 to 90 percent of the adults we encountered, the best we could do with chicks was about 40 to 50 percent. Sometimes they would fly high into the trees or scatter so that we could keep track of only two or three of them at once. Our capture success rate improved with practice (Robinson and Maxwell, 1968).

Once we had a bird, either adult or chick, in hand, we would put it into a cotton stocking, weigh it, examine the stage of feather molt, and record any other information we thought would be useful. Then if it was old enough (over 3½ weeks), we would fit it with a numbered aluminum Michigan Department of Natural Resources band and one to three colored plastic bands. With five colors—red, green, blue, yellow, and white—and two legs, we had plenty of possibilities. Each bird was given its own individual combination, such as "left leg; aluminum over yellow; right leg; yellow over blue." The birds seemed to pay little attention to the bands either on themselves or on their companions. In only two cases did the bands become too tight and cause problems of swelling and infection. Otherwise, banded birds, we believe, behaved the same as unbanded ones.

In the 5 years of regular study (1965-69), we banded 315 spruce grouse and made over 700 different observations of individuals and groups of birds. Since 1969 we have banded 30 additional birds and made another 116 observations.

Radio Telemetry

The 1960s saw the development of miniature radio transmitters, and biologists were quick to see their application for monitoring the movements and behavior of various species of wildlife. Transmitters for ruffed grouse had been developed by Marshall and his co-workers at the University of Minnesota (Marshall and Kupa, 1963), and I thought that they might work well for spruce grouse, especially in helping us find nests and monitor movements of the birds.

In June 1967 I ordered a dozen transmitters and a receiver from Markusen Electronics of Esko, Minnesota. I knew this firm had been doing work for other grouse biologists. As I had not received my order by October and was making a trip to Minnesota for another purpose, I decided to visit the Markusen Electronics factory to get firsthand advice and check on the progress of my radio equipment. I wrote ahead to make an appointment with the head man, Sydney Markusen, himself.

When I arrived at the designated time I found Markusen Electronics was situated in the basement of a modest gray-shingled three-bedroom house, and that Sydney Markusen had gone to the grocery store to pick up a quart of milk for supper, but that he would be back shortly. His staff, one man holding a hot soldering iron, invited me in to wait.

The basement shop contained an upright piano on top of which was an interesting mixture of sheet music and circuit diagrams for transmitters and receivers. Balanced here and there on the laundry tubs were antenna wires and batteries. Shelves were laden with Mason jars containing beets, carrots, and pickles from the recent harvest. Interspersed among the jars were boxes of transistors, crystals, and half-completed transmitters. The soldering man went back to work on a bench in the middle.

After a while Mr. Markusen arrived with the milk and came downstairs. He seemed to be an unexcitable type. He began to check on the progress of my order by examining a list which was thumbtacked to one of the basement pillars along with letters and orders from customers in Africa, India, Alaska, and various other parts of the United States. He told me that I was not very far down the list now and that I could expect my order by Christmas.

Lloyd Fanter

A grouse can carry a small radio transmitter on its back. This aids researchers in studying movements and behavior.

It arrived in late May. When the box came I was hoping that he might have thrown in a jar of those delicious-looking dill pickles either by mistake or as a goodwill souvenir from Markusen Electronics, but no such luck.

The equipment was well made and it worked. A grouse transmitter with its battery weighs about 25 grams and is fitted with plastic "spaghetti straps." The transmitter itself fits on the back of the bird between the shoulders, and a 12-inch piano-wire whip antenna curves backward and upward over it. The spaghetti straps are fitted in a fixed loop around the base of the neck to the breast where the battery is attached. The straps then extend behind the wings to tie snugly to a loop on the rear of the transmitter in the middle of the bird's back. The bird carries the transmitter as it would a small pack sack, with the battery firmly attached between the shoulder straps on the chest.

The range of transmission on the Yellow Dog Plains averaged about half a mile, but it would vary with the topography and whether the bird was in a tree or on the ground. From an airplane I once got a signal from a bird at a range of 3 miles. The batteries would last 3 or 4 months.

On June 2, 1968, I noosed an adult male on his territory at Dead End and fitted him with a transmitter—the first radioed grouse in Michigan, a historic moment. On June 5 he was still there, only about 30 yards from where I had captured him. The signal was working fine and the bird could fly well but I noticed that the harness could perhaps have been fitted a little tighter, with a smaller neck loop and the battery farther forward.

On June 10 the bird had moved 200 yards to the northwest, perhaps off his territory, and he was 20 feet up in a tree. He did not respond to the tape-recorded calls of a female spruce grouse, as most males do at that time of year. On June 12 we found him back on his territory, 15 feet up in a tree. We never saw or heard from this bird again, and sadly suspected that the radio transmitter was responsible for the development of his more passive behavior and ultimately his disappearance.

Through the rest of 1968 and 1969 and off and on through 1973 we attempted to improve the fit of the transmitter harness and eventually radio-tagged a total of 9 males and 20 females. But I was never fully satisfied that birds carrying transmitters were behaving entirely normally.

Of the 29 radio-tagged birds, we lost contact with 9, 1 to 35 days after they were fitted with transmitters. Fourteen of the birds were recaptured and the transmitter was removed, two lost their transmitters and lived on without them, and four died with transmitters on. Of these four, two females became tangled in the harness, one male died with no apparent internal or external cause, and one female was caught in flight and killed by my dog Mandy, who on that day was definitely not man's best friend.

Of four males for which we had "before and after" weights, two maintained weight and two lost weight while carrying the transmitter. Of nine radioed females, two gained weight and seven lost weight. Average weight losses were not statistically significant (*t*-test), but 11 weight losses against 2 weight gains (combining sexes) would occur by chance less than once in 20 times (sign test, Crow at al., 1960). Although some of the birds would be expected to lose weight in summer anyhow, other birds at other times of the year would have been expected to gain weight. I believe the transmitters were responsible for weight losses in many birds.

Survival rates of radio-equipped adult birds from 1968 to 1969 were 1 of 5 males (compared with the non-radioed population rate of 9 of 24) and 1 of 8 females (compared with 5 of 22 in the non-radioed population). The differences are not significant, but I would not want to claim that survival rates were similar between radio-tagged and normally banded birds. For these reasons I did not use data on radio-tagged birds in calculations of mortality.

Our original hope of locating nests by telemetry was tested on three females captured in early spring of 1969 and 1970. One of these, tagged on May 5, was located three times until June 10, all within a 30-foot radius. She apparently made no attempt to nest, as she did not develop a brood patch (an area of bare skin on the belly of the bird, which permits close contact with the eggs and indicates incubation). A second female, tagged on April 8, somehow shed her transmitter, and through blind luck we found her on a nest half a mile from where she had been radiotagged. The third female crossed us up by traveling 3.5 miles, out of range of our searching area, sometime in the spring. We found her in our routine visual search in July. She was carrying a perfectly functioning transmitter. She had no brood but had a brood patch and had probably nested.

Boag (1972) reported that radio transmitter packages affected behavior of captive red grouse, although later studies with red grouse in the field suggested no apparent behavioral differences brought on by radio packages (Boag et al., 1973). Ellison (1973) found that equipment identical to that we used had no apparent effect on the behavior of adult spruce grouse in Alaska, as four of five females nested despite carrying transmitters. Lance and Watson (1977) found red grouse males and nesting females unaffected by carrying radio transmitters, except that two females caught before nesting did not complete nesting. Leon Anderson and George Haas (personal communication) have also used this equipment successfully on spruce grouse in Minnesota, and it has also been effectively used in Alberta (Herzog and Boag, 1977; Keppie and Herzog, 1978). Margaret Herman (personal communication) has successfully used solar-powered transmitters on spruce grouse in Montana.

There may have been something wrong with our technique, although the weight of the transmitter on the smaller Michigan birds could have been a factor. Moreover, we should probably have made attempts to locate birds every day or two, rather than, in some cases, every week or two, as our time permitted. Frequent monitoring may reveal the beginning of a problem which could be alleviated by quick attention.

The transmitters were most valuable to us in obtaining information on chick development and brood survival. Radio-tagging a mother spruce grouse gave us access to her brood. We assumed that development and mortality of the chicks were not affected by a radio transmitter on their mother.

Chapter 4

Through the Seasons
with the Spruce Grouse

As we worked with the spruce grouse for 5 years their habitat became ours. Although we did not subsist from the resources of the Yellow Dog Plains, we began to feel (as well as to observe) the interdependence of the community of life there. Intellectually we knew the human value of pulp wood and knew that even for the good of the spruce grouse, succession must be set back, whether by fire or by chain saw. But we would feel an immediate loss whenever 80 acres of standing jack pines were converted into stumps and slashings. We would worry when spruce grouse were scarce in the spring and would quietly rejoice in another year when their population bounded back again. And we began to sense the pulse of the seasons.

Spring

I arrived on the Yellow Dog Plains shortly after sunrise the morning of April 27, 1967. Spring had come early that year. I drove my car to the crumbling knee-deep remains of the snowdrift that still blocked the Pinnacle Falls Road.

Beside me jack pines, spruces, and a few oaks and red maples reached toward a friendly blue sky. A newly arrived robin, saucy and chirping, flew to the sunshine at the tip of a spruce. He scolded and watched me as I began to walk down the narrow two-rut road into the jack pines.

I was the first one to walk down the Pinnacle Falls Road that spring. There were no footprints or tire tracks that had not been smoothed and nearly obliterated by snow and the waters of its melting. The ground was showing for the first time since mid-November. Behind me the soles of my boots left their peculiar geometric imprints in the moist sand. I felt the refreshing joy of wilderness and a pride in being the first person to walk down this road in 1967. The Yellow Dog Plains belonged to me and the spruce grouse, at least for today.

A short distance down the road I noticed the freshly made three-pronged footprints of a grouse in the sand. I stopped and listened. In a few moments I heard what I hoped to hear—a faint and brief whirr of wings off in the woods. I moved slowly away from the road toward the sound. Leafless stems of blueberry plants rose above their own dead and matted leaves, the leaves of 1966, now returning to the soil. Gray reindeer moss, not yet thawed from last night's frost, crunched beneath my feet as I tried to steal carefully up for a closer look at the courtship display of a male spruce grouse.

The bird was on the ground 50 yards from me when I saw him. He may have seen me too, but he seemed not to mind. I edged into the lower branches of a black spruce to watch. I saw no sign of a female. His display was spontaneous and probably largely beyond his conscious control. Such display would serve not only to attract a potential mate but also to proclaim his territory—a portion of land that he would defend against other male spruce grouse and which he had probably laid claim to last fall.

The bird flew to a jack pine limb about 8 feet high, increasing the speed of his wings, scraping twigs and branchlets, and spreading his tail wide just before he landed. He

Richard P. Smith

A displaying male (bottom) cocks his head to identify a suitable branch to land upon, flies with spread tail to the branch (right), then continues to strut from his perch (top).

37

took a few stiff-legged steps on the limb before flying back to the ground about a minute later. On the return flight, as he was 2 feet above the ground, his body turned suddenly upward, his wings fluttered rapidly, and he descended vertically with closed tail to the ground. There he strutted, his tail opening first on the left side, then on the right, with its feathers audibly rasping against each other, in sequence with his steps. At the end of his strutting walk he rapidly spread his black tail wide, twice, and with scarlet combs inflated, uttered a high-pitched "shik-sheek."

He repeated the ritual of flying to a limb and down again seven times in the next 16 minutes, sometimes returning to different spots on the gound but staying within a triangular opening measuring about 40 × 40 × 60 feet, and using two different limbs 8 to 10 feet high. The sound most audible to my ears was made by his wings hitting small branches as he landed in a pine, but the sound was not loud. The second most audible sound was that of his wings in the air, the third was the sound of his tail swishing, and the quietest sound was made by a standing double-wing beat, made like a ruffed grouse drumming but without either the volume of sound or the extended duration of the tattoo of a ruffed grouse.

At 7:30 he wandered off into the thicker jack pines and half an hour later flew into a tree for a meal of needles. He had not been successful in attracting a female that day.

Spring for spruce grouse, as it is with most birds, is devoted to one function—reproduction. The adult males have, by claiming territories the previous fall, distributed themselves fairly equally, and now their hormone levels, responding to the increasing length of the days, prime them for the ritual of mating.

The females wander in and out of the territories of the males. All of them, including the one-year-olds, are prepared internally by their hormone levels for copulating and egg laying. Their ears are probably well tuned to the "drumming" flights of the males, but externally they appear indifferent. The females seem to become intolerant of one another. Perhaps they too are claiming a nesting territory.

Sooner or later each female copulates with a male, but the relationship between the sexes is very temporary—a few minutes of preliminaries, a minute or so of action, and it is all over. They go their separate ways, the female off to find a nest site, the male remaining on his territory, perhaps with the unconscious hope of receiving the attentions of another female before the season is gone.

Summer

In early summer the dominant animal on the Yellow Dog Plains is not the spruce grouse, not man, not the black bear that feasts there upon berries and ants; it is the black fly. There are about 80 species of these carelessly brazen and hungry insects which hatch from the Yellow Dog River and swarm out over the nearby land in search of a meal. They are joined in June by similar numbers of rapacious mosquitoes in the mornings, deer flies during the day, and no-see-ums in the evenings. The dominant odor during our grouse research summers was that of insect repellent. Once as I bought a half-gallon supply of "Off" for our six-man crew the salesman tactfully advised me that it only required spreading it on with the hands, and that it was not necessary to bathe in it.

One summer Harry Harju showed up with a concoction brewed from a secret formula by an old Finnish immigrant in Newberry. Wearing it, Harry was detectable from 100 yards downwind and 30 yards upwind. This stuff successfully repelled insects, the rest of the crew, and eventually Harry himself. He had to give it up because it was giving him severe headaches and turning his skin yellowish brown. We were pleased with his decision, but concerned about the environmental problems of where and how to dispose of his remaining supplies.

It is probably no coincidence that the hatching of young spruce grouse comes at the peak of insect abundance near the summer solstice. Over centuries of spruce grouse evolution the broods which hatched at that time had the best chance for survival and for passing along in their genes the tendency to mate and lay eggs at the most favorable time. The chicks leave the nest with their mother as soon as their down is dry and they begin to peck at things and to feed immediately. During the first few weeks of their lives insects provide an important source of protein.

A typical summer scene on the Yellow Dog Plains is a watchful female spruce grouse perched on a stump or log with her brood spreading before her, quietly feeding among the blueberry plants. Female spruce grouse are careful and loyal mothers. At times they may brood the young for hours, acting as both stove and umbrella in the cold and rain without feeding themselves. Later when the brood moves and feeds, the mother remains constantly alert to dangers and gives vocal commands to freeze, upon appearance of an enemy, and assemble after its passage. The mother will attack a potential predator or distract it by a noisy "broken wing" display.

Some of the chicks do not live longer than the first few days after hatching, but the survivors grow and learn. They learn what is good to eat and what is not. They learn what they can land upon. In less than a week they can fly away from land-borne enemies.

The adult males molt as their male hormone levels decline with the long days of summer. Their virility falls off and so do their tail feathers. The males remain on their territories only halfheartedly defending them, but then there is no one to defend them against in these languid days. Occasionally, however, a male may feel stirrings of springtime surging through his blood, and the appearance of a female brings on a rather pathetic attempt at a display without a tail. But in late August, as the days grow shorter and new plumage grows in, the males are again ready for action.

It is now that the yearling males first assert themselves. Until late in their second summer most of these birds have assumed a position of neutrality. They have neither proclaimed territories as the adult males have nor laid eggs as the females have. The territorial males tolerated them, provided they kept out of the way, with their feathers meekly compressed against their bodies. But now in late summer these birds are ready to participate in the rivalry for territory and ultimately for mates. Most are no match for an experienced male territory-holder and so these young birds must take the vacant lots—those areas from which the original owner has died, or some less-than-choice terrain that remains unclaimed by the older males.

Autumn

Fall in Upper Michigan is the season of the hunter. In towns and cities the advertisements for food, beer, and used cars are designed to appeal to the sportsman. People on the streets are commonly dressed in hunting clothes, with the Michigan numbered back tag dangling between the shoulders. Hunting is a way of life in the Upper Peninsula.

On a typical October weekend perhaps ten automobiles an hour pass over the somewhat isolated Triple-A road which bisects the Yellow Dog Plains. This is heavy traffic for the Triple-A road. Most of those cars and trucks carry hunters, but few stop there; these are the road hunters who drive one or two hundred miles in a day, gun and ammunition carefully arranged for quick action whenever a grouse appears on the road ahead. Others do not stop because they recognize the unsuitability of the Yellow Dog Plains for their favorite target, the "partridge" or ruffed grouse. They drive on to hunt the mixed hardwood and conifer growth beyond the plains where ruffed grouse are more plentiful.

Thus most spruce grouse on the plains, because they seldom venture onto the Triple-A Road, are relatively safe from hunters. Their greatest human enemy, however, is the inexperienced woodsman, the hunter who often does not know good partridge habitat from bad, cannot tell one grouse from another, and may not care. I heard a report in

1966 of a group of rambunctious youngsters who shot seven spruce grouse, four of which were banded. When informed that their prize bag was made up not of ruffed grouse but of illegal spruce grouse, the boys disposed of all the evidence in a nearby ditch. But such occurrences are rare, and for the spruce grouse on the Yellow Dog Plains, hunting season itself does not present a major problem for survival.

Autumn, however, is a period of hardship for other reasons. Before the first snow covers the ground the spruce grouse digestive system must adapt to a diet of pine and spruce needles. The males must vigorously meet the challenges of establishing and defending territories. In crowded areas perhaps some are unsuccessful, and they may become social outcasts without suitable food or cover. They may succumb to predators or to disease. The adult females must recuperate from the consecutive physiological strains of laying, incubating, caring for their brood, and molting.

Spruce grouse are more gregarious in autumn than at other seasons, and flocks of a dozen or more birds are not uncommon. These flocks are made up of a mixture of ages and sexes, and of birds from different broods.

Winter

It was a crisp morning in January 1962. A male spruce grouse is perched on the snowy branch of a jack pine beside the Triple-A Road, comfortable with a crop full of freshly plucked pine needles. He hears the faint hum of a distant gasoline engine. Winter on the Yellow Dog Plains for many years has been a time of quiet and peacefulness. Even during the logging camp days when men stayed all winter they used relatively quiet hand saws and horses. And when they had moved out in the 1930s their noises left with them. Man's gasoline engine had not yet been adapted for propelling him over snow, and few men would come this far on snowshoes or skis. And so for nearly half of each year, from November until late April or early May, the only man-created sounds a spruce grouse would hear on the Plains were those of occasionally passing airplanes.

But this new sound growing louder and louder is not an airplane. The source is a strange machine which comes around the bend in the deeply snow-covered road. The noise is deafening as it passes beneath the branch of the tree, and the spruce grouse has to control his fright and overcome the urge to fly away. Two men are riding astride rather than inside the yellow and black machine. They shout to each other over the din of the engine and bring the machine to a stop just beyond the bird. One reaches into a packsack on the other's back, bringing out two silver, blue, and red cans which they pop open with a foaming hiss. As they drink the contents, they talk about how many miles they have come and how far they have to go. They discard the cans, which sink into the snow, start the clattering machine up again, and disappear around a bend. Behind them are left the odor of oil and gasoline, a bluish cloud of exhaust, a ribbon of packed snow, and two empty beer cans.

If a spruce grouse were capable of knowing man and his machines and if a spruce grouse could be dismayed, there was a dismayed spruce grouse that January day in 1962 when the first snowmobile came to the Yellow Dog Plains. The peace and solitude of winter were gone, perhaps forever.

I have never liked snowmobiles. They are greasy, smelly, and noisy. But we used a snowmobile to get us in and out of the Yellow Dog Plains for our studies and we fully deserve the disdain of those who prefer winter to be peaceful. During some winters the road was plowed to a point 8 miles from the study area and during others the plowed area stopped 11 miles away. Winter research was cold and inefficient work, what with short days and balky snowmobiles. We had no overnight facilities, so we traveled from Marquette each day.

In contrast to what it is for men, winter for spruce grouse on the Yellow Dog Plains is not a period of great hardship. The spruce grouse's digestive tract has become adapted to the diet of pure pine needles. The adult males maintain control over their territories without frequent challenges and without the strain of active courtship. At twilight, after the evening feeding period, the birds may burrow into the snow, which provides insulation against the heat-robbing subzero night air.

Perhaps it is periods of warm winter weather, rather than cold, that cause difficulties for spruce grouse. Thawing temperatures or a rare winter rain may cause a crust to form on the snow, preventing burrowing and depriving the birds of their blanket when the weather turns cold again. Hungry owls and goshawks must also be reckoned with, but such hazards are not peculiar to winter.

Some birds remain in small flocks and spend much time in the trees, moving infrequently and gaining weight. There is little for a spruce grouse to do in winter but eat and wait for spring.

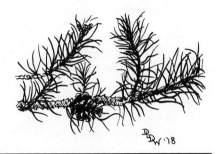

Chapter **5**

Habitat Requirements –
A Place in the Pines

The East

Spruce grouse find their general living requirements in the northern coniferous forest, but they are not uniformly distributed throughout the broad geographical expanse of evergreens. In some places they are rare or absent and in others they are numerous. What kind of habitat best satisfies their needs?

The literature provides a wide variety of answers to that question. Forbush (1927, pp. 24–25) in his *Birds of Massachusetts and Other New England States* described spruce grouse habitat as follows: "In the dense spruce, fir, cedar, and tamarack swamps of the great Maine woods the Spruce Grouse dwells. Where giant, moss-grown logs and stumps of the virgin forest of long ago cumber the ground, where tall, blasted stubs of others still project far above the tree-tops of today, where the thick carpet of green sphagnum moss deadens every footfall, where tiny-leaved vinelets radiate over their mossy beds, there we may find this wild bird as tame as a barnyard fowl."

That word picture painted by Forbush is so vivid it is hard to imagine a spruce grouse in any other habitat. Per-

45

haps in New England dense swampy forests are preferred. Forbush specifically noted that spruce grouse may also be found among firs, hemlocks, and other trees, but rarely in open meadows or clearings. Brewster (in Bent, 1932, p. 131) described the habitat in Maine as "dense matted growths of cedar (arbor vitae), black spruce and hackmatack (American larch)." Brewster pointed out, however (in Bent, 1932, pp. 131–132), that spruce grouse may "wander up neighboring hillsides . . . into neglected pastures choked with intermingling young balsams, red spruces, and white spruces no more than eight or ten feet tall." Other authors cited by Bent (1932, p. 132) note that in Maine the birds may be found "well out in rather wide upland clearings with thickets of raspberry bushes, or even in river- or brook-meadows . . ." They were also reported using lowlands with black ash, birches, and a few larches. In Nova Scotia, Tufts (1961) described spruce grouse habitat as burned-over ridges with "stunted new growth" intersected by wet sphagnum bogs thickly studded with spruce and tamarack.

It seems that in the northeast, wet lowlands are preferred but the birds also use adjacent high grounds. Farther west there seems to be a decreasing dependence on swamps, and an increasing preference for higher ground. In Ontario, Lumsden and Weeden (1963) noted that spruce grouse are found in boreal forests characterized by black spruce and jack pine, especially in places where stands of these two species meet. In Michigan, Barrows (1912, p. 223) described spruce grouse habitat as "spruce timber" and "spruce thickets, frequenting lower and moister lands than the Ruffed Grouse."

Ammann (1963) indicated that Michigan spruce grouse are more often associated with jack pines than with spruces. He lists four kinds of habitat in the state: (1) medium age to old age jack pines; (2) scattered old white spruces, interspersed with mixed young conifers and poplars; (3) medium-age mixed conifer-poplar-birch with scattered small openings; and (4) open bogs with scattered black spruces and tamaracks, interspersed with upland ridges and knolls with medium-age to old jack, red, and white pines.

Our own habitat analysis on the Yellow Dog Plains (Robinson, 1969), the details of which will be given later in this chapter, verifies Ammann's suggestion that jack pines are a favorite habitat and corroborates the Ontario workers' conclusion that a mixture of jack pines and spruces is preferred. Harold Miller (1967) spent time looking for spruce grouse on the Seney Refuge in eastern Upper Michigan. He was not finding many birds until we sent him a description of the jack pine–spruce habitat. He sought out such areas and thereafter had no trouble finding spruce grouse.

In Wisconsin, Grange (1948) gave the following description of spruce grouse habitat: "extensive conifer swamps," (p. 229) " climax or original coniferous forest," (p. 230) "spruce cedar and pine," (p. 231) and "coniferous trees often of the swampland species'" (p. 246). Grange seemed pessimistic about the bird's future in that state, since numbers were declining. Recently, however, I received a letter from David Backus, an ardent grouse hunter from Land O' Lakes, which lies on the Michigan line. He said that spruce grouse are hanging on in Wisconsin adjacent to Michigan. The habitat there seems much like the Yellow Dog Plains, with perhaps less spruce in proportion to jack pine.

Roberts (1936) paid extensive attention to the spruce grouse in his *Birds of Minnesota.* He describes (p. 369) a typical Minnesota haunt as "dense, dark, wet, spruce-tamarack-white-cedar swamps but . . . [the bird] may also be found on the uplands." He noted that in June and July the birds seldom remain in black spruce swamps, showing preference for higher ground covered with white spruces, balsams, and some mixed hardwood. Ground vegetation included sphagnum, Labrador tea, and leatherleaf in the lowlands. In the jack pine–spruce–fir habitat he found wintergreen, bearberry, pipsissewa, reindeer moss, true mosses, and a few sprigs of Labrador tea. Displaying males were found selecting areas of spruce and jack pine with open spaces 30 to 40 feet long by 12 to 20 feet wide.

The West

In Northern Manitoba, Fischer (in Roberts, 1936) found that spruce grouse preferred even-aged jack pine stands 15 to 20 feet tall.

Bent (1932) includes a few descriptions of spruce grouse habitat in Alaska. Here the coexistence of spruce trees and spruce grouse is emphasized. Ellison (1967, pp. 9–10) described Alaskan spruce grouse habitat as follows:

> Territories and activity centers were usually established in moderately dense spruce or spruce:birch stands averaging 40 to 60 feet tall. A few territories were located in very dense, lowland spruce stands where trees averaged 40 feet tall and were dense enough to make walking difficult for a man. Drumming flights were usually performed in small openings 20 to 40 feet in diameter within the above stands. Ground vegetation was always low, rarely exceeding 1.5 feet in height and commonly consisted of mosses, lichens, mountain cranberry, and blueberry.... Nonterritorial males were often located in upland spruce:birch stands to 80 feet tall and with dense understories of grass, alder, and devil's club, a vegetation type apparently not suitable for territories.

Habitat of Franklin's Grouse

Stoneberg (1967) found Franklin's spruce grouse in northwestern Montana on burned-over sites supporting lodgepole pine stands with some Engelmann spruce, subalpine fir, and some western larch in the understory. Stoneberg considered three zones of tree density in his study area, "open," "medium," and "thick." The terms "dense" "denser," and "densest" might have been more appropriate. His tree count ran from 435 to 2500 trees per acre in the "open" zone, to 2500 to 5000 in the "medium" zone, and up to 10,000 in the "thick" zone. Ten thousand trees per acre is about one every 4 square feet. That makes for hard walking.

Some low-growing shrubs grew among the lodgepole pines, including buffalo berry and huckleberries in the "open" zone, snowberry in the "medium" zone and both snowberry and thimbleberry in the "thick" zone. Bearberry and mountain lover grew in all stands.

Ken McCourt (1969) and Rory McLachlin (1970) studied Franklin's spruce grouse in the high foothills of the Canadian Rockies along the Sheep River southwest of Calgary. McCourt analysed the habitat and found that female spruce grouse seem to select cover containing lodgepole pine. Other species present included white spruce, small-toothed aspen, balsam poplar, and willow.

Yellow Dog Plains

On the Yellow Dog Plains we tried to analyse the sort of vegetation the spruce grouse preferred. In 1965 and 1966 we ran 20 randomly selected transects and picked random points along these lines. At each point we sampled trees by the random pairs method, a simple but clever technique devised by Cottam and Curtis (1956) of the University of Wisconsin. What it involves is standing on the sample point and facing the nearest tree. You record its species and diameter. Then, following simple rules, you pick a second tree behind you, record its species and diameter, measure the distance between the two trees, and go on to the next point. From this information you can get species composition, average diameters, and the number of trees per acre, if you sample enough points. We counted only trees larger than 4 inches in diameter at breast height. We also recorded the species, diameter, and height of the shrub or small tree nearest each sample point and noted the ground cover in a 2-foot-diameter circle around the point. We sampled 400 points. This was boring work, but the random pairs method has definite advantages over other sampling methods because you do not have to spend much time at one point, and this was especially important when the black flies and mosquitoes were biting.

Each time we saw a spruce grouse in 1965 and 1966 we went to the spot the grouse was standing on and sampled the vegetation, doing the same things we did at each random point. And so we had two sets of data, one from 400 random spots on the Plains as a whole and one from places where 215 birds had been found. By comparing the two sets of information we could tell what parts of the available habitat the birds selected.

Thirty-two percent of the 430 trees at sites where birds were seen were spruces (29 percent black and 3 percent white spruce), while spruces accounted for only 3 percent of the 800 randomly selected trees. This increase in the proportion of spruces where birds were found was accompanied by a decrease in jack pines. Jack pines constituted 90.5 percent of the trees on the Yellow Dog Plains as a whole but represented only 51 percent of the trees where we found birds. Thus the birds chose places where spruces were likely to be mixed with jack pines.

And there were other differences. Birds were found in areas averaging 134 trees per acre, while the habitat at large contained 181 trees per acre. In the shrub layer, young black spruces were found at 25 percent of the bird sites but only at 4 percent of the random points. Among the ground cover low sweet blueberry, logs and stumps, and trailing arbutus were more prevalent at bird sites than at the random sites. On the other hand, bracken ferns, grasses, and reindeer lichens were more abundant in the habitat as a whole than at spots where the grouse were seen.

Habitat Selection

Why do birds select certain kinds of vegetation to live in? What do they find there that they don't find elsewhere?

Selection of habitat relates to two basic requirements—food and cover—but recognition of appropriate habitat is primarily inherited rather than learned. At least it is with chipping sparrows, which is all we have to go on among birds at present.

Chipping sparrows normally forage on the ground, frequently near pines. Klopfer (1963) reared chipping sparrows from eggs in a laboratory, allowing them no exposure to their normal habitat. When given an equal choice of pine needles or oak leaves to walk upon, the birds spent 67 percent of their time on pine needles and 33 percent on the oak leaves. Captured wild birds, experienced in the ways of pines and oaks, spent 71 percent of their time on pine needles. But learning can play a role in influencing choice of habitat. Another group of chipping sparrows exposed only to oak leaves in the laboratory showed a slight preference for oak leaves. Similar experiments have been conducted with mammals, specifically the prairie deer mouse whose natural habitat is fields (Harris, 1952). Mice reared from birth in the laboratory showed a preference for field conditions over woodland conditions although the preference could be modified somewhat by exposing the young mice only to woodland conditions. It is likely that spruce grouse innately recognize and select the habitat that meets their requirements, and their early learning reinforces the appropriate choice.

Habitat and Cover Requirements

Proper habitat meets the needs of an animal for both food and cover. Cover provides both shelter from bad weather and concealment from predators. We found that mature stands of spruce or jack pine were not favored, despite their superior value as shelter from weather. In such stands, although the canopy is often closed, the lower limbs of the trees have died and fallen away. Often, except for bracken ferns, there is little concealing cover for birds at ground level. Younger stands of jack pine and sparser stands of older jack pines mixed with spruces include trees whose living branches still reach the ground. The foliage of these branches provides concealment, particularly from the horizontal line of sight, and in sparse stands still allows sufficient room for flight. We found adult birds and broods generally using the same cover.

The sphagnum bog which covers the southwestern edge of our study area was frequented by spruce grouse, but while there they spent little time on the ground, which was frequently sodden and covered with dense growth of knee-high sedges. Young broods seldom ventured onto the bog. Islands and points of higher, dryer ground extending into the bog, however, were used frequently. It was my impression that spruce grouse usually avoided low dense cover, such as sedges and bracken ferns which permit them very limited visibility.

In winter the ground cover is snow and the diet of spruce grouse is nearly 100 percent jack pine needles. The birds are more widely distributed, they are often in flocks, and they spend little time on the snow. For these reasons they were hard to find. Instead of searching a plane surface we had to scan the trees. But a few tell-tale tracks in the snow and a dog with a good nose helped. In winter we commonly found birds out on the bog and sometimes in jack pine stands where the ground cover in summer would not have been right for them.

The composition of trees in winter habitat, based on 44 sightings, was 85 percent jack pine and 15 percent black spruce. This compares with summer habitat of 51 percent jack pine and 32 percent spruce. Probably the more arboreal habits of birds in the winter made the foliage on the living low branches of spruces less important. Also, their winter food of jack pine needles probably played a role in their selection of jack pines. The trees were denser where we found the birds in winter, averaging 336 trees per acre, compared with only 134 trees per acre in summer habitat. But talking about trees per acre is misleading here. It might suggest large tracts of trees of different densities, with the birds migrating from sparse tracts to dense ones as the snow comes. Such is not the case. Most of the birds did not move very far between seasons. They would simply more often use the denser clumps of trees present in their home range during the winter.

Habitat and Food Requirements

The spruce grouse finds its food plentiful within its winter shelter on the Yellow Dog Plains. We watched birds feed steadily just before sunset without leaving a single tree. Twenty birds we saw feeding in winter ate only jack pine needles. We examined three crops from accidentally killed birds in winter, and jack pine needles were the only food item we found. This is consistent with the findings of Crichton (1963), who analysed crops of birds from Ontario, where the habitat is similar to the Yellow Dog Plains (Lumsden and Weeden, 1963). Crichton found winter spruce grouse crops to contain 99.9 percent jack pine needles and 0.1 percent spruce needles. Pendergast and Boag (1970) found Alberta spruce grouse to consume 99 percent pine needles and 1 percent spruce needles in winter. Margaret Herman (personal communication) has found Franklin's spruce grouse in Montana commonly eating ponderosa pine needles. This is unusual because the ponderosa pine has needles 4 to 6 inches long, and most researchers have found that spruce grouse feed nearly exclusively on short-needled conifers.

During the seasons when snow is gone, spruce grouse have a more varied diet. We analysed no crops but observed the birds eating the following plants in approximately descending order of importance: leaves and fruits of blueberries, leaves of cowwheat, seeds of grasses, insects, and needles of jack pine and black spruce.

In Ontario, Crichton (1963), analysing spruce grouse crop contents, found that from September until snowfall the birds ate about 50 percent by volume of jack pine needles, 36 percent tamarack needles, 8 percent blueberry leaves, and the rest a variety of materials, including fungi, black spruce needles, and mountain ash berries.

Ellison (1966) analysed 237 spruce grouse crops from Alaska taken at all seasons of the year. In spring the birds ate spruce needles, blueberry leaves, last year's cranberries, oxytrope leaves, crowberries, and lichen apothecia. In summer predominant foods included cranberries, blueberries, and horsetail stems and tips. The birds ate few spruce needles in summer. In September and October they turned increasingly to spruce needles but also ate large amounts of cranberries. They also ate blueberry fruits and leaves, bearberries and horsetail tips and stems.

Pendergast and Boag (1970) found that spruce grouse in the summer in central Alberta commonly eat, in addition to the usual lodgepole pine and a few spruce needles, leaves, flowers and fruit of bilberries and cranberries, fruits of blueberries, seeds of sedges, some unidentified fungi, the spore cases of mosses, flowers and berries of white mandarin, and tips and stems of horsetail.

In both the Alaska and Alberta studies the consumption of conifer needles by spruce grouse fell to nearly zero in July. But by September the birds turn gradually away from foraging on the ground and take to feeding upon needles in the trees (Keppie, 1977). Autumn snowfalls encourage their arboreal feeding habits, but Keppie observed that by November spruce grouse in New Brunswick were feeding nearly entirely on needles, even though the ground was not yet covered by snow.

Jonkel and Greer (1963) examined 56 Franklin's spruce grouse crops collected in northwestern Montana in September and October. Over 60 percent of the diet was conifer needles, principally western larch (39 percent), with the rest distributed among lodgepole pine, fir, and Engelmann spruce. The rest of the vegetable diet consisted primarily of fruits of white mandarin (4 percent), blueberries (4 percent), and snowberries (4 percent). Insects constituted a surprisingly large proportion (over 12 percent) of the diet of the Montana birds. The bulk of this was grasshoppers, but they were apparently found in only a few crops.

In northern Washington, as in Montana, spruce grouse in the fall eat a variety of items. Twenty-nine different genera of plants were found by Zwickel, Boag, and Brigham (1974) in crops of 113 spruce grouse taken by hunters in north-central Washington. This observation led Zwickel and his co-workers to suggest that spruce grouse occupying the western mountains find and eat a greater diversity of foods than those of the more monotonous eastern coniferous forests.

In all of the food habits studies of adult birds, except for Jonkel and Greer's, insects constituted less than 1 percent of the diet even during the season when they were available.

The only work that I have seen on the diet of young spruce grouse is that of Pendergast and Boag (1970) from Alberta. As expected, insects, with their high protein content, play a much more important role in the diet of chicks than in that of adults. Pendergast and Boag found three chicks less than a week old which had consumed only arthropods. In July, 88 percent of the crops of birds in their first month and a half of life contained insects, in August, 50 percent, and in September, 28 percent. Cranberry and blueberry fruits, flowers and leaves, horsetail stems and tips, and sedge seeds also played an important role in the diet of the rapidly growing young birds. Our own observations showed that aphids, ants, blackflies, leaves and fruits of blueberries, leaves of cow wheat, seeds of grasses, and young leaves of bracken fern were eaten by the young birds. We could occasionally get a recently captured young grouse to eat black flies and deer flies while we held it in our hand.

Young birds in Alberta did not begin eating conifer needles until September and not in quantities until October and November. Grit was quite common in the crops of young birds throughout the summer.

Many birds eat small stones, which presumably aid in grinding food in the gizzard. Leopold (1933) cited evidence that red grouse populations in Scotland could be increased by providing quartz grit. Sadler (1961) showed that pheasants obtain minerals from grit, and Pendergast (1969) believed spruce grouse do too. But studies showed that generally less than half of the spruce grouse crops examined in months without snow contained grit (Crichton, 1963; Jonkel and Greer, 1963; Ellison, 1966; Pendergast and Boag, 1970). Grit was most prevalent in October both in Alaska (Ellison, 1966) and Alberta (Pendergast and Boag, 1970).

In Alaska, Alberta, and Ontario, it is common for spruce grouse to seek grit on gravel roads, and during hunting seasons this habit turns out to be fatal for many of them (Ellison, 1974; Lumsden and Weeden, 1963). On the Yellow Dog Plains spruce grouse did not often appear on roads at any season. If they needed grit, it was available during snow-free seasons throughout the area, where the sandy-gravelly soil is commonly exposed by roots of fallen trees and by diggings of various mammals. It is also possible that de-icing salts applied to roads in Alaska, Alberta, and Ontario may provide a mineral attraction for roadside grit that is not present on the Yellow Dog Plains.

Whether or not the amount and quality of food available to spruce grouse in their habitat is an important factor in governing their numbers will be discussed in Chapter 13. Pendergast and Boag (1970), however, suggest that spruce grouse effectively utilize foods available in their habitat and that they do not experience food shortages.

To summarize the general findings of the studies of food and cover selection, the following prescription for habitat seems appropriate for spruce grouse wherever they are found: A good supply of conifer needles, particularly those of jack pine, lodgepole pine, and/or spruces; abundant plants of the genus *Vaccinium,* namely blueberries, cranberries and/or bilberries, with leaves, fruits, and flowers of all of these serving as food; insects for the youngsters; perhaps a scattering of other local plants thrown in, and, for luxury, a supply of fine mineral-rich gravel. All this should be found in a primarily coniferous forest which contains some trees with live branches extending to the ground, a sparse ground cover, and an arrangement of trees in such a way that openings of a few hundred square feet are scattered commonly about. A spruce grouse could ask for little more in life, except perhaps for a little peace and quiet.

Ruffed Grouse Versus Spruce Grouse Cover and
Food on the Yellow Dog Plains

In Michigan the ruffed grouse is the most widespread and
abundant member of the grouse family. It outnumbers the
spruce grouse by at least 100 to 1. But on the Yellow Dog Plains
the spruce grouse prevails. During the summers of 1965–70
we made 652 sightings of spruce grouse and only 25 of ruffed
grouse. Along the edges of the plains, Jon Springer studied
habitat of ruffed grouse. He and his assistants in 1966 and
1967 made 118 sightings of ruffed grouse to only 4 of spruce
grouse. There was practically no overlap in habitat of the two
species. Jon kept vegetation records at each ruffed grouse location and we compared his data with similar data collected at
spruce grouse sites. Ruffed grouse sites contained 57 percent
conifers and 43 percent deciduous trees, including red maples,
white birch, quaking aspen, and sugar maple. On the other
hand, spruce grouse were found at sites with 96 percent conifers and only 4 percent deciduous trees.

In winter some ruffed grouse moved into the coniferous
cover of the Yellow Dog Plains. Such behavior is not surprising. Lewis et al. (1968) cited nine references substantiating
the choice of evergreen cover by ruffed grouse in winter. On
the Yellow Dog Plains the number of ruffed grouse to
spruce grouse seen in winter was 12 to 57, for a ratio of
about 1 to 5. During spring, summer, and fall the ratio was
25 to 652 or about 1 to 26. Ruffed grouse found shelter on
the Yellow Dog Plains but had a hard time finding food.
They normally feed upon buds of aspens, birches, and
maples in the winter (Bump et al., 1947; Svoboda and Gullion, 1972), but these trees were not plentiful on the Yellow
Dog Plains. On February 14, 1968, I followed the tracks of a
ruffed grouse that had recently been feeding on buds of
available deciduous shrubs and small trees on the Yellow
Dog Plains. I examined each plant visited and counted the
number of buds removed by the bird. I also measured the
distance the grouse walked between bushes (Fig. 6). The bird
visited 56 different shrubs, averaging 22 feet between them.
It ate a total of 291 buds, averaging 5.3 per stop. Fifty of the

Figure 6. A ruffed grouse wintering on the Yellow Dog Plains must travel a considerable distance to obtain buds of deciduous shrubs.

shrubs were serviceberry, four were red maple, and two were willow. This bird seemed to spend a lot of energy going from one plant to the next. And what is more, in a single feeding the bird removed 80 to 90 percent of the available terminal buds, which it preferred over lateral buds, and thus severely depleted its food supply over about half an acre. Svoboda and Gullion (1972) described how ruffed grouse in Minnesota could get a complete meal of their favorite and most nutritious food, male aspen flower buds, in a period of less than 30 minutes from a few trees. It is small wonder that the ruffed grouse is not abundant on the Yellow Dog Plains.

Chapter 6

General Behavior

The most striking feature of the behavior of both sexes of the spruce grouse is lack of concern for man as a potential enemy. In books and articles written primarily for hunters the word "stupid" is frequently used to describe this trait, but in literature for bird lovers the word "trusting" is applied. A hunter would apparently not have very deep regrets for shooting a "stupid" bird, but he might feel guilty about shooting one that trusts him. Hjorth (1970) says that only the white-tailed ptarmigan "is more tame to man."

A few examples might serve to illustrate the casual attitude of spruce grouse toward humans. On July 13, 1970, I was conducting a field trip for 30 people enrolled in a summer course at Michigan Technological University. We located a female with her single 3-week-old chick. I captured the mother grouse from a tree with a noose at the end of a 15-foot pole. She fluttered and twisted as she came down, and we untangled her amid the tumult of 30 eager people milling about taking pictures, making jokes, and petting the bird. About 5 minutes later, with the captive mother grouse still in my hand, one of the students held a whole blueberry plant out to her. She obligingly looked it over and picked and ate three or four ripe berries, leaving green ones and leaves alone.

Frequently, recently captured chicks of various ages have eagerly devoured black flies or deer flies that landed on our hands while we were holding the chicks. Perhaps it was cheating somewhat, but by using a tape-recorded call of a female and a stuffed spruce grouse we have often lured a male into a circle, about 20 feet in diameter, of camera-snapping people, and sometimes we could catch the bird in our hands.

Tom Mussehl, a Montana biologist, told me how one day he spotted a male Franklin's spruce grouse on the snow beside the road. He stepped out and noosed the bird and put it into a box in his car. An hour later he released the grouse in a cage at the University of Montana. The bird stepped out of the box, walked about 3 feet, spotted some red berries there, and casually began to feed on them.

I should not give the impression, however, that all spruce grouse are quite so docile. Jerry McGowan, a biologist from Alaska who visited the Yellow Dog Plains with us, believes that the Alaskan birds are more wary than the Michigan birds. It is possible that pressure from hunters in Alaska makes the birds more cautious through learning or selection for the genetically more wary birds. There were a few individual spruce grouse on our study area that were not cooperative. It took us five or six encounters over two summers before we finally captured one particularly wary male in a mist net.

Although spruce grouse show little fear of man, the same is not true of other potential predators. When my Springer spaniel, Mandy, accompanied us, the birds would seem to flush wilder, and once in a tree they would pay little attention to people but would carefully watch every move Mandy made. It was usually necessary to remove the dog from sight before we could capture a bird.

On two occasions grouse frightened by avian predators came to my feet and cowered. On May 4, 1967, I was slowly pursuing an adult hen on the ground near the edge of the bog. She was keeping about a 20-foot distance, just out of reach of my noose pole. Suddenly a barred owl appeared, flying along the bog about 100 feet away. The spruce grouse I was trying to capture scurried quickly toward me and crouched on the ground about 4 feet from me. On another occasion an adult male behaved similarly, apparently preferring to take its chances with me rather than risk capture by a bird of prey which it had spotted but which I never saw. Prawdzik (1963) related a similar occurrence with a ruffed grouse escaping a Cooper's hawk. In that case, however, the grouse burrowed into the snow close to Prawdzik's feet, and allowed itself to be repeatedly caught by him.

How can the tameness of the spruce grouse toward man be explained? Our measurements of the physiology of this bird, discussed in Chapter 10, may shed some light on this subject.

Many grouse have developed the habit of burrowing into the snow. This is apparently an adaptation which takes advantage of the insulating capacity of the snow and conserves metabolic energy for the grouse. Formozov (1946) reported that black grouse confronted by a combination of snow too shallow to burrow into and cold temperatures suffer mortality. He also noted that hazel grouse in cold periods may spend 21 or 22 hours of the day in a snow roost.

I was surprised to learn from other biologists that spruce grouse in Alberta, Montana, and New Brunswick do not tunnel through the snow, although Larry Ellison has told me that Alaskan spruce grouse burrow as our Michigan birds do. I assume that these subnivean roosts are used at night, as with ruffed grouse, but I am not certain.

On February 14, 1968, I examined and measured a few spruce grouse snow roosts. A typical roost is dug in a small opening, at least 8 to 10 feet from trees. This is probably to facilitate a quick escape. In case the roosting bird must make a quick and blind exit from the snow to escape a predator, it does not have to concern itself with immediately crashing into a tree. Some snow roosts consist simply of an entrance hole and an exit hole a foot or two apart, or simply a single pocket. I measured one such pocket. It was 8 inches deep, 9 inches long, and 6 inches wide, and contained a large pile of droppings at the bottom. Other roosts are somewhat extended, and have an open roof alternating with a burrow. Two such roosts are illustrated in Figure 7. Formozov (1946) claims that the holes in the roof are made by the bird's periodically thrusting its head out. At the time these roosts were measured, the total snow depth was 32 inches.

A crust on the snow may prevent birds from burrowing. An old male bird we called Limpy (for reasons we will come to shortly) used the low-hanging branches of a spruce tree frequently, judging from the deep pile of droppings beneath it. The possible influence of a snow crust on survival and reproduction of spruce grouse will be considered in Chapter 13.

Figure 7. Spruce grouse on the Yellow Dog Plains sometimes tunnel beneath the snow.

Chapter 7

Behavior of Male Spruce Grouse

Harold J. Harju, coauthor

Territories

Adult male spruce grouse defend a piece of property against other adult males. The defended area is called a territory, according to the widely accepted definition of Noble (1939). A male remains on his territory, a relatively small area, practically continuously and within it finds all his requirements for living, including food, a place for displaying, and in season, occasional visits from females with which he may breed.

Of what value to the spruce grouse is claiming and defending a territory? Wynne-Edwards (1962) proposes that territorial defense is a means of spacing birds in the habitat and that a territory-owner claims sufficient resources to permit him, his mate, and offspring to live in relative prosperity. Non–territory-holders fail to reproduce, thus reducing the strain of overpopulation and undue competition for resources from others of the same species.

This would work for monogamous birds, and it apparently does for the monogamous red grouse in Scotland (Jenkins et al., 1963). But spruce grouse are polygamous. Every female can find a male and every male will mate with more than one female if he has the opportunity. The females do the egg-laying and rearing of the brood. Even if nonterritorial males did not breed, this would not control reproduction. Thus, as Lack (1966), McCourt (1969), McLachlin (1970), and Ellison (1972) point out, territory probably serves to space out the males to increase the probability of breeding success for a female, both by enabling her to locate a male and by allowing copulation to proceed without undue physical interference from competing suitors. Territorial defense by the males does not seem to control reproduction.

There are two approaches to studying territory. One is to watch the land and record the comings and goings of different owners, a sort of registration of deeds. The second is to watch the birds to see where they go and where they settle down. We used both approaches.

As Chapter 2 recounted in describing the Yellow Dog Plains, a fire in the late 1940s burned a crooked swath ranging from a few yards to 200 yards wide along the edge of the bog. By the 1960s this swath was covered with a growth of jack pines 15 to 25 feet tall, mixed with some black spruces on the wet rim of the bog. The marsh or bog with its scattered clumps of jack pines was used only irregularly by the birds, and on the upland side of the burned area the jack pines were too mature to provide good cover. A few birds used them until 1968, when they were clear-cut, after which the grouse cover was restricted to a strip about 1000 yards long and averaging about 40 yards wide, bounded on the uplands to the northeast by a broad clearing and on the southwest by the bog with its marginal habitat.

A passable two-rut road entered the northwest end of this ribbon of cover and terminated in a triangular clearing measuring about 75 × 75 × 40 feet. In this small clearing the growth of blueberry plants had been suppressed by occasional automobiles turning around. From this clearing the fire crews in the 40s had made a fire lane and road, exposing the sandy and gravelly soil. By the 1960s the soil on the fire lane leading into the jack pines had not yet been overgrown and was covered only with dead needles. This area appeared to be especially attractive to male spruce grouse seeking a territory; indeed, fatally so. From 1965 through 1973 we saw seven different birds lay claim to that choice piece of real estate, and after each tenure the owner was never seen again. We called the turnaround spot at the end of this road "Dead End." Following is a synopsis of events at Dead End territory.

In May 1965 we banded a vigorously strutting male there and never saw him again. The Dead End territory seemed to remain vacant in 1966 but on May 4, 1967, we found a displaying two-year-old there. This bird had been banded as a chick with its mother 3 miles to the east in 1965 and hadn't been seen at all in 1966. He held the territory through two breeding seasons, during which time he was seen within 100 yards of Dead End ten times and nowhere else. In mid-June of 1968 he disappeared, taking our radio transmitter with him.

By November 3, 1968, a new owner had moved in. This bird had been seen twice—once in May 1968, 300 yards southeast of Dead End with another male and two females. His neutral behavior at that time suggested that he was a yearling. He was seen again on August 9, 1968, a mile west of there. When we found him at Dead End on November 3 he was displaying, and we found him there again on February 7, 1969. He was never seen again.

On May 26, 1969, the territory was being claimed by another bird, a handsome fellow with blue and yellow bands. We also had some data on this bird's prior wanderings. He had been seen twice in July and August 1968 at a location about two-thirds of a mile northwest of Dead End, in what we regarded as less than ideal cover—the jack pines were too mature and ground cover too tall. The bird's

A strutting male spreads his neck feathers, presenting a cobra-like effect.

Richard P. Smith

pointed outer primary feathers in early July suggested that he was a yearling in 1968 (Ellison, 1968a). Beginning in May 1969 we saw this bird nine times at all seasons within 100 yards of Dead End and saw him nowhere else. We got to know him well. In May 1970 we took movies of him displaying and frustratedly attempting to mate with our stuffed female spruce grouse.

But on October 16, 1970, a new, unbanded male appeared displaying at Dead End, and we suspected that the bird with the blue and yellow bands was dead after a year and a half's tenure. Eight days later Mandy found his decomposing remains about 10 feet from the edge of Dead End clearing. The intact skeleton and the season of the year suggested that a hunter had shot him and discarded the carcass. And as soon as his territory was vacant, a new bird had moved in.

This new bird was seen only twice, both times in the fall of 1970, although by now our trips to the study area were becoming infrequent. After 1970 he was never seen again.

Then in early May 1971 another male was laying claim to the Dead End territory. We banded him and saw him there five times in spring, summer, and fall, through July 1973.

These were not the only male spruce grouse we saw near Dead End, but they were the only ones that strutted and displayed, with the exception of one instance to be described later. During the period from May 1965 through July 1973 we saw 20 other males in adult plumage within 200 yards of Dead End. Three of these were adult male holders of adjacent territories and seen only at the fringe of the Dead End territory, three were known to be yearlings, one was known to be a bird in its first autumn, and the rest were probably itinerant juvenile or yearling birds. Wandering male spruce grouse were also commonly observed in Alaska by Ellison (1971) and in Alberta by McLachlin (1970).

Southeast of Dead End in the remaining 800 yards of the ribbon of young jack pines there were two other territories. On August 2, 1966, we encountered an unbanded male, which we judged to be a yearling, 250 yards southeast of Dead End. This bird was subsequently seen 17 times, all within 100 yards of that spot, through October 5, 1972. He was seen once out in the bog but all the other times was on dry ground along its edge. This bird lived somewhat over 7 years, and once he established his territory at age 1½ he apparently never left it.

Just beyond and to the southeast a third bird held claim to a territory from May 1968 through May 1971. This bird ranged from 300 yards to 600 yards southeast of Dead End. The bird had been banded as a chick on July 12, 1965, about a mile and a quarter to the northwest, and had not been seen again until he was nearly 3 years old, when he established his territory along the edge of the bog. He lived over 6 years.

The observations made on territory-holders along the ribbon of jack pines near Dead End invite interpretations. First, the territory located right at Dead End seemed to generate a higher than normal mortality for its owners. While the adjacent territory was held for over 6 years by the same bird and the next adjacent one for over 3 years, the Dead End territory had seven owners in 8 years. It is not likely that the birds moved out. None was ever seen alive again, and our observations of other territory-holders indicate that once a territory is established it is claimed for life.

We believe the Dead End site was especially attractive for territorial males because of its generally suitable habitat of young jack pines and spruces, sparse, low-growing cover, and a small clearing which served as a suitable display arena. A perch about 8 feet high on a specific jack pine branch was favored by most of the territory-holders for display. The danger in this territory, however, may also have lain in the clearing. This was a place where hunters exploring new terrain would stop their cars, turn about, and perhaps get out to look around. A spruce grouse defending his territory against a Chevy pick-up could be rudely answered with a load of bird shot. A small glacial mound immediately to the west of the Dead End clearing rises above the surrounding terrain and for this reason may be attractive as a perching place for hawks and owls which might have found a meal available in the form of a strutting spruce grouse. We found remains of a banded nonterritorial male there, apparently killed by a raptor.

Although two adjacent territories may not have had as attractive an arena for display, they also did not possess the enticements to enemies that Dead End did, and thus may have ensured their owners a longer life.

These three territories also gave us an idea of the size of territories. Each of the three territories extended about 200 to 300 yards along the edge of the marsh. With an average width of about 40 yards, territory size was roughly 1.6 to 4.2 acres. These seem to be on the small side for spruce grouse territories. For Franklin's spruce grouse Stoneberg (1967) found male home ranges of 3.0 to 14.8 acres and McLachlin (1970) found a range of 1.2 to 20.7 acres. In Alaska, Ellison (1971) found spruce grouse territories of 2.5 to 34.6 acres.

As a matter of fact the territories of males along the marsh edge near Dead End were smaller than those in other parts of our study area, where good habitat surrounded the birds on all sides. The average size of territories of five marsh edge dwellers was 3.0 acres, while that of seven males seen six or more times on other parts of the study area was 19.1 acres (Table 2). Our large territory sizes compared quite closely with those of spruce grouse in Alberta (McLachlin, 1970) and Alaska (Ellison, 1971).

The edge of the marsh apparently inhibited movements of male spruce grouse. Population densities were at least as high along the Pinnacle Falls Road, and so population pressures probably were not responsible for the small territory sizes on the edge of the bog. McLachlin (1970) noted that visible ecological barriers such as streams and roads may form boundaries of territories. This is apparently the case on the Yellow Dog Plains.

Territory is defined as a defended area, and home range is defined as the area in which an animal spends most of its time. McLachlin (1970) believed that during the period

Table 2. Estimated size of territories of male spruce grouse on the Yellow Dog Plains (only birds with six or more sightings are included)

Bird number	Number of sightings	Acres
	Along bog edge	
65–3	7	6.2
65–87	9	1.5
66–54a	18	1.7
68–20	9	1.5
68–71	7	4.2
Average	10.0	3.0 ± 1.0^a
	In broad habitat	
65–27	9	20.5
65–73	6	9.9
66–8	27	18.5
66–12	9	18.3
66–13	6	18.5
66–47	12	24.7
68–34	6	23.2
Average	10.7	19.1 ± 1.8^a

[a] Mean ± standard error.

from mid-May to mid-September the two are synonymous for adult male Franklin's grouse in the Alberta mountains. We believe the same holds true virtually year round for adult male spruce grouse on the Yellow Dog Plains. Of five males for which we had made six or more sightings, including at least one winter (November 1–March 31) sighting, four were found within their summer territory in the winter. The fifth bird was located in January about 200 yards from his summer range, to which he returned by the following May. Margaret Herman (personal communication) found that spruce grouse in the mountains of Montana regularly move 2 to 3 miles between summer and winter range.

While some male birds are strongly attached to a territory and seldom if ever leave it, others seem to be wanderers. Most wanderers appear to be young birds, but not all young birds are wanderers. Ellison (1971) found some yearlings displaying on territories in their first spring. He suggested that there is a whole range of territorial behavior among the male spruce grouse population, from that of the intense compact territory holders such as we found along the marsh at Dead End to that of the more-or-less nomadic individuals wandering over a few square miles of the habitat. Increasing maturity probably influences a bird toward the more stable and sedentary existence of a small territory.

Courtship and Territorial Displays

When spring comes to the Yellow Dog Plains a male spruce grouse is a feathered bundle of sex hormones begging to express themselves. The hormones are calling for two actions—other males must be repelled and females must be attracted and mated with. But at the same time a myriad of external stimuli play upon the sex drives, which must not override the basic instinct for self-preservation. Sunshine, rain, snow, wind, the sound of another male, the sight, posture, and sound of a female, the time of day, hunger, and perhaps the memory of a recent escape from a

A territorial male spruce grouse climaxes a display sequence by spreading his tail fully for a brief moment and uttering a high-pitched "shik-sheek."

Richard P. Smith

goshawk may all interact to influence the sort of posture and activity the bird engages in. And so what comes out of this bundle of feathers is a kaleidoscopic array of behavior patterns containing a number of common identifiable elements but without entirely predictable sequence or composition. Thus our interpretations of what spruce grouse are communicating to each other through their displays, utterings, and rattlings are probably extreme simplifications. The following descriptions and interpretations will warrant revisions as methods of studying behavior become more sophisticated. Because the displays of male spruce grouse have been reported quite thoroughly by other authors (Lumsden, 1961; MacDonald, 1968; Hjorth, 1970) we shall describe them only briefly here.

Puffing up or "Oblique" Posture

The lowest intensity of display by a male is erecting the body and tail feathers and the combs. This was often brought about upon first sight of a spruce grouse of either sex or upon detection of any disturbance. Puffing-up generally preceded any other display.

Ground or Branch Pecking

Pecking decisively at the ground or a branch often follows the puffing-up display, and seems to be the next step
in a gradient of increasing intensity of display.

Strutting with Tail-swishing
and the Challenge Note or "Squeak Call"

This performance usually starts slowly, the tail opening
on alternate sides, gradually increasing in tempo until it
ends 5 to 10 seconds later with a full spread of the tail
done twice quickly and simultaneously accompanied by a
high-pitched double vocal squeak. We considered this to be
a "challenge" note, It was frequently made at us, as well as
at other spruce grouse of both sexes. It seemed to be associated both with territorial defense and with courtship.
The challenge note was sometimes given without strutting
beforehand but always with the double spread of the tail.

The Head Jerk

Upon approaching within a few feet of a female, the
male crouches down, puffed up with his combs fully inflated and brilliant. He twists his head jerkily back and
forth about 10 times in 3 or 4 seconds. This presents his
scarlet combs to good advantage, especially if viewed from
the front, where they contrast against the dark tail. The
head jerk is apparently designed to break down any final
resistance the female may be demonstrating. It does not always work, however. The head jerk appears to be entirely
sexual, as we have seen males do it only when a female is
present.

Threat Call

This is a deep-pitched throaty rattle, which Hjorth has
termed the "throaty hissing cantus." This sound is uttered
over a period of 2 to 3 seconds with an initial quick note,
followed by a longer one of about half a second, then
gradually shorter ones accelerating to a rate of about 7 to 9
per second. We heard males utter this call only in the pres-

ence of other males or in response to recorded male sounds. According to Welty (1975), this is the lowest-pitched vocal sound made by any bird, having a frequency of about 80 cycles per second, about E just below the bass clef in musical notation.

Drumming While Standing

The male spruce grouse occasionally performs a quiet and abbreviated version of drumming such as the ruffed grouse does. We watched birds while standing make two wing strokes, each producing an audible thump. Franklin's grouse make three or four strokes (MacDonald, 1968). Our motion pictures of one bird show two wingbeats given in 0.40 seconds. We have seen spruce grouse do the standing drum between drumming flights when other males are in the vicinity, and also when courting a female at a range of about 15 feet.

Drumming Flight

The behavior of a male spruce grouse performing his drumming flight near the Pinnacle Falls Road in 1967 was described in Chapter 4. The drumming flight, because of its dramatic nature, is one aspect of the biology of spruce grouse that has been reported by many observers. The drumming flight of a spruce grouse does not produce the volume of sound that a drumming ruffed grouse does, being audible to a human at a range of only about 100 yards under good conditions. A ruffed grouse can be heard for a distance of up to 1 mile (Bump et al. 1947). Several accounts have been reviewed by Hjorth (1970), describing a number of variations in the drumming flight of the spruce grouse. These include:

a) beating the wings rapidly (drumming) on an ascending flight and descending quietly;

b) drumming at the top of a flight, about 14 feet high, with ascent and descent quite normal;

c) flying from a branch, descending a bit, drumming, then ascending to another branch;

d) drumming in an ascending flight, spiraling three or
four times around the trunk of a tree, and landing
on a branch 20 feet up;

e) descending from a branch until 4 to 6 feet above the
ground, then swinging into a nearly vertical position
with tail spread, and descending on drumming
wings to the ground.

The latter, along with the reverse of it, that is, flying
upward to a limb and drumming while descending a foot
or two onto a limb, were the only types of drumming
flights which we saw on the Yellow Dog Plains. In observations of perhaps 50 different males we never saw any
fancy spiraling or dipping between branches. It is possible
that the differences in drumming flights seen by different
reporters could be variations invented by individual birds,
but it is also possible that they could represent regional
"dialects" in the visual language of the birds.

The Franklin's spruce grouse of the Rocky Mountains
definitely speaks its own dialect in its drumming flight. A
male, upon descending from a branch, produces a loud
double clap in flight by striking his wings together above
his back. This seems to be the most notable difference between the displays of the Franklin's grouse and those of the
other race or races of spruce grouse (MacDonald, 1968;
Stoneberg, 1967; McLachlin, 1970).

We believe that the drumming flight is used primarily as advertisement, both for territorial defense and for attracting a
female that is not in sight. Once in mid-June we watched a male
and female feeding and resting together, with the male sometimes strutting and head-jerking for the female. After a few
hours she suddenly flew away. A few seconds later the male
flew in the same direction. Unable to locate her, he began a
near-frantic series of drumming flights in a vain attempt to
woo her back. We frequently also observed drumming flights
in response to the presence of other males and to the recorded
sounds of both males and females. But a drumming flight just
did not seem to be the thing for a male to do when he was alone
with a female on his territory.

Fighting

We saw several fights between males on the Yellow Dog Plains. Stoneberg (1967), MacDonald (1968), and McLachlin (1970) observed Franklin's spruce grouse fighting. As is usually the case, no fatalities or serious injuries to the combatants occurred. An occasional lost feather and deflated pride seemed to be the only immediate consequences of defeat.

The fights we saw on the Yellow Dog Plains have been described in the following account:

Usually if both birds are on the ground and neither retreats, they fight after uttering several threat calls. In fighting, the birds circle each other, maintaining a distance of about five to ten feet. Finally one, usually the resident male, makes a rush at the other, his neck extended forward and wings out to the sides, tips nearly touching the ground. This often causes the intruder to flee. If it doesn't, the two males rush at and attempt to strike each other. Sometimes the two will fly or leap a few inches into the air before coming together. In such cases the beak, feet, and wings are all used to strike each other. When two or more males compete for a female they may attack each other from the strutting posture. Such attacks are usually flight attacks. It may take several flight-attacks to cause a sexually aroused intruder to flee. (Harju, 1969, pp. 26, 29)

Stoneberg (1967) noted that the attacks of a male Franklin's grouse were directed toward the head and breast of a mounted male. Our mounted male was decapitated after several attacks by males. Lumsden (1961) felt that the red combs on an intruder were important in releasing an attack, and indeed both McLachlin (1970) and Stoneberg found that the attacking bird concentrated his attack on the combs and head region, not giving up until feathers, combs, and skin had been removed, even though the defenseless stuffed bird had been knocked on its side. This suggests that spruce grouse which retreat early in combat are probably behaving quite sensibly.

One tape recorder, with which we played grouse calls to the males, was rectangular, measuring 2.5 × 4.5 × 8 inches. It was black and gray with a bright red cylindrical "stop" button located near one end. When we left the tape recorder playing on a territory for 3 to 10 minutes, the territory-owner would occasionally attack the machine, invariably pecking the red button first. A newer machine, the same size but a gray-brown color and with an orange rather than red button failed to induce similar attacks, although it played the same tapes. It is likely that the red combs serve to release the pecking behavior in an attack (much as the red feathers of the breast of the European robin release the attack response by other males of the same species [Lack, 1943]), provided there are other clues, such as sounds suggesting the presence of another spruce grouse.

Many disputes between adult male spruce grouse were settled without physical combat. An example took place on April 18, 1968. The snow was nearly gone; a second consecutive early spring. At 6:45 A.M. we encountered a banded adult male 20 yards north of the Sand Road. He was limping because a band was too tight and his left leg was swollen. (We later caught this bird, replaced the band and he lived another 2½ years.) The tape of a female precopulatory call was played, and the male (now dubbed Limpy) responded strongly with several drumming flights and a standing drum.

Later we heard another male making drumming flights to the south of us. At 8:00 A.M. Limpy confronted this male, which carried two red bands (R/R), about 60 yards south of the Sand Road. There was a vigorous exchange of drumming flights, but at no time did R/R get north of Limpy. Once R/R landed 6 feet south of Limpy, then retreated "sneaking," with Limpy in pursuit, going slowly enough not to catch up with the challenger.

When we played a female call, R/R responded with a flight to a limb and Limpy stood on the ground giving two or three standing drums. The same thing was repeated by both birds three times. In 10 minutes R/R flew off southward; meanwhile, Limpy had flown into a tree, where he remained 5 to 8 minutes. He began a series of drumming

flight performances, each one carrying him in a northeast-
erly direction back toward where we had encountered him
displaying earlier.

This seemed to be a reasonably clear-cut example of territorial defense without physical contact. Both Limpy (Bird
No. 66–8) and R/R (Bird No. 66–18) had had territories
since 1966 in that vicinity, and they lived there until 1970
and 1971, respectively. Their territories abutted along an
east-west frontier of about 400 yards which ran parallel to
the Sand Road, a narrow unvegetated logging road that
served as a display arena. Limpy seemed to claim the Sand
Road; R/R in 18 observations was never seen closer than 50
yards south of it. Limpy in 27 sightings was seen once 100
yards south of the Sand Road but aside from that never
more than 60 yards south.

On May 5, 1968, we watched a confrontation of three
males near Dead End. It was a bright warm day at the peak
of breeding. Bird 65–87 had been occupying the Dead End
territory for over a year. Bird 66–54 had been holding the
adjacent territory immediately to the southeast since August
1966. A new adult male (68–1) had been banded in
January 1968 on a small island of dry ground out in the
bog 100 yards south of Dead End. On April 27 we had
seen him standing on a rotten log just about 50 yards
southeast of Dead End, in the traditional Dead End territory. On May 5 at 9:45 A.M. we found 65–87, the resident,
occupying the same log. There were no other birds in sight.

We placed our mounted female 30 yards from him, 20
yards southeast of Dead End clearing, and played the precopulatory female call on our tape. He immediately responded and attempted copulation with the mounted
female. A few minutes later other male visitors arrived, the
veteran, 66–54, walking in from the adjacent territory, and
68–1, the new bird, flying in from the west.

Both visitors landed close to what we thought was the
boundary between the territories of 65–87 and 66–54. We
had never seen 66–54 quite this far northwest and 65–87

had never been seen farther southeast. The new bird was treated rudely by both territory-owners; he was driven back west by 66–54 in a flying pursuit but avoided actual combat. Later he sneaked back in and this time was chased east by 65–87. The new bird was not seen again for six months, when we found him in October, displaying 50 yards west of Dead End.

During the course of the chases that day in May we moved the stuffed female across the territorial boundary, thus reversing the roles of champion and challenger, with the territory-owner enjoying the domination and rights and privileges of his position. The new bird, which seemed to be claiming a marginal territory during a year of high population, apparently did not have a chance.

But all our examples were not as easily interpreted. Two weeks earlier, on April 24, 1968, we found 65–87 at 7:30 A.M. right at Dead End, the heart of his territory. A half-inch of snow covered the ground and it was still snowing. The bird was strutting when we first saw him. We presented a stuffed male to him, getting no response, except that he flew to a limb 15 feet high. Presenting a stuffed female caused only a puffing-up and a few pecks at the branch before he retreated to a new and higher perch and stopped displaying altogether.

Maybe the snow accounted for his lack of interest. But McLachlin (1970) found that snow did not hamper the display of Franklin's spruce grouse. On May 18, a cool cloudy day, we presented a new stuffed male to the same bird. He immediately attacked it, pecking it and knocking it over. We put out the stuffed female and he attempted to copulate with it.

Males were tested acoustically with all of the sounds we recorded in the spruce grouse repertoire. Males normally showed responses to only four of the sounds; the male threat call, the display-flight, the challenge note, and the aggressive call of the female (Table 3). We considered a response to be occurring when the sound induced any type of behavior.

In April and May only a stuffed female was required to stimulate precopulatory behavior by males and only a stuffed male was required to stimulate aggression by territorial males. Toward the end of the breeding season (early June), both the sight and recorded sounds of the female were needed to stimulate precopulatory behavior, and sight and sounds of the male were required to stimulate aggressive actions by males. In late summer, during the peak of molting, a mounted female, sounds, and movement of the stuffed bird were required to stimulate precopulatory behavior by males. A stuffed male, sounds, and movement of the stuffed bird were required to stimulate aggression by males in late summer.

Table 3. Responses of male spruce grouse to recorded sounds

	Sound			
Categories of response	Threat call	Display-flight	Challenge note	Hen aggressive call
No reaction	14	10	13	18
Submission	4	4	0	0
Alert posture	16	0	0	0
Alert posture and threat call	15	0	3	0
Alert posture, threat call, attack	15	0	0	0
Strutting	0	10	12	29
Display-flight	0	10	0	8
Challenge note	0	0	12	52
Copulation	0	0	0	23
Total number of tests	*64*	*34*	*40*	*78*

Males paid no attention to a human holding the stuffed male and moving it, as long as the threat call was being played. Often birds that were not responsive to the sound alone would become aggressive when the stuffed male was passed in front of them. On two occasions males were lured close enough on the ground to be caught by hand as they tried to attack the stuffed male. Another time a male bird became so aggressive toward a stuffed male that, trying to strike the stuffed bird, he fell off the branch he was on. Four males exhibited a submissive response to the threat call. All four had been banded the year before as chicks. Two of the birds fled on the ground when the threat call was continued, and the other two remained motionless in trees. It seems likely that all four birds had not established territories.

The behavior of male spruce grouse, to summarize, involves territorial and sexual displays peculiar to their sex and their species. Both territorial and sexual displays are spectacular, with the bird utilizing the scarlet combs, plumage patterns, and vocal and mechanical sounds to communicate to their fullest potential. There is variation in vigor, however, within and among individuals according to the time of year, the type of stimulus being received, and the ownership of territory. Some nonterritorial males apparently must wait for a vacancy before establishing a territory and presumably becoming part of the breeding population.

Chapter *8*

Behavior of Female Spruce Grouse and Broods

Donald E. Maxwell, coauthor

Vocalizations

The female spruce grouse is usually a quiet bird, Her markings blend in well with her surroundings, and spectacular displays are foreign to her nature, except when she must defend her brood. Probably because the behavior of female spruce grouse is more subtle than that of the male, it has received much less attention from biologists.

Females during late summer, fall, and winter communicate very little with vocal sounds. They occasionally utter a very low feeding call, a low-volume, relatively low-pitched descending whistle that lasts perhaps half a second and may be given in sequence of two to four calls. Aside from that, unless alarmed, they remain quiet.

As breeding season approaches, a female becomes more vocal. She occasionally gives a long series of clucks, loud at first, then decreasing in volume, lasting about 4 or 5 seconds. This is sometimes followed by three or four high-pitched whines. MacDonald (1968), 'Harju (1969), McCourt (1969), and Herzog and Boag (1977) all report having observed female spruce grouse responding aggressively to this call. MacDonald recorded such a call when a female Franklin's spruce grouse attacked a mounted female of her species, and found that this call, when played back, attracted both sexes, males displaying with drumming flights and females approaching on foot, apparently with aggressive intent. Ellison (1971) has used this call to obtain a census of male spruce grouse in Alaska, and Harju took his tapes of his call of the female spruce grouse, which we recorded on the Yellow Dog Plains, to Wyoming, where he played them for male blue grouse, which responded with sexual displays. Apparently the call has an aphrodisiac effect for more than one kind of grouse. Females did not react to any of our recorded male sounds, although this may have been because most of the females we tested had broods and therefore had little receptivity to males.

Table 4 shows the results of playing tape-recorded female and chick calls to female grouse. Hens on nests and those with young broods did not respond to the female aggressive call, although one female with a 6- to 7-week-old brood did respond with her own aggressive call. All other aggressive responses by females took place in the spring before incubation. Herzog and Boag (1977) have conducted more conclusive tests with the female aggressive call. These will be discussed in a later section of this chapter.

Table 4. Responses of female spruce grouse to recorded sounds

Categories of response	Sound	
	Hen aggressive call	Chick distress call
No reaction	7	9
Brooding call	0	10
Assembly call	0	10
Alarm call	1	15
Alarm call and distraction display	0	24
Aggressive call	7	0
Aggressive call and approach	2	0
Total number of tests	*17*	*68*

William L. Robinson

A female spruce grouse strolls in spots of June sunshine among blooming dwarf dogwood.

After the young have hatched, the female uses a variety of sounds to communicate with her brood. These include a brooding call, an alarm call, a warning call, and an assembly call.

The brooding call is a quiet clucking with a slightly increasing pitch which the hen begins to utter as the chicks are hatching from the eggs. It may serve as a device for imprinting her voice upon the chicks, as is apparently the case with young mallards and young wood ducks (Manning, 1967). The call is given at the rate of about 1 per second during feeding and traveling, until the chicks are several weeks old.

The alarm call is a series of clucks given at a rate of 5 to 8 per second, with frequency increasing as the apparent degree of danger increases. A "trill," a series of very rapid clucks (28 per second) may be uttered interspersed among the other clucks. The alarm call is given upon approach of a potential predator.

We heard female grouse produce a "warning" call only twice, both times in response to a flying avian predator. It is a quick nasal, low-pitched descending sound which has the effect of making the brood become alert and motionless.

The assembly call was also a nasal descending note, uttered at a rate of about 3 per second and lasting a few seconds. This serves to reassemble a scattered brood after danger or disruption has passed. Harry Harju became quite skilled at issuing the assembly call vocally through his nose, and we were sometimes successful in assembling chicks for capture before their mother was ready to have them reassemble, much to her frustration.

Mating Behavior

Harju (1971, pp. 380–381) witnessed the mating act on May 5, 1968, on the Yellow Dog Plains. The rather passive behavior of the female is evident from his description:

Immediately prior to copulation the male approached the female very slowly and deliberately in the strutting posture with his head cocked to one side, probably to expose the billiant red eye combs. The approach was made indirectly, in a series of short, sidling struts at an angle to the side of the female, from the front toward her rear. The male slowed considerably as he neared the female, and seemed to be assessing her response to his display. As he drew near the female (within 6 ft) he suddenly made stamping movements with his feet, lowering the front of his body slightly as he did. His head was then snapped from side to side, one or two times at first, followed by a pause, then several times in succession, exactly as described by Lumsden [H. G. Lumsden, Displays of the spruce grouse. Canadian Field Naturalist 75(3): 151–160] for Spruce Grouse in Ontario. The rectrices were swished open and closed while this "head-jerk" was being performed, and the wings were flicked out to the side, perhaps to provide balance. The hen during all this display appeared very little interested, and did not move a great deal, nor did she make any apparent movements to attract the male.

Immediately after giving the last of several head-jerk displays, the male strutted from the front of the female around to a position just behind her. The female then responded by crouching low on the ground with her back to the male. Her wings were out-stretched and held slightly above the level of the back, with the primaries spread widely apart. The body feathers of the hen were somewhat ruffled in appearance and the tail was closed and shifted over to one side to expose the cloaca. This response is very much like the receptive posture of female Sage Grouse (*Centrocercus urophasianus*).

The male, once the female had assumed the receptive posture, stepped on her back and grasped the feathers of the back of her head in his beak. The wings of the male were extended to the ground on either side of the female, probably to maintain balance. His tail was lowered in an attempt to make cloacal contact. The male then made pushing movements with his feet against the upper back region of the female, with his neck bent forward and pulled down so that his throat was nearly on his breast. Once cloacal contact was established, the treading movements on the female's back continued for approximately 10 sec, after which the male dismounted. He then strutted away in the same vigorous manner displayed in precopulatory behavior.

The female after copulation exhibited postcopulatory behavior similar to that displayed by many hens of the Galliformes [H. G. Lumsden, The displays of the sage grouse, Ontario Dept. of Lands and Forests Research Report 83]. Once the male had stepped off her back, the female moved forward several feet with most of her feathers ruffled, shaking them vigorously as if she had taken a dust bath. Her tail was alternately spread and closed, and her head was in a more vertical position than it was in the receptive posture. The feather-shaking lasted about 15 sec, after which the female spent a short time preening.

The male continued to show a high degree of response to sexual stimuli after copulation; i.e., he strutted vigorously, gave several challenge calls, and twice performed display-flights in response to recorded female calls. The female showed no further response.

Territorial Behavior of Females

Do females claim a plot of ground and defend it? Mac-Donald (1968), Harju (1969), and McCourt (1969) reported seeing females behaving aggressively toward each other in the breeding season, but could not tell whether they were defending a territory against other females or whether they were simply showing intolerance. If females defend a specific area, such behavior would tend to spread the breeding females out in the available habitat and at times of high grouse population force some females into unsuitable habitat where they might not locate a male or where they might fail to nest successfully (Wynne-Edwards, 1962).

The picture was not clear to us. We never saw a female spruce grouse attack either a live female or a mounted female, although females did approach our tape-recorded calls of another female with aggression possibly the objective. McCourt's (1969) observations of Franklin's spruce grouse were similar to ours, but MacDonald (1968) witnessed a female of that race uttering aggressive calls while physically attacking a mounted female.

We found that whether or not actual fighting occurred, females tended to avoid one another in the spring. Table 5 shows the sociability of female spruce grouse, that is, how many we found alone and how many we found in the company of other spruce grouse. In the winter period (January 21–March 31) 7 of 11 females seen were accompanied by other females, but in April the females were avoiding each other. From April through May and most of June, the only females (4 out of 30) seen with other females were always accompanied by courting males. It was not until June 25 that we saw two females, both of which had failed in their reproductive attempts, together without a male. Ellison (1973) made 150 sightings of spruce grouse females in the spring in Alaska and never saw two together.

Table 5 also illustrates the contrast in sociability of females between the early April period and the late April and early May period, the peak of mating, when 64 percent of the females were seen with males, though never alone with other females. During this period in 1968 we saw seven banded and one or two unbanded females along the 1000-yard Dead End strip. They seemed to be spaced quite evenly. Six of the females were seen in territories of the three males which lived along the 1000-yard strip of young jack pines.

Of the seven banded females, only one was not seen again. The other six all showed up with broods in late June or July within 200 yards of where they had been seen in April and May. We found two of them on nests, both within 100 yards of where they were seen in early May. This indicates that nesting takes place in the area the females inhabit in early spring.

Table 5. Sociability of female spruce grouse

Period	Number of females seen	% alone or alone with brood	% with other adults	% with other females
January 21–March 31	11	19	81	64
April 1–April 20	5	80	20	0
April 21–May 15	25	36	64	16[a]
May 16–June 25	32	84	16	6
June 26–July 20	107	89	11	5
July 21–Aug. 31	96	71	29	13

[a]Four of 25 females were in the company of other females but in those cases a male was also present; thus, no females were seen only with other females during this period.

The even spacing of breeding females and their apparent avoidance of one another strongly suggested some form of territorial defense among females, but we were not certain of it. In most bird species the male is the chief defender of the realm. But is the spruce grouse (and possibly other species of grouse) different?

Recently researchers at the University of Alberta (Herzog and Boag, 1977) demonstrated quite conclusively that female spruce grouse do indeed defend their domain against other females of their species during the nesting season. They played a tape of a female aggressive call to many females, adults and yearlings, and observed their responses. Some adult females began responding aggressively to the call in late winter, but as spring progressed and the other adults and yearlings settled into their nesting home ranges they all became aggressive toward the intruding tape-player. Most of the birds which had retreated from the call earlier in the year were immature birds; a few of them were adults which had not yet settled into a nesting territory.

Herzog and Boag noted, as we did, that the female aggressive call is rarely uttered without provocation, and suggested that actual fighting among females may be quite rare. Instead, territorial disputes are resolved quietly and quickly by retreat of the nonresident bird, or even more simply by females avoiding other females as soon as they are alerted to their presence by seeing them or by hearing sounds other than the aggressive call, sounds such as wingbeats and feeding calls.

Herzog (1978) found that incubating females responded aggressively to the taped female call when they were feeding. He postulated that territorial defense serves to ensure a nesting female with adequate food reserves, in particular, the tender, calcium-rich young needles of mature spruce trees, to sustain her through the nesting period. The calcium would replace that spent in egg production, although Zwickel and Bendell (1972a) caution about assuming that calcium levels are actually depleted in the female's body. We have seen incubating females feeding on the newly emerged needles of black spruce, and similar behavior has been observed in Alaska (Ellison, 1966) and Alberta (Pendergast and Boag, 1970; McCourt et al., 1973; Herzog, 1978), the latter authors being the first to suggest the importance of the calcium in the young spruce needles as a potentially essential nutrient and therefore an important component of a female's territory.

The spruce grouse, it appears, is unusual among birds. The male defends one territory, and the female defends another. The result is a distribution of individuals among available resources and a dispersal of those grouse without territories, perhaps into new terrain. It remains, however, for researchers to learn whether the aggressive females which claim a territory early are more successful at breeding and passing along their genes than the timid outcast females. Does claiming a territory confer a selective advantage upon those who do so? Do the females of other polygamous species of grouse, less amenable to close observation, show the same sort of territorial behavior as the spruce grouse?

Laying and Clutch Size

After a hen has copulated she goes off to her territory to begin laying eggs. We really do not know how much advance preparation of the nest site she does, but we suspect very little. One nest we found had only one abandoned egg in it. The site was fairly typical, beneath the bent-over stem of a small broken jack pine. There was no build-up of gathered materials, only a small rounded depression in the ground litter of needles and blueberry leaves apparently made by the settling motion of the hen as she laid the egg. McCourt et al. (1973) found that until incubation began the nest of a Franklin's grouse was also very simple.

Nests were built up as incubation progressed, a result of the setting hen's pulling nearby materials under her. We never saw a female carrying nesting material. The outside diameter of six nests we measured at hatching time was about 8 to 10 inches and the depression which contained the eggs was about 5 to 6 inches in diameter and about 1 to 2 inches deep. The materials in the nests were dead pine and spruce needles, blueberry stems, and a very few feathers, all materials from the immediate vicinity. The feathers were not plentiful enough to have any insulating effect. When the hen was off the nest the eggs were left uncovered, as is the case with ruffed grouse (Bump et al., 1947), but a female Franklin's grouse observed by McCourt et al. (1973) usually covered her eggs with litter upon leaving the nest.

Most spruce grouse nests were built beneath overhead cover, in the form of low evergreen branches—spruce, jack pine, and in two cases, white pine. A site immediately adjacent to the trunk of a tree or a stump was selected by four of the nine nesting birds we found. The other nests were beneath low growing branches and in one case beneath green slashings of jack pines left by pulp cutters the previous fall at the edge of a broad clear-cut area.

Growing around the nests were blueberry plants, starflower, dwarf dogwood, trailing arbutus, and mosses, typical plants of the forest floor in spruce grouse habitat.

Only one of the nests we found was in the heart of a male spruce grouse's territory, and that was the only nest near which we saw a male. All other nests were either outside male territories or at their seldom-visited and ill-defined fringes. Ellison (1971) found 18 spruce grouse nests, all outside the territories of the males. There is probably good reason for this. It is unlikely that a male spruce grouse would allow an incubating female much peace and quiet, and his conspicuous presence at that season could attract predators to the nest. In contrast, rock ptarmigan females nest on the male territory apparently without continual harassment (MacDonald, 1970). When we found the nest located on a male territory, on May 22, 1968, our friend Limpy was strutting about the nest, displaying, and another interested male was about 20 yards away. On May 26 we rechecked the nest and found the female on it; Limpy, the only male now present, was about 100 yards to the east. On our next visit, 11 days later, we found the nest destroyed, probably by a red fox, judging from the appearance of the scattered eggs (Bump et al., 1947). The female had escaped, and we found her later. Of the eight active nests we found (the ninth was the abandoned single egg), this was the only one in which the eggs did not hatch. It may have been a coincidence; or the fact that this nest was near the center of activity of a displaying male may have increased its vulnerability.

Describing the number of eggs in spruce grouse clutches should be a rather simple matter arrived at by properly identifying nests and counting the eggs they contain. Unfortunately, an early authority, perhaps none other than John James Audubon (Rand, 1947), failed to do one of these things and his mistake has been faithfully copied by bird encyclopedists to the present time.

The following paragraph from Rand (1947, p. 127) summarized early accounts:

Audubon in 1834 gave the clutch size as 8 to 14 eggs: Bendire in 1892 gave 9 to 13, rarely more, usually about 11, exceptionally 16; Baird, Brewer, and Ridgway gave 8 to 18 (also saying that it was imagined by the common people that when more than 10 eggs were found in the same nest they are the product of two females); Reed in 1904 gave 6 to 15; Bent in 1932 for the eastern races gave 10 to 12 as the usual clutch size saying that 14 to 16 have been found, and sets of less than 8 are probably incomplete; but for the northwest race, *C. c. Osgoodi,* Bent gives the clutch size as 5 to 8; Forbush in 1927 gives 8 to 16, usually about 12, as the clutch size; and Roberts in 1932 gives 8 to 15 eggs. Chapman in 1921 gave the clutch size as 9 to 16 eggs, but in his 1932 edition changed it to 6 to 7.

We could add to this list Coues (1903), 9 to 16 eggs; and Barrows (1912), 8 to 15 eggs per clutch; and probably many others, including the recent *Game Birds of North America* (Rue, 1973). In only two references listing more than 10 eggs per clutch was there given an indication of the number of nests actually seen and these two, with 12 and 13 eggs, represented only two nests.

Tufts (1961) (who must be considered the champion spruce grouse nest finder of the pre-radio telemetry era) found 39 nests in Nova Scotia. Thirty-seven of these contained between 4 and 7 eggs and one contained 10. Ellison (1972) found 21 nests in Alaska, with a range of 4 to 9 and an average of 7.54. Keppie (1975) reported 21 nests of Franklin's grouse in Alberta, containing 2 to 6 eggs, with an average of 4.9. Of seven complete clutches we found on the Yellow Dog Plains three nests contained 5 eggs, three contained 6, and one contained 7, for an average of 5.7 eggs per clutch. We did find two very young broods with 8 chicks, so it is likely that a few clutches of 8 eggs were laid. Because of occasional adoption of older chicks, which we shall describe later, one cannot assume that the number of chicks in a brood represents a minimum number of eggs in a clutch, such as Rand (1947) suggests.

It is likely that the older weakly substantiated reports of

clutch sizes greater than 10 are wrong and that Audubon's error has been perpetuated. The average clutch size is actually 5 to 7 eggs, although it does seem that those of Alaskan spruce grouse (Ellison, 1972) are consistently larger than those reported from birds over the rest of the spruce grouse range.

Is a female spruce grouse physiologically capable of producing only a set number of eggs? Some birds, which can lay only a fixed number of eggs, are called "determinate" layers. But most birds are "indeterminate" layers, continuing to produce eggs if the clutch is not complete, that is, if the recently laid eggs are continually removed. Welty (1975) reviewed a number of reports of indeterminate laying. One involved a yellow-shafted flicker, a bird normally having a clutch size of 6 to 8 eggs, which laid 71 eggs in 73 days when each new egg was taken away leaving only one nest egg. Among the grouse family, 11 female willow ptarmigan, which normally have a clutch size of 8 or 9, were induced by removing eggs to lay an average of 16.8 eggs per female, with one bird laying 27 eggs (Host, 1942). Charles Peterson of Iron Mountain, Michigan, kept a few wild spruce grouse in captivity. Two hens produced, under conditions in which eggs were removed, 10 and 5 eggs respectively. The production of 10 eggs by one female suggests something more than determinate laying but something considerably less than indeterminate production of eggs.

We found only one nest on the Yellow Dog Plains in which laying had not been completed by the time we came across it. This nest was discovered on June 2, 1968, when it contained 4 eggs. On June 5 it contained 5 eggs, which turned out to be the complete clutch. So we have no field information on the laying rate. One of the captive females mentioned above, however, laid 10 eggs, beginning on May 10 and ending June 1. The other laid 5 eggs from May 28 through June 7. The average appears to be about 1 egg every 2 days, although in one 3-day stretch the bird that laid 10 eggs laid 1 each day, but 6 days elapsed between her second and third eggs. McCourt et al. (1973) found a laying rate of 1 egg per 1.4 days in a Franklin's grouse nest.

We weighed and measured some eggs and found the average of 14 eggs to be 42.1 mm (1.66 in) long by 32.5 mm (1.28 in) across at the widest point. Fourteen eggs from captive birds averaged 41.3 × 30.1 mm (1.63 × 1.19 in). Our measurements were very similar to those presented by other authors (Bent, 1932; Roberts, 1936). Measuring eggs is not very exciting biology, but it was mildly interesting to find that the spruce grouse lays larger eggs by 5 to 10 percent than its cousin the ruffed grouse (Bump et al., 1947), which is a larger bird than the spruce grouse by about 10 to 20 percent. The clutch size of the ruffed grouse ranges from 9 to 14 eggs, compared with the spruce grouse clutch of 4 to 9. In the last week of incubation our 14 spruce grouse eggs averaged 19.4 grams in weight, with a range of 18 to 22 grams. Fourteen fresh eggs from two captive females, however, averaged only 19.1 grams.

Spruce grouse eggs, according to Bent (1932), are "the handsomest eggs of any of the grouse." The eggs we found were smooth and had a slight gloss. The background colors varied from a cinnamon brown to a cream color, and they were spotted with darker, irregularly shaped dots of chocolate brown, often with the broad end of the egg more generously marked than the narrow end. The eggs did look handsome to us. In fact, considering the amount of searching required to find a nest, they looked positively beautiful.

Incubation

It is difficult to imagine a bird that sits more faithfully on her nest than a female spruce grouse. Bump et al. (1947) described an incubating ruffed grouse which allowed crews of men to work within a few feet of her without flushing and another ruffed grouse that continued to incubate during a forest fire and allowed a spray of water to be played over her. Impressive, but my pride in the spruce grouse prompts me to say, "That ain't nothin'."

In June 1966 we received word that a pulp cutter had found a spruce grouse nest. Between his feet at the base of the jack pine he was cutting he had noticed a female spruce grouse on her nest. Out of respect for motherhood he withdrew his· chain saw after cutting one-third of the way through the tree. A chain saw is a very noisy contraption, and sawdust and exhaust spew out of it in various directions. The distance from the saw cut in the tree to the head of the nesting bird was, as I measured it, 10 inches. The tree beside the nest was spared and eventually it was the only one left standing. All the others for acres around were felled, limbed, and cut into 100-inch bolts, while the faithful mother watched. The nest hatched successfully on June 27.

The combination of protective coloration and the tendency for an incubating hen to remain on the nest throughout almost all manner of threats to its safety make spruce grouse nests very hard to find. In five seasons of hard searching with crews of up to seven people we found only nine nests. Perhaps partly crazed by exhaustion, black flies, and mosquitoes I found myself occasionally making rash promises of rewards to anyone in the crew finding a nest.

In 1968, three people joined our crew as part of a National Science Foundation program of research participation for high school teachers. This meant more nest hunters, but their schools did not get out until mid-June and by that time the nesting season was nearing an end. The three recruits from the more urban parts of the Midwest had hardly unpacked their bags in Marquette before we had them on their way to the Yellow Dog Plains. They had enrolled in a graduate research course and an A was promised to anyone finding a nest.

Within half an hour Bob Sullivan of Flossmoor, Illinois, who had never seen a jack pine, much less a spruce grouse before, called me over to determine whether the brownish bird he was looking at was a female spruce grouse on a nest. It was. I was jubilant that he had located a nest—and none too soon, as it was hatching at the time—but deep down I wondered if he had really earned that A in biological research. I was afraid he would take his A and go home or spend the rest of the summer fishing, but he didn't. He

Incubating females are well camouflaged and seldom fly unless they are touched by an intruder.

stayed and prepared a good paper on blood parasites and white cell counts of spruce grouse.

We did not obtain much information on the exact length of the incubation period. The one incomplete clutch we found was completed between June 3 and June 5. It hatched on June 26, indicating an incubation period of 21 to 23 days. A clutch from a captive female was placed in an incubator, which developed a fluctuating temperature in 3 days, after which the eggs were removed and placed under a domestic bantam hen. They hatched in 23 days (including the 3 days in the misbehaving incubator). McCourt et al. (1973) observed a Franklin's spruce grouse nest which hatched in 23.5 days, but Pendergast and Boag (1971a) recorded a 21-day incubation period for a captive spruce grouse. Apparently there is a variation in the length of the incubation period and this variation could reflect individual differences in incubating attentiveness (McCourt et al., 1973).

Incubation is one of the least exciting aspects of spruce grouse behavior to watch. The birds sit so still and so quietly that the blink of an eye becomes a major event sending the observer's pencil scurrying across the paper. It was dull, but we would not have known how little an incubating female moves unless we had watched several. Almost all her time for 23 days is spent covering the eggs, maintaining a nearly constant warm temperature, while inside the eggs, chicks are slowly developing. Stillness probably serves to prevent the distribution of her odor. My dog Mandy, with an experienced nose, once passed 6 feet downwind from an incubating female without detecting her. McCourt et al. (1973) found incubating spruce grouse to spend about 97 percent of their time on the nest. The few feeding excursions we saw were brief and not very predictable. At 21 days one female was off the nest when we arrived at 7:45 P.M. and was back on again at 8:50. This same bird left the nest at 4:10 P.M. on the next day, returned at 4:30, then left again at 4:50, fed 50 feet away, returned at 5:15 P.M. and remained until the chicks hatched and left the nest at 10:45 the next morning. Herzog (1978) observed incubating female Franklin's grouse to leave the nest for 11 to 23 minutes three or four times per day, usually in early morning and evening.

About a day before hatching, movement inside the eggs becomes audible. The young are pipping at the eggs and the female becomes restless. She frequently pecks beneath herself and begins her very soft clucking, the brooding call. Whereas prior to the pipping of eggs the mother spruce grouse had been careful to defecate many yards away from the nest she now begins to leave the large "clocker" droppings nearby. She may also feed adjacent to the nest on blueberry leaves which had been providing some concealment.

We watched the hatching of six nests. In warm dry weather chicks from the three nests whose eggs began to pip in the afternoon were off the nest by between 10 A.M. and 1 P.M. the next day.

A cloth blind was constructed about 8 feet from a nest in June 1968. Cold wet weather probably influenced the behavior of this banded yearling female bringing off her first brood. There were five eggs in the nest. Following is a chronology of Maxwell's observations of this nest:

June 25—windy, cool, cloudy
09:15
We moved female off nest and found two eggs with pipped holes, two with small cracks and one, the smallest egg, still intact.
09:30–09:48
Female is back on the nest calling, giving brood calls, 3 to 5 at a time, about 30 seconds apart, often shifting about on the nest. Heard a chick call.
10:25
A chick came out from under the female. She pushed it back beneath her. She had been holding her weight off the eggs for most of the past hour.
10:30–11:17
A quiet period, female sometimes closing her eyes.
11:18–11:35
Rambunctious chick again comes out from under its mother, unsteady but dry, gets pecked gently on the head and returns beneath the mother.
12:00–12:55
Three dry chicks emerge from under female for a few minutes at a time, peck randomly at leaves and twigs.
13:30
I checked under female to see how many chicks had hatched. One egg was still intact, other four hatched. Female would not move but pecked my hand three times.
14:14
A light sprinkle of rain has begun.

14:50–15:12

Still light rain. Female feeding vigorously on blueberry leaves and buds within 18 inches of nest. Chicks moved off nest beneath her.

15:15

Female back on nest brooding young.

15:45

Rain is coming harder. Everything, including me, is becoming thoroughly soaked.

15:55

I leave.

June 27

09:25

Still raining hard and by all indications has been all night. Temperature about 50°F. Female still on nest with chicks under her. Her back is drenched, with feathers wet and stringy and bare skin showing.

09:40–10:49

Female once moved with chicks 2 feet off nest, feeding 3 minutes on blueberry leaves, then returned to nest brooding chicks.

10:50–15:50

Female moves slowly from nest with four chicks. Fifth one is left dead in the nest. At 15:50 she is about 100 feet from the nest. It is still raining and she is brooding chicks 95 percent of time.

June 28

08:15

Fine, cold drizzle falling, temperature 40–50°F. Female 200 feet south of the nest, still brooding four chicks.

The significant features of our observations of this female include her persistence in brooding the young despite hunger and the obvious discomfort she must have been experiencing. With the cold wet conditions the metabolic cost of maintaining body temperature must have been high. Unfortunately we did not weigh her. In addition, leaving the nest was done quite gradually, with two false starts of a few feet and subsequent return.

The young apparently adapted quite readily to feeding on blueberry leaves and buds when insects were unavailable, and they began feeding, after some random pecking practice, within a maximum of about 22 hours after hatching. They did not depend on the female to show them food. This is similar to what Zwickel (1967) observed with young blue grouse.

This female was seen once again on July 19 with a brood of three. After that she was never seen again. An orphan brood of three, presumably her young, was found in the vicinity a week later, and one of these, a female, lived for at least 2 years.

Renesting

Renesting is the behavior carried out by some birds which, upon destruction of their first clutch of eggs by a predator, lay a second set of eggs in a new location. Renesting has been reported for most species of grouse (Johnsgard, 1973), but is not very frequent among any of them. Ellison (1968b) verified renesting by a radio-tagged spruce grouse in Alaska after she abandoned a clutch of six eggs. The second clutch, laid 180 yards away, also contained six eggs, of which three were infertile and two were removed by a predator. Keppie (1975) also reported a Franklin's grouse renesting within a few days of destruction of a first nest with a single egg.

We had no direct evidence of spruce grouse renesting on the Yellow Dog Plains, but strongly suspect that two late broods were the result of second nest attempts. In 1966, 16 broods hatched between June 17 and 28, with the average date of June 23. One female was found on July 13 with a 2- to 3-day-old brood, making her chicks nearly 2 weeks younger than the youngest of the other broods on the study area. This female had been seen with a courting male on May 15 and thus probably began nesting at the usual time in mid-May. She apparently had an early failure but was successful in renesting. In 1969, eight broods hatched between June 16 and 20. A ninth brood hatched on July 17, our latest hatching date ever recorded, and probably a renest. Spruce grouse did not commonly renest on the Yellow Dog Plains, judging both from the synchrony of hatching and from the number of nestless and broodless females seen in the late incubating and early brood seasons.

Leaving the Nest

The chicks begin exploring their environment as soon as they can walk but their obedience to their mother and her control over them keeps them within a foot or two of her until she is ready to leave the nest. The leaving is gradual, a matter of feet per hour on the first day, sometimes with brief returns to the nest. The eggshells are left behind along with any unhatched eggs, and once abandoned the nest is never used again.

The Role of the Mother Spruce Grouse

Once the young have left the nest the female plays a few important roles. She serves as a sentry, a defense force, an incubator, and an umbrella. Her sentry duties are nearly continuous. She is forever alert, usually perching upon some elevated object for a good view of the terrain. She herself may feed as she stands guard but she remains watchful through each bite. When danger approaches she utters the alarm call which causes the chicks to freeze or go into hiding, and when the danger has passed she announces the all-clear and reassembles the brood.

If the danger is close and persistent she may attack the intruder, at least if it is human, actually striking him or her with her wings and pecking, or, more frequently, she may put on a distraction display. This is often a combination of "broken wing" feigning and a "sneak" display. In the latter case the female crouches low with feathers and wings held tightly to the body, much like a bird hiding from an avian predator. When the intruder approaches her, she sneaks rapidly off 15 to 20 feet, where she awaits the intruder. When the intruder again gets close she sneaks off ahead again, and so on. Then, just when the intruder is expecting another sneak, she may launch a flying direct attack. Often by this time the brood has been left safely behind, and the intruder's attention has been focused on the mother and upon himself. All of the female's action is accompanied by tail-fanning and loud clucking. The female spruce grouse may keep this up for hours.

The female spruce grouse is quite persistent in distracting an enemy and is also adept at reassembling her entire brood after a disturbance. Edminster (1947) notes that mother ruffed grouse frequently move out even though their entire brood has not reassembled after scattering to escape danger. Such behavior is not characteristic of spruce grouse. Once, when we pursued and captured a 5-week-old brood of five chicks, they strayed hither and yon over about 40 acres. The following day they were all together again with their mother.

Her job as an incubator seems to last only a few days after hatching. During those few days she may brood the chicks for up to 45 minutes at a time. After that the young birds rarely touch their mother.

Is brooding related to the weather? That is, does cold wet weather cause young birds to spend more time keeping warm under their mother than they would if it were warm and dry? We don't have many observations, but on the day after hatching nest 68–2, that cold wet event described earlier, the female brooded the chicks 96 of the 104 minutes we watched, or about 92 percent of the time between 8:25 A.M. and 12:44 P.M. There were only three feeding periods, each only 2 to 3 minutes long. The day after nest 68–4 hatched, the weather was warm and bright. This brood was observed for 235 minutes, between 9:15 A.M. and 1:20 P.M. The female brooded these birds 138 minutes, or only about 59 percent of the time. Ninety-seven minutes, or 41 percent of the time, was spent feeding, and the other few minutes were spent moving without feeding. These results are similar to those obtained by Zwickel (1967) with blue grouse.

Is cold wet weather harmful for young grouse? This question can be argued, with some authors suggesting a poor crop of grouse is brought on by a cold wet spring (Ritcey and Edwards, 1963; Boag, 1966) and others claiming it makes no difference (Bendell, 1955; Zwickel, 1967). Although Zwickel (1967) found that young blue grouse had less time for feeding in cold wet weather, he found that survival of two broods he observed was not affected, with seven of seven young from one brood and three of four from another brood surviving.

Our own results with spruce grouse are inconclusive. The female that brooded five chicks on the warm sunny day abandoned three of them on the next day. The female that hatched five eggs in the rain lost one chick before she left the nest. She was not seen from June 28 until July 19, by which time her brood had declined from four to three. Another female hatched a brood of six on June 13 in a light drizzle. The rain continued for 2 days. We found the female alive, two dead chicks near the nest but no trace of the other four chicks. Thus we do not have an answer to the question whether cold wet weather at hatching time harms young spruce grouse.

What does the mother spruce grouse not do? She does not show the young ones food, nor does she bring food to them. She does not usually lead them in feeding. Generally the brood fans out ahead of her. Occasionally, however, she will lead the brood to a new area, often by flying ahead, calling, waiting for the chicks either to fly or walk to her, flying ahead again, and so on.

We never saw fighting between two females with broods, but we rarely saw two broods associating with each other. The mutual avoidance of hens for one another probably continues to act throughout the summer, although they range somewhat widely. This is consistent with what Ellison (1973) found with Alaskan spruce grouse. Until late July, the broods remain remarkably discreet, with practically no interchange of members.

Within the broods, tolerance for one another is the rule. Despite frequent situations in which competition for a choice morsel or a prime dusting spot might arise, we never saw the members of a brood display antagonism toward one another or establish any sort of dominance hierarchy. Such peaceful behavior has also been described among wild blue grouse chicks (Zwickel, 1967).

Of the various groupings of spruce grouse found on the Yellow Dog Plains in summer, females with broods are the most mobile. They do not cover great distances but compared with single males and single females, the mothers and broods are the travelers. The longest movements we recorded were as follows: a female with a 3- to 4-week-old brood of five covered two-thirds of a mile in 5 days. Another brood of five chicks 3 to 5 weeks old, covered two sides of a triangle about half a mile and three-quarters of a mile on a side and part way back again in a 2-week period. Another brood covered a home range about five-eighths of a mile long by 200 to 300 yards across. At the other extreme, one brood in 1967 remained all summer in a 10-acre "island" of uncut cover surrounded by cuttings—a circle only 220 yards in diameter.

We found six broods on consecutive days and found they had moved an average of 292 yards overnight, with a range of 150 to 450 yards. Movements usually took the birds on a zigzag course so that they remained within a radius of 600 yards. By contrast, ten adult males seen in June and July on consecutive days had moved only an average of 155 yards with a range of 50 to 300 yards. A single broodless female moved only 100 yards overnight.

Of 26 broods for which we had at least two sightings, the average greatest distance across their home ranges was 509 yards and the largest was 1760 yards. Although variation is great, an area of about 500 × 300 or 400 yards, or 30 to 40 acres, seems adequate for the needs of a brood of spruce grouse. In 1965 there were 23 broods on our 2-square-mile (1280 acres) study area. This comes to about 56 acres per brood, somewhat larger than the home range estimate of 30 to 40 acres. The broods were not evenly distributed over the study area, however, but had some overlapping home ranges and many gaps between brood ranges.

Combined Broods

We never saw a brood less than a month old with more than 8 chicks, but in late July and early August 1965 and 1967 we found two broods with 11 to 14 chicks. These large broods were the result of combining young from at least two broods under the guidance of a single adult female.

On July 29, 1965, we found an unbanded adult female with 14 chicks, all about 5 weeks old. We did not find other adult females in the vicinity from whose broods chicks were known to be missing. The female with the large brood was found again in July 1966 and in 1967 with broods of 2 and 4 chicks, respectively.

On July 28, 1967, we found another female with 11 chicks, 5 to 6 weeks old. On the next day she had 12 chicks and by August 11 she had accumulated an entourage of 14 chicks and 2 persistently displaying adult males. We know with certainty that 2 recruits into this large brood had defected from their own brood of 5 between August 1 and August 10. The brood of 5 banded young was seen on August 1 about 50 yards from where the brood of 12 had been seen July 31. On August 10 we found the brood of 5, now down to 2, still with their mother about 500 yards to the southwest. On August 11 we found 2 of the missing young with the brood of 12, which now had 14. This large brood had moved only about 150 yards.

The mother of this big brood in 1967 had been seen in late July 1965, with a brood of 3; in late July 1966, with a brood of 5; and was seen again in July 1968 with 4 chicks. Thus accumulation of large broods does not appear to be habit-forming or a persistent trait among certain females.

In both of the large broods described above there was no antagonism shown among chicks or between the female and the chicks. On July 22, 1969, however, we witnessed what was apparently an unwelcome adoption. We encountered a female with a brood of 7 chicks about 5 to 5½ weeks old, each weighing about 200 grams. Along with this brood was a chick weighing 148 grams, about 4 weeks old, and marked with red dye on its wings. This was a bird from another younger brood that we had captured and marked a few days earlier about 150 yards away. The chicks in the large brood paid little attention to the newcomer, but their mother was quite relentless in trying to chase the small chick away. Over a period of about an hour or so she chased the young bird 10 to 12 times a distance of 3 to 10 feet. But the chick was as persistent in hanging around as the female was in pursuing it. We never saw this large brood again. We did, however, see several times the brood that the red-dyed chick had originally abandoned, and, through August, she had not returned to her own mother and brood. On September 25, a fourth of a mile south of the area this brood had frequented, I encountered the original mother of the runaway chick; then, a few minutes later, I found another female about 20 yards away. Its bands told me that it was the long-lost chick, now a female in her first autumn plumage, and probably having not the slightest idea that the other bird nearby was her own true mother.

Response of Broods to Predators

One summer Rudolph Emerick (1968) presented mounted avian predators to spruce grouse broods on the Yellow Dog Plains to observe their response. Famous experiments by Tinbergen (1939) showed that young turkeys instinctively recognize the moving silhouette of a flying hawk as distinguished from that of other birds. We wanted to test whether young spruce grouse would hide or take other defensive action when confronted by a mounted predator, or whether recognition of predators must be learned.

Emerick used a goshawk mounted in a standing position, a short-eared owl in standing position with wings held slightly out from the body, a snowy owl in standing position looking much like the cigar advertisement, and a snowy owl with outstretched wings. These were chosen because they happened to be available from the dust-covered bird collection of Northern Michigan University. Emerick presented one or more these specimens to females and their broods, which ranged from 2 to 7 weeks old.

Emerick, upon finding a brood, would wait with predator shrouded until the brood became accustomed to his presence. Then he would either place the mounted predator in the chicks' path and remove the shroud or hold the base of the mounted raptor in his hand and move it. Distances from predator to chicks ranged from 3 to 25 feet and from predator to hen, 3 to 12 feet.

In presentations to 44 chicks, only 22 chicks showed any alarm at all about the mounted raptor, and their mothers reacted only 13 out of 21 times. Of 22 chicks shown a stationary short-eared owl, only 9 showed a response. Eight of them strutted with head up and neck feathers ruffled, 1 retreated, and the others appeared indifferent to the mounted owl. Of 11 chicks shown a stationary goshawk, 1 strutted, 1 retreated, and 9 did not respond. The standing snowy owl caused all 4 chicks seeing it to strut, and the "flying" snowy owl, propelled on a long pole, caused all 4 chicks it passed over to flush into cover. Movement of the predator was apparently important in eliciting stronger responses from both chicks and their mothers. This corresponds with conclusions of Hartley (1950), although Hartley noted that recognition of owls by wild songbirds does not depend on movement.

It was somewhat surprising to us that so few chicks and adults seemed to be concerned about a mounted goshawk standing near them. Often small songbirds, chickadees, juncos, and white-throated sparrows, would scold and mob the stationary goshawk, while the spruce grouse brood would stroll indifferently about within a few feet of the rather menacing looking but long-since harmless raptor. Either the spruce grouse were not as astute as the songbirds in recognizing a motionless potential enemy, or they were observant enough to distinguish between a stuffed bird and a live one. Since the adult males had difficulty distinguishing between a male spruce grouse and a black and gray tape recorder with a red button, I suspect that their ability to recognize a potential predator is less well developed than that of songbirds. Emerick's tests were quite preliminary but they suggest possibilities for further ethological studies comparing responses of different species to predators.

In observing the birds' response to real avian predators, we saw a hen with a brood a few days old fly in pursuit after a kestrel which had passed about 25 feet from her. On two other occasions a female crouched and hid from kestrels. The upright alert posture was shown by a female and her brood for a soaring raven.

Orphan Chicks

Is motherhood necessary? Surely a female spruce grouse must have better things to do in tending to her own survival than fretting all day over a bunch of troublesome chicks. But we assume that her instinct to act as a sentry and to warn against and distract predators confers a selective advantage for her offspring, and that this behavior, like the benefit of her protective coloration, is passed along to her female offspring, and this is how spruce grouse continue to exist. But some chicks from broods left motherless at an early age were able to survive.

In the course of our studies we came across 13 chicks, members of different broods, ranging from 3 to 6 weeks old that had been, for various reasons, left without a mother. Table 6 summarizes our observations of these orphans. Of eight banded orphans two, or 25 percent, survived until the following year. This compares with an 18 percent overall return of all banded chicks in subsequent years. The figures are very small but they at least show that the loss of a mother for a spruce grouse chick only 3 weeks old is not necessarily fatal to the chick.

The two surviving banded orphans may, however, have displayed peculiar dispersal habits. The male was seen at

Table 6. Observations of orphan spruce grouse chicks

Estimated age of chicks	Number of chicks	Date of observation	Possible mother	Were chicks banded?	Fate
21 days	4	July 16 1965	65-44; had brood of 6 on July 12. Found crippled, 100 yds from brood on July 16.	Yes, 3 of 4	Three not seen again. Fourth, a male, lived for 2 years, seen 3 times.
21 days	2	July 10 1968	68-19, died July 8 or 9.	No	One seen passing within 5 feet of a female without a brood. No response from either party. Not seen again, to our knowledge.
21 days	2	July 17 1968	Unknown.	No	Not seen again, to our knowledge.
5½ weeks	3	Aug 8 1968	67-11, not seen after July 11. Had 3 chicks this age in this vicinity.	Yes	Two not seen again. Third, a female, was seen 5 times again through October 1969
6 weeks	1	July 26 1968	67-37, not seen after July 22.	Yes	Had moved 50 yards from where banded with mother on July 22. Not seen again.
6 weeks	1	Aug 7 1967	Unknown.	Yes	Not seen again.

the age of 8 months, in March, about 1100 yards southwest of his brood home range. At 11 months he was back in his old brood range and at 24 months was in a new adult home range 900 yards southeast of his brood home range.

The female at 9 months (April) was seen about 800 yards southeast of her brood home range, at 12 and 13 months (July and August) had moved 2.25 miles east, and did not bring off a brood (although she had developed a brood patch and presumably nested). But in October of her second year she had moved 2.5 miles back, close to her brood home range.

Both of these movements are peculiar because they indicate a return to the area of the brood home range after an initial dispersing movement. We have no other records of birds which have "changed their mind" about dispersing and returned to their brood range. Is it possible that the mother may have some influence on the permanence of dispersal of the young? That is, unless the chicks have someone indicate to them something like, "Get out and stay out" they don't stay out?

Brood Break-up and Dispersal

The break-up of broods in late summer and fall is not very dramatic. We do not have much data on the actual times and travels of dispersing young birds because we did not spend much time on the Yellow Dog Plains in mid to late August. We described earlier the transfer of two chicks from one brood into another large brood in early August. On August 29, 1969, radio transmitters were put on two members of a brood and their mother in hopes of following their dispersing movements. Two weeks later we found not a trace of any of them. We hired an airplane and flew all over the northern part of the county listening for them, to no avail. On September 29 we found the mother carrying a transmitter with a broken antenna, but we never saw her chicks again.

In the fall we commonly found flocks of 4 to 12 spruce grouse and usually these flocks included immature birds. Are these flocks just broods? We examined the composition of nine flocks seen between September 30 and November 3. Two of the flocks were too large, 10 to 12 birds, to be single broods, and seven of the nine flocks we saw included at least one adult male, two of which were known banded adult males. A flock of five observed on November 3, 1968, contained a banded adult male; an immature banded male dispersing 1 mile from his brood home range with, as it turned out, 2 miles left to go before settling down; an unbanded immature male, and two banded immature females from separate broods. This flock was a mixture of ages, sexes, and families. If flocks are composed of dispersing

Table 7. Movements in miles of female spruce grouse banded as chicks[a]

	Distance from brood range (in year 0) to first sighting in a subsequent year		Distance between locations in consecutive years after year 1			
	Interval (years)		Interval (years)			
Bird	0–1	0–2	1–2	2–3	3–4	2–5
66-29	0.5					
66-39a	1.3					
66-44		3.1				
66-45	3.7		0.1	0.0	0.1	
66-64		0.7				
67-11	2.4					
67-15	2.9		0.0			
67-27	2.5					
67-37	2.9					
67-43	3.7		0.9			0.1[b]
67-47	1.0					
68-60	1.3					
68-68	0.5					
69-26	1.0		0.0			
	Average = 1.96 ± 1.18[c]		Average = 0.17 ± 0.32[c]			

[a]Distances were obtained to the nearest eighth of a mile by measuring distances on aerial photographs with a scale of 4 inches to the mile and were later converted to decimals.

[b]Bird 67–43 was banded in 1967 and seen in 1968, 1969, and 1972.

[c]Mean ± standard deviation.

birds, a higher proportion of unbanded birds, moving in from off the study area, might be expected. Of the 61 birds in nine fall flocks, 37 percent were unbanded, compared with 31 percent unbanded birds we encountered in August. This suggested that some birds from outside the study area were moving in, since the proportion of unbanded birds would be expected to decrease rather than increase as we continued to capture and band them. Ellison (1973) found that late fall flocks of spruce grouse in Alaska persist only a few days. We had no good information to test whether Michigan flocks are also temporary.

Table 8. Movements in miles of male spruce grouse banded as chicks[a]

	Distance from brood range (in year 0) to first sighting in a subsequent year		Distance between locations in consecutive years after year 1		
	Interval (years)		Interval (years)		
Bird	0–1	0–3	1–2	2–3	1–3
65-37	0.7				
65-41		0.9			
65-49	0.6				
65-59	0.4		0.6		
65-87	3.0				
65-88	0.7				0.1[b]
66-30	0.6				
66-39b		8.0			
66-50	0.6				
66-53	0.1				
67-25	0.4				
67-29	0.9		0.3		
67-30	0.1				
68-51	1.4				
68-56	0.5		0.4	0.1	
68-66	4.0				
	Average = 1.43 ± 2.04[c]		Average = 0.30 ± 0.21[c]		

[a]Distances were obtained to the nearest eighth of a mile by measuring distances on aerial photographs with a scale of 4 inches to the mile and were later converted to decimals.

[b]Bird 65–88 was banded in 1965 and seen in 1966 and 1968.

[c]Mean ± standard deviation.

How far do the birds disperse? Of 170 chicks banded we saw 31, or about 18 percent, in subsequent years. Our return rate of 18 percent was quite high, but McCourt (1969) got returns of 18 out of 69, or about 28 percent. Bendell and Elliott (1967) found only 2 percent of their immature blue grouse in subsequent years, and Choate (1963) obtained about 11 percent of banded juvenile white-tailed ptarmigan. We did not know the sexes of most of the young birds when we banded them, but the 31 birds we saw again included 16 males and 15 females. (One of the females was returned to us by a hunter who did not know the location where he had shot it.)

Data on movements of these birds are shown in tables 7 and 8 on pages 110 and 111. Fourteen females averaged 1.96 miles between their brood site and the area where they were first seen in a subsequent year. The 16 dispersing males averaged 1.43 miles between their brood range and first subsequent location. This includes one bird that traveled 8 miles. Without that extreme case, the other 15 males averaged 0.99 miles. McCourt (1969) also found that female Franklin's grouse tended to disperse farther than males, although his distances of disperal in the Alberta foothills tended to be only about half of what we found on the Yellow Dog Plains.

Actual dispersal distances are probably greater than the figures given because undoubtedly many birds moved completely off the study area and were never seen again. The example of a bird traveling 8 miles suggests that this was likely.

Chapter 9

Growth and Plumages

Robert Delongchamp and Craig Sunne, coauthors

Growth and Development of Chicks

From those handsome spruce grouse eggs come beautiful chicks. Scientific analysis aside, a newly hatched spruce grouse is a lovable little creature. Its round body is covered with a soft yellowish-orange down with dark brown patterns on its wings and back. Behind its bright exploring eye a short black stripe curves over the cheek to the ear region. The crown is covered by a nearly round rich brown cap which is outlined by a thin line of black. A spruce grouse chick is helpless enough to require some mothering but not so helpless that it is a totally and incessantly demanding nuisance as nestling robins and crows are.

For the first day or two the chicks' feeding efficiency is low, as they learn to discriminate ants from gravel, and black flies from their toenails. During this time they live on the reserves of egg yolk which they carry with them. Their weight may drop 2 or 3 grams from the 16 to 18 grams they weigh at hatching, but thereafter they grow rapidly (Fig. 8). Some of the weights in Figure 8 are from birds

113

which hatched from observed nests and are therefore from chicks whose ages are known. The others are from birds whose age upon first capture was estimated by comparing their plumage development with that of known-age birds. Such birds were counted only if they were captured and examined at least twice; they are known-interval chicks.

In 2 weeks a chick doubles its weight and in the next 10 days it doubles it again. It again doubles its weight in the next 7 or 8 days. By the time it is a month old it weighs about 140 grams. It is half grown (240 grams) by the time it is 6½ weeks old, and by early October (15 weeks) many of the young are as large as the adults.

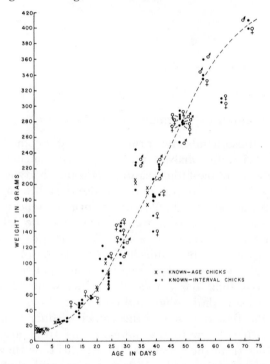

Figure 8. Spruce grouse chicks grow rapidly, as this graph shows. "Known-age" chicks are those from nests which we saw hatch, while "known-interval" chicks are those from broods captured and weighed more than once and whose age at first capture was estimated by comparison with known-age chicks.

The rate of growth of male and female chicks appeared to be about equal through the first 6 weeks or so. Thereafter, the males, which as adults weigh more than females, tended to continue a rapid rate of growth as females slowed down. Figure 9 shows spruce grouse in various stages of development.

5 DAYS OLD

17 DAYS OLD

DAY OLD

Figure 9. Appearance of growing young spruce grouse at 1 day, 5 days, and 17 days. Chicks can fly at 6 days of age.

Chicks younger than 6 weeks had no distinguishing external sex characters. We individually marked some chicks less than 3 weeks old with dye. Once spruce grouse chicks are 3½ weeks old they can carry numbered leg bands. The sex of chicks 6 weeks and older could be told by observing their newly developing breast feathers, which are black in the males and barred in the females (Ellison 1968a). Thus we knew the sex of chicks in their first 6 weeks only by recapturing them when they showed up later. We would then work backwards through our records to obtain information on their weights and plumage development.

We attempted to sex chicks in their natal down and postnatal plumage. We recorded all sorts of data on patterns of markings on the head, color and size of comb, length of tarsus, length of beak, length of tail feathers, and brightness of the feet. Since development of characteristic plumage of female gallinaceous birds is apparently controlled by oestrogen (female sex hormone) levels (Voitkevich, 1966) and since the ovaries of very young spruce grouse are unlikely to be active, perhaps it was unrealistic to expect the birds to demonstrate sexual differences at such a young age. Young males looked just like young females. One technique which we did not adequately explore, however, is the one used by poultry hatcheries to separate newly hatched cockerels from pullets. This involves inspecting the cloaca for a rudimentary phallus found in the males (Masui and Hashimoto, 1933; Alder, 1935; Thompson and Black, 1935). Whether such a technique would work on spruce grouse is not known.

We had trouble locating information on when young grouse begin to fly. Edminster (1947) said young ruffed grouse can fly 20 to 30 feet at 12 days. Townsend (in Bent, 1932) reported that young spruce grouse can make short flights at 10 or 12 days. Our observations are as follows: We encountered two 4-day-old broods and one 5-day-old brood in which none of the chicks could fly. One 6-day-old chick (known-age) could not fly, but chicks from another brood with practically identical weight and wing feather development and which we assumed were also 6 days old could fly about 6 feet. All chicks in a known 7-day-old brood could fly 10 to 15 feet. Nine-day-old chicks were flying well and known-age 13-day-old chicks could fly 150 feet horizontally and 40 feet high. This is about as far and as high as the adults ever fly; chicks, however, lack the stamina to make very many such flights in rapid succession as adults can.

Our conclusion was that spruce grouse chicks fly at 6 or 7 days and are therefore very precocious in that trait, although this feat is not unrivaled among birds. Young hazel grouse of northern Europe fly at 4 days (Welty, 1975) and the Malau megapode, a peculiar tropical bird which hatches out of an incubating compost heap maintained by the male, can fly at hatching (Weir, 1973).

Growing spruce grouse go through plumage changes typical of gallinaceous birds. The *natal plumage* is down. This down is gradually replaced by the *juvenal plumage*, which is rather drab tan, brown and black barred, and lasts the bird until late in its first summer. At that time the bird begins to assume the attractive *first-winter* or *postjuvenal plumage*, which closely resembles the *adult* or *nuptial plumage* acquired in the second summer. The adult plumage is replaced annually thereafter.

The 10 remiges or primary flight feathers, those attached to the "hand" part of the wing, also undergo changes typical of other grouse. The seven inner primaries are present at hatching. The eighth emerges on the fifth or sixth day, the ninth at about 19 days, and the tenth at about 23 days. The first set of primaries, even though seven of them are present at hatching, are not regarded as part of the natal plumage but as part of the juvenal plumage, because they remain with the bird for 1 to 3 months. The ninth and tenth juvenal primaries are retained through the winter and into the second summer. Figure 10 charts the progress of wing molt with age of chicks.

The first (innermost) primary is lost at about 14 to 20 days, and its replacement begins to grow in almost immediately. The rate of molt of primaries varies among broods and among individuals of the same age but in general occurs at a gradually decreasing rate, with an interval of about 4 to 5 days between dropping each of the first three primaries to about 8 to 10 days between dropping the last few primaries.

McCourt and Keppie (1975) came up with a simple and accurate method of telling the age in days of young Franklin's spruce grouse chicks. They simply measured the length of the seventh juvenal primary. This feather grows at a fairly constant rate up to about 30 days. That feather is

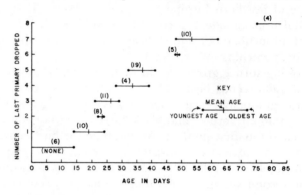

Figure 10. The progress of molting of wing primaries in spruce grouse chicks. The numbers in parentheses indicate the number of chicks examined at each stage of molt.

the shortest at hatching and it grows to the greatest length during its 30-day tenure. We compared measurements of juvenal primary 7 of our known-age chicks with those of McCourt and Keppie and found them to be amazingly close. It appears that measuring the seventh primary is an effective way of estimating age of spruce grouse chicks up to about 30 days (Fig. 11).

Beyond 30 days McCourt and Keppie (1975) used the length of the ninth juvenal primary and the seventh postjuvenal (first winter) primary. More variation occurs with juvenal primary 9 (Fig. 12) as the birds get older and our data for postjuvenal number 7 were not plentiful (only 12 measurements). The method of using the length of juvenal 7 until it reaches 85 mm (about 3.3 in), then using juvenal 9 until it reaches about 100 mm (4 in), seems to be a reasonably accurate and simple way to tell age up to 50

A male spruce grouse displays in May in a small clearing.

The beauty of the female spruce grouse lies in her subtly mingled patterns of brown, gray, black, and white.

A twelve-day-old chick pauses while feeding among the blueberries in early July.

This spruce grouse nest was situated beneath a fallen jack pine top. The site, clutch size, and scarcity of insulating materials are typical of a spruce grouse nest.

When jack pines are clear cut spruce grouse habitat may be rejuvenated, but it is barren for many years.

days. Beyond that, the variation of the length of postjuvenal 7 in our Michigan birds is considerable, and on the
basis of the few birds we have measured we would not have
confidence in estimating age to within a week.

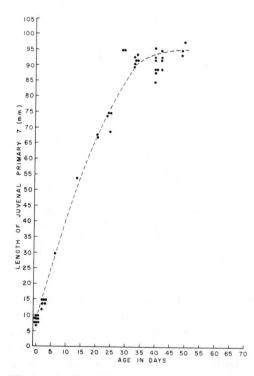

Figure 11. The length of juvenal primary 7, because it grows rapidly and
at a steady rate for 30 days, can be used as a good indicator of age of
young spruce grouse chicks.

Young spruce grouse apparently molt a little faster than
the blue grouse (Zwickel and Lance, 1966) and the ruffed
grouse (Bump et al., 1947). Spruce grouse chicks generally
hatch a week or two later than ruffed grouse in northern
Michigan. A speeded-up molt may be an adaptation of the

young spruce grouse to complete their summer molt before
the rigors of autumn set in.

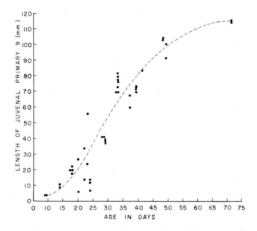

Figure 12. Juvenal primary 9 grows less predictably than number 7, but its
length can be used to approximate the age of spruce grouse chicks after
juvenal primary 7 reaches 85 mm.

Molting of Adults

After the mating season, adult spruce grouse undergo
what is almost poetically called the postnuptial molt. This
involves complete but fortunately gradual replacement of
all their feathers. Molting places increased energy demands
on a bird both for manufacturing new feathers and for
maintaining body temperature with an incomplete insulating layer (Payne, 1972). Figures are cited in that study of
increased metabolic rates for molting in various species
ranging from 5 percent to 46 percent. In spruce grouse the
molting period extends over about two months in the
summer. Its timing has probably evolved to come after the
stresses of breeding and during the warmest period of the
year. Accordingly, spruce grouse on the Yellow Dog Plains
can meet the increased metabolic requirements and have
some surplus energy and material with which to increase
body weight during the molt.

In the postnuptial molt of grouse the ten remiges are dropped and replaced in sequence, beginning with the one nearest the body. In the postjuvenal molt of grouse in their first summer only the first eight of these feathers are replaced, leaving the outer two as older feathers, often with pointed tips, and sometimes not quite matching the eight new feathers. Awareness of this fact makes it possible for wildlife biologists to distinguish birds of the year from older birds in hunters' bags in the fall and thus estimate the production of young. These techniques are widely used with a variety of species of grouse (Taber, 1969). Ellison (1968a) described such a method for distinguishing adult from young Alaskan spruce grouse, where the adults have a distinctly rounded outer (tenth) primary and the adjacent primary has little or no brown edging. Juveniles have a distinctly pointed primary with heavy mottling or a wide brown edging. We examined many banded birds on the Yellow Dog Plains in various seasons and found that Michigan spruce grouse did not conform very well to the patterns of the Alaskan birds. For example, in the summer of 1968, of nine male birds of known age which had not yet undergone summer molt, five adults and one yearling had rounded outer primaries, but two adults and one yearling had pointed primaries.

In October, however, the new primaries are young, and we found that sheathing at the base and wear of the tips could be used to tell new flight feathers from old ones and thereby distinguish juvenile from adult spruce grouse. A suitable ageing technique remains to be developed for spruce grouse in other seasons in the eastern parts of their range.

In the summer we made notes on the progress of the wing molt on 75 males, 46 females with broods, and 26 females without broods. Typical of most grouse, male spruce grouse begin and end the molt ahead of the females (Johnsgard, 1973). Figure 13 illustrates the timing of molting of males and females with broods on the Yellow Dog Plains. Females without broods were intermediate between males and mother hens in the timing of their molt.

Figure 13 shows that the first five primaries are dropped quite rapidly, especially among the males, over a period of 2 to 3 weeks, but the shedding of the last five may extend through 7 or 8 weeks. Boag (1965) found blue grouse with a rate of about one per week for the first six feathers and a slower rate for primaries 7 to 10.

We did not have enough data to relate the timing of the molt to weather in different years or to compare the molting process of known-age adults with known-age yearlings. We also had little data on the stages of the molt that take place in late August and September; but by October all

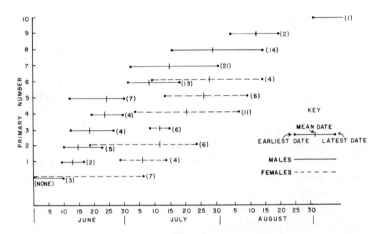

Figure 13. Male spruce grouse undergo the molt three to four weeks before females with broods. This chart shows the averages and ranges of dates when the wing primary feathers are dropped. Females without broods molt at dates intermediate between males and brood females. Numbers in parentheses indicate the number of birds examined at each stage of molt.

adult birds we examined had all new wing primaries, and the young birds had completed development of postjuvenal plumage.

There has been little published information on molting times of adult spruce grouse, but Stoneberg's thesis (1967) contains some data on molt of adult Franklin's spruce grouse in Montana. The same pattern of females lagging behind males is apparent and the dates of molting appear remarkably close to those in the Michigan birds. For example the mean date for shedding the third primary by females in Montana was July 9, while in Michigan it was July 12; in Montana males have shed their sixth primary on the average by July 11, and in Michigan by July 9.

The molt of the large tail feathers (rectrices) is much more rapid than the gradual shedding of the flight feathers. For this reason, not many of the birds we captured were in intermediate stages, that is, having some old and some new tail feathers. We found that the shedding sequence is from the outside in, as Stoneberg (1967) found in some of his spruce grouse. This is typical of most species of grouse (Johnsgard, 1973). The last date on which we found a male with a complete set of old tail feathers was June 27. The first date we found a tail-less male, that is, one that had shed all his old tail feathers, was July 3. We found partial sets on June 27, and July 3, 8 and 17. But during that period 15 males were recorded as having shed all of their old rectrices. Thus, the shedding of tail feathers for an individual bird probably takes place over a period of perhaps a week or so, and for the population over a 3-week period. By mid to late August most males are resplendent with new body feathers and a shiny new tail, and many of them at that time begin to display their finery in establishing a new territory or protecting an old one against newly confident yearling birds.

Females without broods shed their tail feathers between July 27 and August 4, according to a few sightings of tail-less birds. Females with broods may undergo a more gradual tail molt. We saw none without tail feathers, but our records are very scant for late August and September, when such a molt takes place.

Chapter **10**

Physiology

Heart Rates, Breathing Rates, and Temperature

It may be pretentious to entitle this chapter "Physiology." Our methods were extremely crude by comparison with such modern techniques as radio telemetry, physiographs, and radioactive tracers. We made some measurements of heart rates and breathing rates of 123 spruce grouse, and took their temperature, while we temporarily held them captive.

We were interested in physiology as it related to populations of grouse. By measuring heart rates and temperatures we might be able to tell whether we had sick or healthy spruce grouse, and if the population declined we might know the reason why. Heart rate can be an indicator of metabolic rate (Owen, 1969), related to how fast a bird is using its available energy. Although there is room for improvement, we know of no other published data on temperature, heart rates, and breathing rates of spruce grouse. We also feel that these factors, which roughly describe this bird's physiology, may reflect its somewhat peculiar behavior.

From June through August 1968 we collected data from 73 adults and 50 chicks ranging from 17 to 53 days old. We placed each captured bird head first in a short cotton stocking (this was known as "socking it to the bird"), which provided a restraint for easy handling and served to calm the bird after the stress of capture. We waited at least 5 minutes after capture before taking measurements. Heart rate was determined by placing a stethoscope against the breast and counting ventricular beats during a 15-second interval. Breathing rates were obtained by counting the inhalations in a 15-second period, as indicated by pulsations of abdominal feathers. Heart and breathing rates were recorded until counts in a 15-second interval did not vary by more than about 10 percent.

Cloacal temperature (the cloaca is the chamber just inside the vent which accepts the products of the urinary, genital, and digestive systems before the bird voids them) was measured with a mercury thermometer inserted to a depth of about an inch for adults and equivalently less for younger birds. It was left in for 3 minutes or until a constant temperature was obtained, and was read to the nearest 0.2°F. Air temperatures during most of our measurements ranged from 60° to 80°F.

Calder (1968) properly recommended that collection of data on respiratory and heart rates be made under standardized conditions with the bird neither restrained nor inverted, and in contact only with the floor of the cage. Our methods violate Calder's recommendations, but are similar to those employed by Long (in Bump et al. 1947) with ruffed grouse. Our data therefore may be of value in comparing physiological parameters of spruce grouse and ruffed grouse under similar stressful conditions.

Table 9 summarizes the data from chicks of three age groups and for adult males and females. Expected trends occur, in which body temperatures increase and breathing and heart rates decrease with age. No significant differences occurred between sexes in temperatures and breathing rates, but a statistically significant difference did occur between heart rates of adult males and adult females, with the males having a slower rate. Long (in Bump et al., 1947) also found that adult male ruffed grouse have slower heart beats in both excited and resting conditions than adult females. He also found that body temperatures of the sexes were similar, but unlike us he found breathing rates of adult males more rapid than those of adult females.

Table 9. Cloacal temperatures, breathing rates, and heart rates of captured spruce grouse[a]

Age and sex	Weight[b] (grams)	Temperature °F	°C	Breathing rate (breaths per minute)	Heart rate (beats per minute)
Chicks					
17–21 days	54–85 (4)	104.5 ± .58	40.2 ± .32 (3)	108.0 ± 6.32 (5)	368.4 ± 37.27 (5)
22–42 days	76–225 (35)	106.5 ± 1.24	41.4 ± .69 (32)	102.7 ± 22.45 (32)	375.9 ± 49.98 (31)
43–60 days (male)	254–330 (5)	106.3 ± .40	41.3 ± .22 (5)	91.6 ± 13.22 (5)	310.0 ± 35.78 (5)
43–53 days (female)	260–310 (8)	106.4 ± 1.66	41.3 ± .92 (8)	95.6 ± 20.84 (8)	320.1 ± 41.77 (8)
Adults					
Male	483 ± 19 (31)	107.5 ± 1.05	41.9 ± .58 (28)	76.4 ± 23.93 (32)	182.9 ± 36.37 (28)
Female	424 ± 28 (34)	107.4 ± 1.05	41.9 ± .58 (39)	77.0 ± 29.12 (41)	220.8 ± 46.26 (39)

[a]Figures given are the mean ± standard deviation. Sample size is given in parentheses.
[b]For chicks the range of weights is given; for adults the mean weight ± 1 standard deviation is given.

Table 10 compares cloacal temperatures, breathing rates, and heart rates of the spruce grouse and the ruffed grouse, the latter from data given by Long in the above-mentioned study. The ruffed grouse data was collected from captive birds restrained much as the spruce grouse were restrained. The values for both ruffed grouse and spruce grouse were considerably above resting heart rates and breathing rates calculated by formulas presented by Calder (1968), and may be accounted for by the stressful conditions under which measurements were made. I found the relative values between spruce grouse and ruffed grouse interesting, however. The spruce grouse, despite its smaller size, appears to have a slightly lower body temperature and a much lower heart rate than the ruffed grouse. This is contrary to the general trend, in which temperature and heart rates of birds increase with decreased body size. (It is possible, however, that Long may have been counting both auricular and ventricular heart beats in the ruffed grouse, in which case the reported values should be divided by 2.) Breathing rate is apparently more rapid in the spruce grouse than in the ruffed grouse, possibly indicating shallower breathing in the former species.

The relative values for heart rate and temperature for the spruce grouse and the ruffed grouse seem consistent, suggesting significant differences between these two birds in their responses to potential dangers encountered in the environment. The ruffed grouse is typically a nervous bird with an excitable personality. The spruce grouse, on the other hand, is an imperturbable bird. It tolerates close approach by man and usually flies only a few yards into a tree to escape a potential predator. The placid behavior of the spruce grouse may be a reflection of its generally low-key physiological makeup, suggested by its heart rate and temperature.

Table 10. Comparison of average weights, cloacal temperatures, breathing rates, and heart rates of spruce grouse and ruffed grouse[a]

	Average weight (grams)	Temperature (°F.)	Breathing rate (breaths per minute)	Heart rate (beats per minute)
Males				
Spruce grouse (28–32)	483.4 ± 19.3	107.5 ± 1.1	76.4 ± 23.9	182.9 ± 36.4
Ruffed grouse	615	107.7	67.7	306.5
Females				
Spruce grouse (34–41)	424.0 ± 28.3	107.4 ± 1.1	77.0 ± 29.1	220.8 ± 46.3
Ruffed grouse	535	107.7	64.0	366.7

[a]Figures given for spruce grouse are the mean ± standard deviation. Sample size is given in parentheses. Data for ruffed grouse are from Long (in Bump et al., 1947).

Weights and the Annual Weight Cycle

We weighed 83 adult females and 85 adult males. For these purposes we considered birds that were in their second calendar year and older as adults. The average weights of birds known to be in their second year were not significantly different from those of older birds. We weighed spruce grouse by hanging them in a stocking from a spring

scale that was accurate to within 5 grams. We had no samples in November, December, or February, and we pooled
the weights of three females obtained in March with two
weighed in April to get a larger sample and probably a
more realistic figure. Figure 14 shows the average weights
of spruce grouse through the year.

The general pattern indicates that birds of both sexes are
heaviest in late winter and early spring, and lightest in June
after the strains of the breeding season. The birds on our
study area followed a weight pattern similar to that of
spruce grouse in Alberta (Pendergast and Boag, 1973) and
Alaska (Ellison, 1972).

The Alberta birds are, on the whole, larger than their
Michigan counterparts at equivalent times of the year, with
females averaging about 50 grams and males averaging
about 80 grams heavier. And the Alaskan birds are heavier
again than the Alberta birds by 30 to 50 grams. Allen's
Rule, which states that members of a species tend to be
larger with increasing latitude, seems to apply to the spruce
grouse.

Males in Michigan and Alberta outweighed the females in
every month except May, when the hens are laden with de-

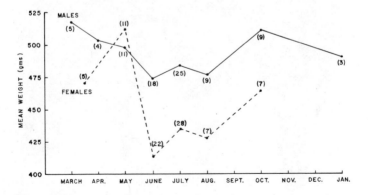

Figure 14. Male spruce grouse on the Yellow Dog Plains outweigh
females at all times of the year except in May, when the females are
laden with developing eggs. Numbers in parentheses indicate the
number of birds weighed.

veloping eggs. In Alaska adult females outweighed males in March, April, May, and October, although only in May was the difference more than 10 grams.

Pendergast and Boag (1973) analysed anatomical reasons for weight changes in spurce grouse by weighing a variety of organs from collected birds. They found that the body weight of spruce grouse was higher in winter than in summer because of combined increases in weight in the muscles, which probably have intramuscular fat depositions, and the digestive tract and its associated organs, including the crop, the stomach (ventriculus), the pancreas, the caecum, and the large intestine. Among females the peak weight in May was accounted for by the large size of the reproductive tract with its developing eggs, in addition to enlargement of the musculature and the gastrointestinal structures.

Greg Septon

Spruce grouse from the northern edge of their range are larger than those from the southern edge, following Bergmann's Rule. The pair on the left is from Alaska and the pair on the right is from Wisconsin.

Do having a brood and undergoing the stresses of motherhood affect the weight of females? None of the females we weighed in June or early July lacked a brood patch. All but one of the females on the Yellow Dog Plains that we handled had apparently attempted to nest. But do those spruce grouse which fail to raise a brood regain weight sooner than the mothers tied down with family duties? Table 11 shows that in June, July, and August females without broods tended to be a few grams heavier than those with young but the differences were not large and were not statistically significant (*t*-test).

Table 11. Comparison of average weights in grams of female spruce grouse with broods and without broods[a]

	June	July	August	Average, June–August
With brood	413 ± 22.5 (9)	430 ± 24.0 (19)	415 ± 35.0 (3)	424 ± 25.2 (31)
Without brood	418 ± 26.3 (7)	439 ± 18.1 (7)	440 ± 18.0 (3)	431 ± 23.3 (17)

[a]Figures given are the mean ± standard deviation. Sample size is given in parentheses.

Diet and Digestion

To anyone who has ever tasted pine needles, the thought of eating them as a steady diet for 5 or 6 months is somewhat distressing. My admiration for the spruce grouse increased when I discovered their ability to make a living and even to gain weight by eating jack pine needles. But spruce grouse are not the only grouse that feed on needles. The blue grouse subsists through the winter primarily on needles of firs, hemlocks, and pines (Beer, 1943; Hoffman, 1961; King, 1973), and the big capercaillie of northern Europe eats prodigious quantities of Scotch pine needles, to the extent that the trees are damaged; the bird is sometimes regarded as a nuisance (Lindroth and Lindgren, 1950; Zwickel, 1966).

How much must a spruce grouse eat in winter to maintain itself? Pendergast and Boag (1971b) found that captive birds weighing about 550 to 600 grams were eating about 40 grams (dry weight) of lodgepole pine needles per day while losing weight at a slow rate. Forty grams dry weight is about 85 grams of needles off the tree[1], or about 105 cc[2], which is a substantial amount (20 percent of total body weight) but quite possible. Ellison (1972) reported contents from a single spruce grouse crop weighing 70 grams.

In 40 grams of needles there are about 213 kilocalories. Pendergast and Boag found that the birds extracted a little less than 30 percent of this energy: the rest passed on through the digestive tract. So the energy requirements of spruce grouse necessary for maintenance are somewhat above 63 kilocalories per day, and it follows that in order to get these calories from pine needles they must eat over 85 grams (fresh weight) of needles. But Ellison (1972) reported daily consumption of 90 grams, *dry weight,* of spruce needles for captive spruce grouse in Alaska, and the birds continually lost weight and died, eating needles from the same trees wild birds thrived upon. He speculated that the trials of captivity imposed an unnaturally high metabolic stress on the Alaskan spruce grouse, which seem to be more excitable than those from other parts of the range.

Despite the weight losses shown by captive birds in Alberta and Alaska, however, we know that wild spruce grouse do survive the winter quite handily eating needles. They not only obtain sufficient energy but they apparently also get enough nutrients such as proteins and minerals. Protein is often considered the most critical factor in vegetation used by wildlife as food, and its availability is often regarded as an indicator of quality of food (Dasmann, 1964). Some researchers (Treichler et al., 1946; Bump et al., 1947; Hoffman, 1961) have specifically suggested that protein is most important in the maintenance and growth of grouse.

Pine needles do not provide abundant protein. We found protein levels of about 8 to 9 percent of dry weight of needles of jack pines from the Yellow Dog Plains (Gurchinoff

---

1. Based upon our own data (Gurchinoff and Robinson, 1972), which show jack pine needles to have about 55 percent water content.

2. Based upon needle volume-dry weight data from spruce grouse crops of Pendergast (1969).

and Robinson, 1972). This figure is near the top of the range of protein levels of 3.15 to 9.4 percent reported by other workers from needles of several species of conifers (White, 1954; Hoffman, 1961; Wells and Metz, 1963; Madgwick, 1964; Ellison, 1966; Boag and Kiceniuk, 1968; Pendergast and Boag, 1971b).

These protein levels compare poorly, however, with those recommended for domestic poultry (24 percent; National Research Council, 1966), and with those found in most summer spruce grouse foods. For example bilberry (a close relative of the blueberry) leaves contain 14.3 percent protein, bilberry flowers 18.3 percent, the green fruit 11.7 percent, and ripe fruit 10.1 percent (Pendergast and Boag, 1971b). Nevertheless, spruce grouse survive by eating needles in large enough quantities to meet their energy and nutrient requirements (Pendergast and Boag, 1971b; Ellison, 1972).

Mineral content of lodgepole pine needles was analysed by Pendergast and Boag (1971b) and of white spruce by Ellison (1966). Although these levels were also low on a percentage basis compared with recommended diets for chickens, spruce grouse probably meet their mineral requirements in the same way they meet their energy and protein requirements, by eating a lot (Pendergast and Boag, 1971b; Ellison, 1972). In some locations they also eat grit from which they may derive some minerals.

In addition to eating large quantities of food, spruce grouse show some discrimination by selecting needles from certain trees. Steve Gurchinoff and I (1972) found that they browsed on certain individual jack pines that had significantly higher protein and mineral levels than neighboring trees. Ellison (1972) found that Alaskan spruce grouse fed on spruce needles which had a lower crude fiber content than those from other available trees. His penned birds showed similar selection, choosing spruce needles with lower fiber content. Selecting needles with less fiber might increase feeding efficiency, but Ellison pointed out that the fiber content of spruce needles was 23 to 25 percent, while that of lodgepole pine needles fed' on by spruce grouse in Alberta was 42 percent (Pendergast and Boag, 1971b) and wondered whether such selection was explainable. We have already noted elsewhere (Chapter 8) that incubating females on the Yellow Dog Plains would feed on the tender needles of growing spruce twigs, which are quite rich in protein (16.8 percent) and calcium 0.43 percent) (Pendergast and Boag, 1971b), and would have obvious benefit for a brooding mother.

There is some debate whether grouse are able to digest woody parts of plants. In grouse the intestinal caeca (the two blind tubes leading from the junction of the small and large intestines) are well developed compared with those of most other birds. In spruce grouse they are 25 to 40 cm (10 to 15 in) long (Pendergast and Boag, 1973). Their greater development in birds that eat more fibrous materials led Leopold (1953) and Farner (1960) to suggest that they play a role in digesting cellulose. Suomalainen and Arhimo (1945) were able to demonstrate the breakdown of some cellulose by bacteria cultured from caeca of capercaillie, black grouse, and hazel grouse. But Pulliainen et al. (1968) found no evidence of cellulose decomposition by willow ptarmigan. McBee and West (1969) found that willow ptarmigan eating woody twigs and buds fill and empty the caeca only once a day and that of the two products, a paste-like material and a fibrous roughage, which come down the small intestine from the gizzard, only the paste is sent into the caeca. The woody roughage passes down into the large intestine and presumably out without being digested. Bacterial action ferments the paste in the caeca and, according to McBee and West, may provide up to 30 percent of the daily energy requirements of captive birds and perhaps half of that for free-ranging ptarmigan.

But the question of whether the "paste" contains cellulose and lignin and if so, whether these woody components are acted upon by the bacteria, remains unanswered. Pendergast and Boag (1971b) analysed materials going in and coming out of spruce grouse and concluded that lignin was not digested by their captive birds, although they concede that their birds, which were partly fed on poultry rations, may not have been fully adapted to a very fibrous diet. Moss and Parkinson (1971) suggested that among red grouse the ability to digest lignin depends upon conditioning of the digestive tract. Fenna and Boag (1974), upon studying the anatomy of the digestive tracts of spruce grouse and Japanese quail, concluded that the intestine permits quick voidance of indigestible food while the caecum works upon the digestible material, extracting nutrients. Such a system, they suggest, saves weight, a universal concern of birds.

If conditioning of the digestive tract is important for spruce grouse converting to a winter diet, the birds make the change gradually. In September and October, before snow comes and while their other sources of food are still available, they begin to feed increasingly on conifer needles (Jonkel and Greer, 1963; Crichton, 1963; Ellison, 1966; Pendergast and Boag, 1970).

As mentioned earlier, the weight of the digestive tract varies with the seasons. Pendergast and Boag (1973) found that the gastrointestinal tracts of captive spruce grouse kept on a diet of commercial poultry pellets failed to show seasonal variation in weight and length, while those of wild birds eating their normal diets were larger in winter than in summer. The diet of nutrient-poor needles is apparently responsible for enlargement of the digestive tract in winter.

Longevity

In nature most birds meet with violent death before the symptoms of senility set in. Thus few if any birds die of old age, and physiological longevity is therefore difficult to define. Of the 315 spruce grouse we banded, only a few lived more than 5 years.

Our three oldest birds were males. One of these was banded as a chick on July 12, 1965. We subsequently saw him 13 times, the last time on May 3, 1971. Another was banded on June 23, 1966, when he was at least a year old.

He was last seen on May 17, 1971. Both of these birds were at least 6 years old. The oldest one, however, was a male which we captured and banded as at least a yearling on August 2, 1966. We saw this bird a total of 18 times on his territory. He finally disappeared after October 5, 1972, after living a minimum of 7½ years.

Our oldest female spruce grouse was banded as a chick on August 11, 1967, was seen ten times, and disappeared after October 1, 1972, living 5½ years. Two other females lived over 4 years.

Our observation of a 7½-year-old spruce grouse is similar to maximum longevities of sage grouse, ruffed grouse, and sharp-tailed grouse summarized by Johnsgard (1973) and longer than the reported life spans of red grouse, white-tailed ptarmigan, and greater prairie chickens (Johnsgard, 1973).

In summary, the general metabolism of the spruce grouse is tuned at a rather low key and the bird's easygoing temperament may reflect its metabolism. The physiological details of its digestion remain to be worked out, but the spruce grouse seems well adapted for a summer diet of various leaves and fruits and for a winter diet of conifer needles, which are always plentiful in its habitat. The life span of the spruce grouse seems similar to or perhaps a bit longer than that of most other grouse. Perhaps the doctor's advice to take it easy and live longer has been heeded by the spruce grouse.

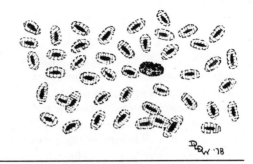

Chapter **11**

Diseases of the Spruce Grouse

Mark J. Leider and Thomas L. Jones, coauthors

The evening is still and muggy for late June, and thousands of tiny "no-see-ums" are leaving their larval casings and emerging from pockets of brown water in the bog. Swallows, chimney swifts, and dragon flies are capturing some, but many escape. A female spruce grouse incubating her eggs is soon surrounded by a sizzling and pesky swarm of the tiny insects. One lands upon the bare comb above her left eye. The insect's blade-like mandibles immediately slash through the outer layer of skin, and the sharp spines of its maxillae abrade the new wound. An injection of saliva provides an anticoagulant which allows the blood to flow freely. The labrum forms a trough in the wound and suction pulls the blood of the bird into the body of the no-see-um. Soon its belly is filled and the no-see-um flies heavily but quickly to a resting spot at the sheltered base of a spruce tree.

Within the blood which the no-see-um has sucked from the spruce grouse there are not only red and white blood cells and plasma, but a few unusual cells—cells living inside

the red blood corpuscles and nearly engulfing their
nuclei—blood parasites. These are one-celled animals related to those causing malaria and sleeping sickness in humans. These parasites found in the blood of spruce grouse
and other birds have been named *Haemoproteus.*

Some of the *Haemoproteus* are more numerous and larger
and darker than others. They are the ones containing the
female genetic material. The smaller and lighter parasites
carry the male genetic substance. The membranes of the
red cells subjected to the stomach fluids of the no-see-um,
soon burst. The blood parasites, now in a new environment,
respond quickly. Within a few minutes, each male cell concentrates its nuclear material into a small mass, grows a
long flagellum, and is now capable of swimming about in
the plasma among the pieces of blood cells in the stomach.
When this mobile cell encounters its female counterpart,
the two join and their nuclei fuse to form a single cell, a
round zygote. In hours the zygote enlarges and elongates
into a horseshoe shape, burrows into the wall of the digestive tract of the insect, and reshapes itself into a sphere, the
oöcyst. As days pass, changes take place inside this sphere.
Microscopically it looks like an orange dividing internally
into 20 or 30 segments, with genetic material being equally
apportioned among the segments, which are called sporozoites. About a week after the no-see-um had fed on the infected bird, the sporozoites mature. Looking like slender,
minute bananas, they emerge through the skin of the
oöcyst and travel to the salivary glands of the insect, which
all this while has probably been unaffected by the rather
unexciting development of blood parasites within its body.

When this no-see-um gets hungry again, and when the
weather is right, it flies, seeking another meal of blood
which it finds in another spruce grouse. The no-see-um
burrows in among the bird's feathers, which may be thin
now during the molt. The feeding no-see-um injects its anticoagulant saliva plus the sporozoites of *Haemoproteus* into
the tiny wound on the neck of the bird, and so into the
blood stream. The sporozoites make their way to the lungs

of the bird, where they remain to divide several times over during the next 2 weeks. The results of this division are gametocytes, male and female, which re-enter the blood stream of the bird, each one choosing a red cell, the gametocyte grows within this cell and in about 1 week has nearly surrounded the nucleus. Some of the *Haemoproteus* gametocytes may be siphoned out with a new insect bite, and the cycle for them begins again. Others remain in the blood of the bird until it dies.

That is the life cycle of *Haemoproteus canachites,* worked out by Fallis and Bennett (1960) from a captive spruce grouse in Ontario.

Haemoproteus is only one of many kinds of parasites and diseases of birds. Wildlife biologists have expended considerable effort attempting to identify diseases which may be a cause of periodic declines in grouse populations. Herman (1963b, p. 341) noted that "Without a doubt, this family of birds (Tetraonidae) has been subjected to more investigations of disease than has any other family of wildlife species." The search has been for a single agent causing the "grouse disease" which was believed to be responsible for periodic population declines. What have been the results of these investigations?

After reviewing the literature, Herman (1963b) concluded that no single infectious agent is responsible for widespread disease in grouse. Bump et al. (1947, p. 404) reached a similar conclusion: "Although about 50 parasites and a number of disease conditions have been observed in ruffed grouse, none have been conclusively associated with any widespread decrease in the numbers of these birds over the entire range." They pointed out that a parasite identified as causing mortality in one part of the range of the ruffed grouse is not present in other parts of the range, and that "no disease recorded to date seems, therefore, to make a serious bid for the title of the 'grouse disease' in America . . ."

Nevertheless, we did not want to dismiss the possibility of some kind of disease as a factor acting upon spruce grouse populations on the Yellow Dog Plains. We concentrated our pathological analyses on the blood, since drawing blood samples did not require sacrificing the birds. We never encountered a grouse that was visibly ill, although if a bird in the wild had become sick and had died quickly, we might not have found it. We considered a hypothesis, however, that blood parasites might make the birds ill and thus increase their vulnerability to predation or cause them to seek unnatural habitats where they might not survive as well.

Some 96 different birds were sampled in 1966 and 1967, followed in 1968 by blood sampling of a further 135 grouse. We attempted to relate the load of blood parasites a bird was carrying to its temperature, its heart rate, its general disposition, and the habitat it was found in.

We drew blood from birds by piercing the ankle of the bird just above the hallux (the hind toe) with a sterile lancet. A drop of collodion was then applied to the wound to prevent infection and further bleeding, and the bird was released. A blood film was made on a slide, stained, and examined under a microscope. We found four kinds of blood parasites: *Haemoproteus, Leucocytozoon, Trypanosoma,* and microfilariae. Samples were considered negative if we found no parasites in 15 minutes of careful searching.

The following descriptions of *Haemoproteus* and *Leucocytozoon* are based on Fallis (1965):

Haemoproteus is the genus name for a group of one-celled animals that live part of their life cycle in the abdomen of a biting midge or "no-see-um" or a louse-fly, migrate to the insect's salivary glands, and get into a bird when the insect bites the bird. Once in the bird, they undergo asexual reproduction probably a few times over a period of a few weeks, then each individual parasite, now called a gametocyte, invades a red blood cell. Infection in the bird is apparently chronic (Dorney and Todd, 1959). Pathology of *Haemoproteus* is uncertain.

Leucocytozoon is the genus of another kind of one-celled animal with a similar insect-bird life cycle. The insect in this case, however, is a black fly, and once *Leucocytozoon* gets into the bird it takes only about a week to do its reproducing and get into the red cells. Infection is apparently permaent. Heavy *Leucocytozoon* infections are known to cause high mortality rates among ducks and geese (Herman, 1963a).

Trypanosoma is a genus of one-celled flagellated animals that swim in the plasma of the blood of vertebrate animals. In humans and cattle some species of trypanosomes cause sleeping sickness. Trypanosomes are apparently not pathological in birds (Bump et al., 1947; Erickson et al., 1949; Dorney and Todd, 1959; Levine, 1961) and may be more properly considered parasites of insects such as mosquitoes, black flies, and deer flies, in whose bodies they may become numerous and cause damage (Bennett, 1970).

Microfilariae are the microscopic larval forms of nematode worms, which are roundworms of visible dimensions that infect various organs of the body. They are found free in the plasma, and are the largest of the blood parasites. Their length is about 20 times that of a red blood cell and their width about the same as the length of a red blood cell. Knowledge about their life cycles in grouse is very sketchy. Microfilariae have been commonly found in adult grouse (Clarke, 1935; Fowle, 1946; Erickson et al., 1949; Brinkmann 1950; Dorney and Todd, 1959; Stabler et al., 1967; Jones and Robinson, 1969). They are apparently live-born from an adult worm, but to our knowledge no one has made identifications linking larval and adult worms. Microfilariae are generally not very abundant in the blood. Pathological effects on their avian hosts are believed to be minimal or none (Bump et al. 1947; Erickson et al., 1949; Dorney and Todd, 1959). Table 12 is a list of blood parasites that have been described from spruce grouse.

The spruce grouse in the Yellow Dog Plains carried light to average loads of blood parasites (Table 13). Our heaviest infection of *Haemoproteus* was 265 gametocytes per 10,000 red blood cells, with an average of 64. Dorney and Todd (1959) found a range of 2 to 150 per 10,000 cells in ruffed grouse; Fowle (1946) reported 10 to 270 in blue grouse; but Bendell (1955) found up to 5,000 infected cells per

10,000 cells, and Garnham (1966) found pigeons with half their red cells carrying *Haemoproteus* parasites.

Likewise, *Leucocytozoon* infections in our spruce grouse were low to moderate, with 2 to 40 gametocytes per 10,000 red cells, with an average of 12 in adults, and 2 to 125 per 10,000 red cells in chicks. This compares with 10 to 20 per 10,000 in blue grouse (both adults and chicks) in British Columbia (Fowle, 1946; Bendell, 1955). Fallis and Bennett (1958) mentioned that their highest parasitemia in ruffed grouse (33 parasites per 10,000 red blood cells) was equivalent to the lowest rates of infection found in ducks. As mentioned earlier, young ducks and geese are known to die from *Leucocytozoon* infection.

We attempted to see whether an increase in blood parasite load would cause an increase or decrease in heart rate,

Table 12. Blood parasites found in spruce grouse

Location		Reference
	Haemoproteus	
Ontario		Fallis and Bennett, 1960
Alaska		Stabler et al., 1967
Michigan		Jones and Robinson, 1969
	Leucocytozoon	
Ontario		Clarke, 1935
Alaska		Stabler et al., 1967
Michigan		Jones and Robinson, 1969
	Plasmodium	
Alaska		Stabler et al., 1967
	Hepatozoon	
Alaska		Stabler et al., 1967
	Trypanosoma	
Ontario		Clarke, 1935
Alaska		Stabler et al., 1967
Michigan		Jones and Robinson, 1969
	Microfilariae	
Ontario		Clarke, 1935
Alaska		Stabler et al., 1967
Michigan		Jones and Robinson, 1969

breathing rate, or body temperature of spruce grouse. We calculated correlation coefficients (r), which reveal how closely one factor changes as another factor increases or decreases. For example, a correlation coefficient can tell us whether the heart rate increases or decreases with blood parasite load.

We compared rates of infection by *Haemoproteus*, *Leucocytozoon*, and a combination of the two with heart rates, breathing rates, and temperatures in adult males, adult females, and chicks in three age groups. We did not attempt correlations with *Trypanosoma* and microfilariae because of their low rates of infection and their assumed nonpathogenicity. Of the 27 r values calculated, 24 indicated that there was no statistically significant relationship between the number of parasites a spruce grouse was carrying and its heart rate, temperature, or breathing rate. The only significant correlations were found among adult males.

Table 13. Blood parasites found singly or in combination in 80 adults and 55 chicks of spruce grouse, summer, 1968

Parasite	Number of occurrences	
	Adults	Chicks
None found	9	12
Haemoproteus only	8	0
Leucocytozoon only	5	20
Trypanosoma only	9	4
Microfilariae only	4	0
Haemoproteus, Leucocytozoon	2	0
Haemoproteus, Trypanosoma	7	0
Haemoproteus, microfilariae	2	0
Leucocytozoon, Trypanosoma	2	19
Leucocytozoon, microfilariae	5	0
Trypanosoma, microfilariae	5	0
Haemoproteus, Leucocytozoon, Trypanosoma	5	0
Haemoproteus, Leucocytozoon, microfilariae	2	0
Haemoproteus, Trypanosoma, microfilariae	3	0
Leucocytozoon, Trypanosoma, microfilariae	4	0
Haemoproteus, Leucocytozoon, Trypanosoma, microfilariae	8	0

Temperature and heart rate were higher with increased infections of *Haemoproteus* (r = 0.527 and 0.570, respectively), and heart rate was higher with increased occurrence of a combination of *Haemoproteus* and *Leucocytozoon* (r = 0.734).

Thus for most birds we were not able to show any relationship between blood parasite load and heart rate, temperature, and breathing rate. But what about the adult males? Are the blood parasites actually affecting their physiology?

Since the red blood cells are primarily concerned with transporting oxygen throughout the body, one might assume that this function could be impeded by a parasite within the red cell. Increases in heart rate might be expected to compensate for reduced oxygen availability. In the adult males with the heaviest infection, about 190 cells per 10,000 were carrying *Haemoproteus* and 5 cells per 10,000 were carrying *Leucocytozoon*, indicating that only about 2 percent of the cells were affected.

From our data, arguments could be made either to support or to refute the conclusion that blood parasites were affecting the physiology of the adult males. A correlation coefficient establishes no cause-and-effect relationship, and might only describe a coincidence. A researcher arguing that blood parasites have no effect on spruce grouse would point out that in the adult males with the heaviest infection only about 2 percent of the cells were affected. This small percentage of reduction in oxygen-carrying capacity probably would not be measurable in heart rate or temperature under the uncontrolled conditions in which we worked. One could point out that no other studies have shown *Haemoproteus* to be pathogenic. Bendell (1955) found blue grouse with up to 50 percent of their red cells carrying *Haemoproteus* gametocytes without noticeable symptoms or increased mortality.

Our parasitized birds were found in cover indistinguishable from that used by nonparasitized birds, indicating that if the birds were sick they were not sequestering themselves. We found no difference in survival rates between birds with infections of *Haemoproteus* and *Leucocytozoon* and birds that showed no infection (Table 14). Approximately equal proportions of infected birds and uninfected birds were found in subsequent years.

And finally, since adult females and young were not measurably affected by equally high parasitemias, the results with adult males could be a statistical artifact, a spurious correlation.

On the other hand, the correlation could reflect a real influence of the blood parasites on the condition of adult males. The species of *Haemoproteus* might be different from those described in other birds, and gametocytes of this species may have a stronger effect on oxygen transport in the host. The spruce grouse may be more susceptible than other species to adverse effects of *Haemoproteus*. The adult male spruce grouse, which were more actively molting than the adult females during our summer sampling period, may be more susceptible to parasitism at that time. Sullivan

Table 14. Comparison of survival rates of spruce grouse carrying *Haemoproteus* and/or *Leucocytozoon* blood parasites with those not carrying them

	Parasitized[a]		Not parasitized	
	Number sampled	Number known surviving	Number sampled	Number known surviving
Chicks				
1966	9	2	24	5
1967	8	3	5	2
1968	25	3	2	0
Total	42	8	31	7
Adult females				
1966	10	7	2	1
1967	5	2	2	2
1968	15	6	9	5
Total	30	15	13	8
Adult males				
1966	9	4	15	9
1967	3	1	2	2
1968	14	8	6	1
Total	26	13	23	12

[a]"Parasitized" refers to any *Haemoproteus* or *Leucocytozoon* found.

(1968) counted white blood cells in the blood of spruce grouse, the same birds we sampled, and found highly significant correlations between the blood parasite load and white cell counts, and significant differences in average white cell counts between birds with parasites and those without them. This held with adult males, adult females, and young birds. Sullivan's work strongly indicates that blood parasites do produce a response in their host, at least in the production of white blood cells, particularly lymphocytes.

The question whether blood parasites adversely affect spruce grouse remains unanswered. More study needs to be done under controlled conditions, with sampling done at regular intervals and at constant temperatures. The characteristics of parasitized and nonparasitized blood should be compared.

Even if some spruce grouse are adversely affected by blood parasites, the number is probably quite low, and it is not likely that blood parasites were responsible for a great deal of mortality of spruce grouse on the Yellow Dog Plains.

We have practically no data on pathological conditions, aside from blood parasites among spruce grouse in our study area. This is partly because we made no effort to collect it by sacrificing and internally examining spruce grouse (which are protected in Michigan) and partly because we were unable to find either ailing or freshly killed birds whose infirmities or deaths had not been caused by violent agents such as goshawks and shotguns. Herman (1963b) suggested that disease does not seem to be a major cause of mortality in grouse populations. Most researchers who are attempting to identify reasons for fluctuations in numbers are turning their efforts from seeking possible single causes of population regulation toward considering a whole complex of factors, including the genetic characteristics of the population, which influence birth rates and survival and interact with a variety of behavioral and environmental agents, such as territoriality, weather, food availability, competition, predation, and disease.

Chapter 12

Predators of the Spruce Grouse—Friend or Foe?

In late April, winter had challenged spring on the Yellow Dog Plains and had dropped an inch of new snow in the night. The bright new snow covered the gray and grainy drifts which lay stubborn in shadows among the jack pines. In the openings, recently bare, bright sunlight was piercing the frigid air, converting the snow on the blueberry shrubs and brown and splintered brackens into sparkling drops of water.

On Sunday morning in such a setting, Tom Jones and I were walking southward, east of the Pinnacle Road. As I emerged from a stand of tall jack pines a large bird flew swiftly and powerfully toward me; then, when only a few yards away, swerved. Its silhouette and size told me it was a goshawk. I felt the glare of its intense orange eye before it darted into the pines and continued northwesterly. In its talons it was carrying something dark which I thought at the moment was perhaps half a muskrat, but against the bright sky it was hard to tell. We were a mile and half from muskrat habitat.

147

Three hundred yards farther south I think I found the answer. The fresh feathers and blood of a male spruce grouse were scattered over the snow as if by an explosion, in a circle 12 feet in diameter. We found two plastic bands attached to the severed right foot; the aluminum band on the left leg had apparently been carried past me by the goshawk a few minutes earlier. Although the evidence was only circumstantial, it seems likely that the spruce grouse had been performing its courtship routine when it had been rudely interrupted by the hungry goshawk. The hawk, judging from the quantity of feathers lying about, had done a great deal of plucking and probably some eating on the spot before it had decided to take the rest of its lunch with it.

From this observation it would be easy to conclude that the goshawk is an enemy of the spruce grouse; and indeed an individual spruce grouse most certainly should not trust a goshawk. But whether the goshawk or any other predator is the enemy of the spruce grouse as a species is subject to debate.

It appears that predation is the most common cause of mortality among ruffed grouse (Bump et al., 1947; Dorney, 1963; Rusch and Keith, 1971) and spruce grouse (Ellison, 1974). The question remains, whether the predators are removing a "surplus" which would not survive to breed anyhow, or whether the population would actually increase if it weren't for the predators. The answer to this question is apparently sometimes yes, sometimes no. There will be more discussion of the possible effects of predation on the spruce grouse population on the Yellow Dog Plains in the following chapter.

Nest Predation

Of the nine nests we found on the Yellow Dog Plains, two were molested by predators. One clutch of six was completely destroyed by a red fox. In the other case we found a nest with four whole eggs and a fifth broken and partly eaten egg with only the head of the embryonic chick remaining. The hen was still incubating the four eggs; we removed the remains of the broken one. On the next day there were only three eggs left in the nest, with no sign of the fourth one, and the shell of one of the remaining three eggs had a quarter of an inch hole. The following day only two eggs were left. Fortunately for their occupants, they hatched on that day and the chicks departed. Yolk smears on the lower trunk of a nearby spruce led us to believe that a red squirrel had been enjoying a daily breakfast of well-incubated grouse eggs. Bump et al. (1947) reported occasional red squirrel predation on eggs of ruffed grouse. In addition to the two nests mentioned above, we found a lone broken egg from a nest we could not find. This egg had been eaten by an unidentified mammal.

Predation of Birds

We found remains of 17 spruce grouse that had been eaten by predators (Table 15). To identify predators we used a variety of methods. A mammalian predator usually bites through the bases of the large feathers, and an avian predator frequently plucks the large feathers of its victim. A weasel frequently hides uneaten prey beneath a log.

Table 15. Predators of spruce grouse on the Yellow Dog Plains, 1965–70

| | Number of spruce grouse killed | | | |
Predator	Male	Female	Sex unknown	Total
Red fox			1	1
Coyote		1		1
Weasel		1		1
Unidentified mammal	3	1	1	5
Goshawk	1			1
Barred owl			1	1
Unidentified hawk or owl	4	1		5
Unknown	2	—	—	2
Total	10	4	3	17

Fresh spruce grouse feathers at a fox den in June and spruce grouse toes in owl pellets also give us good circumstantial evidence of predation.

No single kind of predator was identified as being responsible for a large number of dead spruce grouse. It is likely, however, that the goshawk and the great horned owl (and possibly the barred owl), which live on or near the study area year round, made most of the kills in the "Unidentified Hawk or Owl" category. Among the mammals, the coyote was the most common predator on the study area, judging from tracks and droppings found. The single record of a grouse kill by a coyote was made when we surprised a coyote and it ran off with a female spruce grouse in its mouth. None of the predators found on the Yellow Dog Plains relied primarily on spruce grouse for food. There would not be enough birds to last very long, and their scattered distribution would probably require a predator specializing in spruce grouse to expend too much energy to hunt them down. Herzog and Boag (1978) suggest that spacing of spruce grouse in their habitat through territorial behavior may be an evolved adaptation which reduces the chance of success of their predators.

Rusch and Keith (1971) found that predation was by far the most important source of ruffed grouse mortality in a carefully studied population in Alberta. About 31 percent of the birds killed were taken by mammalian predators (coyote and lynx), and 69 percent were killed by raptors (great horned owl, goshawk, red-tailed hawk, and broad-winged hawk). In the same population Rusch et al. (1972) found that as great horned owls shifted their diet more heavily toward snowshoe hares and away from grouse, survival of young ruffed grouse improved and the population increased. Snowshoe hare populations were high on the Yellow Dog Plains in 1965–66, then declined strikingly, remaining low until 1967–68, when they began a slow increase. Our predation records are not numerous enough to tell whether predators on the Yellow Dog Plains were shifting their food preferences to grouse when the hare population crashed. In 1965 we found remains of two predator-killed spruce grouse, in 1966 we found five, 1967–69, three per year, and in 1970, one.

Eng and Gullion (1962) found that goshawks preyed disproportionately higher on drumming male ruffed grouse. We found 10 preyed-upon males to 4 preyed-upon females (Table 15), having made 399 sightings of live males to 345 sightings of live females during the study. The probability of finding 10 males and 4 females from that population does not differ significantly from chance, although a trend may be indicated. The preponderance of male spruce grouse in predator kills may reflect either greater vulnerability of males to predation because of their conspicuous behavior and choice of display arenas, or greater probability of finding the remains of a male because its plumage is more visible to us. The fairly rapid turnover of adult males on the Dead End territory (Chapter 7) suggests that on that territory adult males suffered higher mortality than the population as a whole, but the adjacent male territory-holder lived to be 7 years old, considerably longer than average.

Probably the best way to obtain data on the extent of predation on a population is to study simultaneously both the predators and the prey, instead of passively watching the prey animals disappear and guessing at what caused their demise, as we did with the spruce grouse. Unfortunately, predators often work at night, cover large expanses of terrain, and avoid humans. With the help of radio telemetry, however, the details of predator behavior are gradually being worked out, and as they are, more knowledge about the influence of predators on prey species will be gained.

To sum up: a variety of predators will eat spruce grouse or their eggs when the opportunity presents itself. The predators include owls, goshawks, red foxes, and coyotes, with none of these apparently depending upon spruce grouse as a significant part of its diet. Although predation is the most commonly identified cause of death of spruce grouse, it is not clear whether spruce grouse populations would be much higher without predators. The role of predators in influencing quantity and quality of grouse populations requires more study.

Chapter 13

Population Ecology

For years ecologists have been probing the mysteries of how animal populations are able to increase and decrease, with so very few populations reaching abundances of epidemic proportions and so very few, under natural conditions, declining to the point of extinction. What are the factors that cause populations to fluctuate yet keep the numbers of a species within certain reasonable bounds? This was one of the questions we were exploring with the spruce grouse on the Yellow Dog Plains. The spruce grouse has been maintaining itself in Michigan at fairly low levels for 60 to 70 years (Ammann, 1963). Its populations go up and down, but it does not go to extinction, nor does it become abundant. Why?

The grouse family has attracted the attention of many ecologists attempting to develop a general theory to explain population regulation. This is because grouse have economic value as game birds, they are known to show wide fluctuations in abundance, and they are fun to work with. Some grouse populations are cyclic, that is, showing regular peaks of abundance at 9- or 10-year intervals, but others are stable, and some may fluctuate quite unpredictably

(Keith, 1963; Weeden and Theberge, 1972; Zwickel and Bendell, 1972b). Bendell (1972) thoroughly reviewed the literature on grouse populations and was unable to formulate a general explanation applicable to all members of the grouse family, much less to populations of other animals.

The information most useful in promoting an understanding of grouse populations comes from research in which a broad array of biological and physical environmental influences are measured closely, along with the numbers, behavior, and physiology of the birds. Studies which follow populations through more than one peak and valley probably hold the greatest promise for identifying principles responsible for regulating grouse numbers. Such studies include those of red grouse in Scotland by Jenkins, Watson, and Miller, of ruffed grouse by Guillion in Minnesota and by Keith and his co-workers from the University of Wisconsin, of spruce grouse by Boag and his students in Alberta; and of blue grouse by Zwickel and Bendell in British Columbia.

Our spruce grouse work on the Yellow Dog Plains lacks the time span and perhaps the thoroughness of those studies, but it may contain some tidbits of information that, at best, will contribute to our knowledge of grouse populations or, at worst, will simply add to the confusion. I agree with Bendell (1972) and Watson and Moss (1970) in believing that we are still a long way from accepting any general theory to explain how the numbers of animals in nature are controlled.

Habitat

If a species persists in an area year after year, the habitat there must meet at least the minimal requirements of the species. If the habitat is not suitable, a bird can express its dissatisfaction in one of three ways. It can move out, not reproduce, or die (or execute some combination of the three, provided the third does not come first). Of course, not all habitat is equally suitable. In good habitat the birds may attain some maximum density and in marginal habitat the population may be sparse or the birds may occur only occasionally. But even in the best habitat birds rarely over-populate the range to the extent that they deplete available food.

The Yellow Dog Plains, although it covers only about 25 square miles, is apparently a good spruce grouse habitat. The number of birds on our 2.5 square mile study area in the spring ranged from about 30 to 58 birds, for a density of about 12 to 24 birds per square mile. This is a little lower than densities of 20 to 30 birds per square mile on the Kenai Peninsula of Alaska (Ellison, 1974), similar to 12 to 23 per square mile in southern Alberta (McCourt, 1969; McLachlin, 1970), and higher than 8 per square mile found in northwestern Montana (Stoneberg, 1967). Nowhere in their range do spruce grouse attain the breeding densities of 80 or more per square mile reported for ruffed grouse (Johnsgard, 1973).

On the basis of our Yellow Dog Plains studies and casual searches elsewhere in the Upper Peninsula, Michigan spruce grouse densities, where they occur, seem to be about average. This suggests that the quality of habitat in Michigan is adequate, but that the statewide population of spruce grouse is not high because proper habitat is found only in a few locations.

In describing changes in size of the spruce grouse population on the Yellow Dog Plains we used as a base the formula $r = b - d$, which simply says the rate of growth (r) of a population equals the birth rate (b) minus the death rate (d). If there are more births than deaths, the population increases; if the deaths exceed births, the population declines. Then we have to add birds that move in during a given time period, the immigrants (i), and substract the birds that disperse out, the emigrants (e), so the formula (for those who like formulas) is now $r = b - d + i - e$

An analysis of the rate of growth of a population should take into account the above-mentioned factors and explore the elements contributing to them. In populations such as those of most birds, which breed only once a year, the problem is somewhat simplified because we are able merely to add the number of newly hatched young to the population rather than having to integrate mathematically for continuously changing adult populations and reproductive rates, as is necessary in many rodent and insect populations.

Characteristics of the Breeding Population

Numbers of breeding birds, their sex ratios, and their age ratios varied from year to year on the Yellow Dog Plains. Table 16 shows numbers and sex ratios of the breeding population in April and May. Peak populations were reached in 1965 and 1968. Lows occurred in 1967 and 1969. In 1970, although we lack good quantitative data, our observations indicated a recovery taking place. We felt another peak was reached in 1971, and again in 1974, with a decline in 1975. A 3-year cycle of peaks appeared, but the troughs could come either the first or second year following a peak.

Were the differences in population sizes chance fluctuations around a base level or were there significant differences between years? Over five seasons the average breeding population was 46 birds. A statistical test (Chi-square) showed that such fluctuations would be expected by chance a little less than 1 out of 10 times, which is not regarded as statistically significant. But when the high year of 1965 was compared with the low year of 1969, a nearly significant

Table 16. Minimum breeding populations of spruce grouse on the Yellow
Dog Plains study area

Year	Males	Females	Total	Sex ratios (Males per 100 females)
1965	26	32	58	81
1966	28	17	45	165
1967	19	22	41	86
1968	20	33	53	60
1969	19	13	32	146
Average	22	23	46	96

difference was obtained (Chi-square = 3.83, when a value of 3.84 indicates a difference at 0.05 probability). Thus the nearly twofold difference between spruce grouse numbers in a high year and in a low year would barely be expected by chance alone. The discussion in this chapter assumes that biological factors rather than random mathematical fluctuations are responsible for the observed annual differences in numbers of spruce grouse.

Although there was considerable variation in sex ratios from year to year, the ratios did not differ significantly from 100 males per 100 females. Because spruce grouse are polygamous it is unlikely that the deficiency of males in 1965, 1967, and 1968 reduced the breeding of females. Similar variations around an even sex ratio also occur in Washington (Zwickel and Brigham, 1970) and Alaska (Ellison, 1974).

Determining age ratios was somewhat difficult. We had no reliable way of distinguishing yearlings from older birds by plumage. The criteria based upon wear, shape, and coloration of the outer two primaries described by Ellison (1968a) for Alaskan spruce grouse and for Franklin's grouse in Washington (Zwickel and Martinsen, 1967) did not work well in winter and spring on our known-age Michigan birds in the field. Similar difficulties were encountered by McLachlin (1970) in Alberta. Because we banded almost all of the adults and a large proportion of chicks each year on the study area we had reliable age information for most years for over half of the breeding birds present (Table 17). A banded bird was recognized as an adult (at least 2 years old) either because it was banded as a chick and its age was known, or because it was banded in adult plumage as either a yearling or older bird, then caught in subsequent years, and therefore regarded as an adult. Because adults were found to be quite faithful to their established home range (Chapter 7) it is likely that almost all of the unknown-age females were yearlings and unknown-age males were either yearlings or 2-year-old birds establishing territories.

During the peak year of 1968 the smallest percentage of

known adults was present, and during the low year of 1969 the largest percentage of known adults was present. Another way to look at the data is to see how many banded chicks are recovered in the breeding population the following year (Table 18). Because many chicks probably leave the study area and many others enter it during their first fall and winter, the recovery of banded chicks is not a true reflection of survival, but it does represent at least a minimum survival rate and may reflect relative survival of an age class. It is probably reasonable to compare these minimum survival rates from year to year.

The highest breeding population (excluding 1965, when we had no banded birds to start with) was in 1968, when 27 percent of the immature birds banded in 1967 were seen. During the other three years only 6 to 10 percent of the chicks banded the previous year showed up. The recovery of banded chicks in 1968 was significantly higher than in 1966 and 1969 and from 1966, 1967, and 1969 combined.

The high proportion of birds in their first year carried through the winter (Table 18) was combined with a low proportion of known adults (Table 17) in 1968. The low spruce grouse populations of 1967 and 1969 contained high proportions of known adults. In 1966, a moderate

Table 17. Age structure[a] of breeding populations of spruce grouse on the Yellow Dog Plains study area

	1966	1967	1968	1969
Males				
Adult	9	15	9	12
Yearling	2	2	3	2
Age unknown	17	2	8	5
Percent known adult	*32*	*79*	*45*	*61*
Females				
Adult	8	11	12	8
Yearling	0	1	6	2
Age unknown	9	10	15	3
Percent known adult	*44*	*50*	*36*	*62*
Both sexes				
Percent known adult	*38*	*63*	*39*	*61*

[a]"Adult," as used here, refers to birds 2 or more years old.

year, there was 'a low proportion of known adults, but in 1965 we had not covered the Pinnacle Falls Road unit very thoroughly and we probably had neglected to capture and band several adult birds that showed up in 1966 as unknown-age birds.

In 1970, although our visits to the study area were reduced, we believed that a population recovery had begun. At least ten broods were produced on the study area (compared with nine in 1969) and we found birds more easily than in 1969. Of the 20 different adult or yearling birds encountered in 1970, 10 (50 percent) were known adults, and we found 2 of the 29 birds (7 percent) which we banded as chicks in 1969. Although our sample sizes are very small, the age distribution was intermediate between high and low years and probably reflected the population recovery which was occurring.

Our demographic observations strongly suggest that the size of the breeding population of spruce grouse is largely influenced by recruitment of yearlings. This is consistent with the results of many other studies of grouse (Bendell, 1972).

The annual variation in recruitment of young birds into the breeding population each spring appears to be quite independent of reproductive success the preceding spring and summer. The total number of chicks present on the study area during the summer was relatively constant from

Table 18. Recovery of banded chicks after their first winter

Year	Number of chicks banded in previous year[a]	Number of banded yearlings present	Percent of chicks as yearlings	Size of breeding population
1966	36	2	6	45
1967	32	3	9	41
1968	30	8	27	53
1969	40	4	10	32

[a]As an example, there were 36 chicks banded in 1965, of which 2 were present in 1966.

1965 through 1968, but spring breeding populations varied widely. Details of chick survival will come later.

Although it appears that survival of young spruce grouse through their first winter is a very important factor in determining the size of the breeding population, it is not the only factor. Nor does the identification of the age group and the critical season give us an answer to the question of what causes variation in survival of young birds in different years. More long-term study is required to identify what specific environmental or innate factors play the key roles in deciding life or death for these young birds.

Egg Production

We found nests in only 3 of the 5 years of study and found only a total of nine nests, with an average complete clutch size of 5.7 eggs. Of the nine nests observed, seven hatched successfully. As mentioned earlier (Chapter 12), one nest was found abandoned with a single unincubated egg. The unsuccessful nest was destroyed, probably by a red fox. Another was partly depredated by a red squirrel. Thirty-nine of the 40 eggs in the completely incubated nests hatched, for an egg fertility rate of 97.5 percent.

Of the seven complete clutches found, two were laid by known yearlings and contained 5 and 6 eggs, one was laid by a hen known to be at least 2 years old and contained 5 eggs, and four nests laid by birds of unknown age contained 5, 6, 6, and 7 eggs, respectively. No difference in clutch sizes attributable to age of the female were apparent from these few observations.

Although not all females brought off broods, we think that all of them except one at least laid eggs. We found brood patches on all females we examined in late May and June, with the exception of one of the three females on which we had placed a radio transmitter in the prenesting season. Zwickel and Bendell (1967b) found that the presence or absence of a brood patch is a reliable indicator of whether or not captive female blue grouse attempt to nest. They also found that about 98 percent of wild blue grouse laid eggs. It appears that similar characteristics hold for the spruce grouse. A reasonable figure for egg production would be to multiply the mean clutch size (5.7) by the number of females present in May. Multiplying by the fertility rate (0.975) then gives the number of fertile eggs. We did not have enough data to determine whether there are year-to-year variations in clutch size or fertility.

Chick Production

The number of chicks produced from the eggs depends upon their fertility and the survival of eggs against predation or abandonment. Our data on nest predation and abandonment were extremely scanty. It appears, however, that on our study area egg losses constitute a high proportion of loss of total potential production of chicks.

Once the female has left the nest with her brood, the probability of her losing all her chicks is quite low. From 1965 to 1971 we saw 40 broods away from the nest at least twice from June through August, and of these only one female had lost her entire brood (she had only one chick when we first encountered her). Therefore it seems that after a mother hen has led her brood away from the nest, total loss of a brood is rare, and broodlessness is caused more by the loss of eggs or of very young chicks than by deaths of chicks older than a few days. Similar observations have been made of blue grouse (Zwickel and Bendell, 1967b).

Considerable annual variation occurred in the proportion of female spruce grouse with broods (Table 19). From 67 to 88 percent of the females seen produced chicks. These figures are higher than the 41 to 60 percent reported for Franklin's spruce grouse in Alberta (McCourt, 1969), but lower than the 80 to 90 percent reported for Alaska spruce grouse (Ellison, 1974). These figures assume equal probability of seeing a female whether or not she has a brood. McCourt (1969) believed that the probability of seeing a female with a brood, because of her aggressive behavior, is higher than that of seeing one without a brood, but Ellison

(1974) assumed that there was no bias in locating hens with or without broods. We tested for a bias by comparing the proportion of broodless females seen more than once in a summer with the proportion of females with broods seen more than once in the summer. The assumption is that the chances of seeing a bird a second time is equivalent to the chance of seeing it the first time. Sixteen of 23 broodless hens (70 percent) were seen a second time, and 37 of 72 hens with broods (51 percent) were seen a second time. The difference is not statistically significant; thus, while it does not conclusively show that females without broods tend to be more readily seen, it does show that females without broods are at least as likely to be found as those with broods. I believe that our figures on the proportion of females found with and without broods are probably accurate, within reasonable limits.

Nine banded females known to be yearlings were seen in the summer during the June 20–August 20 period, when successful females are accompanied by young. Four of the 9 yearlings had broods, compared with 32 of 39 females known to be adults, and 24 of 30 females of unknown age. The difference in reproductive success between known yearlings and known adults is not quite statistically significant at 0.05 probability. McCourt (1969) also found slightly higher reproductive success among older female Franklin's spruce grouse.

Table 19. Production of spruce grouse chicks on the Yellow Dog Plains study area, based upon brood sizes when first seen away from the nest

Year	Number of females	Number of females with broods	Percentage of females with broods	Total number of chicks	Average number of chicks per brood
1965	32	23	72	82	3.6
1966	17	15	88	75	5.0
1967	22	15	68	75	5.0
1968	33	22	67	75	3.4
1969	13	9	69	30	3.3

The average size of broods (the largest number of chicks seen with the female after leaving the nest) tended to be slightly smaller among yearlings and unknown-age birds than among birds 2 years old and older. In 1968, when we had the largest sample size, 4 yearling females averaged 3.25 chicks, 11 unknown-age hens had an average of 3.18 chicks, and 7 older birds averaged 3.86 chicks, but a t test revealed no significant differences between brood sizes.

Are we accusing the young females of not doing their share of reproducing? In 1968, when there was a high proportion of young birds in the breeding population and after which the population declined, 4 of 6 known yearlings produced broods, while only 7 of 12 known adults brought off young. Eleven of 15 unknown-age females had broods. It appears, then, that the known yearling birds contributed their share to reproduction in 1968, a generally poor reproductive year, with 13 chicks from 6 yearling females, compared with 27 chicks from 12 females known to be adults. Although in general yearling hens are apparently not as prolific as older females, the population decline which occurred on our study area in late 1968 cannot be attributed to their inadequacy in producing offspring.

Redfield (1975) observed that a high percentage of females with broods and large early brood sizes are associated with increasing populations of blue grouse. In our study the highest percentage of females with broods (88 percent) and high brood size (average of 5.0 chicks per brood) occurred in 1966, a year that was followed by a decline in population. The lowest proportion of females with broods (67 percent) occurred in 1968, a high population year, which was followed by a decline. The largest total number of chicks was produced in 1965, also a year followed by a decline. No consistent pattern or correlation between summer brood sizes and spring population the following year could be found.

Since recruitment of yearling birds is an important factor in determining the size of spring populations, survival of young after the summer brood season must be an essential ingredient in determining the size of breeding spruce grouse populations.

Survival and Mortality of Chicks

Table 20 shows brood sizes recorded in the first and second months of life. A high rate of survival of chicks would produce brood sizes which approach the clutch size of 5.7. In 1966 an average brood size of 5.0 chicks was maintained into August, but in 1968 the late July–August average was only 2.9 chicks. Taking into account all years of the study, early mortality, as with most species of grouse, was fairly high. An average drop occurred from clutch size of 5.7 to 4.0 chicks in the first month, but in the second month average brood size dropped only from 4.0 to 3.7 chicks. Both clutch and brood sizes are lower than those of spruce grouse in Alaska, where clutch sizes average 7.5 and July broods average 5.2 chicks, with August broods only slightly lower (Ellison, 1974).

We had little information on survival and mortality in autumn, although it seemed that birds were quite easily found through October. The November–December period seemed

Table 20. Average spruce grouse brood sizes[a] on the Yellow Dog Plains study area

Year	Average brood size[b]	
	June 15–July 19 (0–4 weeks old)	July 20–August 19 (4–8 weeks old)
1965	3.8 (12)	3.6 (12)
1966	5.2 (10)	5.0 (11)
1967	5.0 (7)	4.1 (9)
1968	3.2 (11)	2.9 (11)
1969	3.0 (5)	3.8 (5)
Weighted average	4.0 (45)	3.7 (48)

[a]Based upon brood size when last seen during the period.

[b]Numbers in parentheses indicate the number of broods the average is based upon.

to be critical, as we could usually tell subjectively in January, by how many birds we found, approximately what the level of the forthcoming spring population would be. Our data from January through April likewise were limited, but we found no striking circumstances in that period which indicated that high mortality was occurring.

Causes of mortality might include diseases and parasites, malnutrition, predation, and exposure to unfavorable weather. Our studies of blood parasites (Chapter 11) from 1966 to 1968 showed that although blood parasites were common among the birds, their levels were generally low. Leider (1969) concluded that blood parasitism was not an important factor in mortality rates. A few studies of other species of grouse have identified disease as contributing substantially to numbers of deaths but most workers now agree that it is not a mortality factor of serious consequence (Bendell, 1972).

Food quality and quantity (Chapter 10) has not been shown directly to limit spruce grouse numbers on the Yellow Dog Plains (Gurchinoff and Robinson, 1972), in Alaska (Ellison, 1972) or in Alberta (Pendergast and Boag, 1971b).

Predation is a rather mysterious agent of disappearance of birds (Chapter 12). Predators strike quickly, usually when no one is looking, and frequently leave little measurable trace of their work, especially if it involves consuming a small bird which goes down feathers and all. The question of to what extent predation controls numbers of grouse remains somewhat conjectural (Bendell, 1972).

It has been suggested by many workers that bad weather has a serious effect on grouse populations, depriving grouse of food, causing the death of young chicks, and affecting the viability of eggs and chicks hatching from them (Bendell, 1972).

A currently prevalent viewpoint holds that all of the extrinsic factors such as weather, predation, and food may work to regulate populations only if they are allowed to do so by intrinsic processes—processes that operate within the grouse populations. These intrinsic factors include genetic differences in resistance between increasing and decreasing populations, aggressive interactions in dense populations, and territorial defense, all of which may send the less fortunate birds packing or render them susceptible to predators, bad weather, starvation, and disease. There are many difficulties in identifying and verifying the interactions of intrinsic and extrinsic factors, but progress is being made.

On the Yellow Dog Plains early brood size of chicks was closely correlated with June temperatures (Fig. 15). Temperature data were taken from Marquette, 35 miles distant, but the temperature trends there are probably similar to those on the Yellow Dog Plains. The correlation coefficient ($r = 0.887$ p <0.05) shows a significant correlation between early brood survival and June temperature. It might be surmised that wet weather would further increase the effect of cold on mortality of chicks, but adding rainfall data

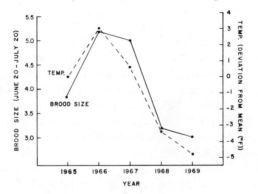

Figure 15. It appeared that there was a close relationship between early survival of spruce grouse chicks on the Yellow Dog Plains and June temperatures, but direct cause and effect was not conclusively shown.

weakened rather than strengthened the correlation. Since weather is quite easy to measure and to formulate correlations upon, we may be guilty of over-rating the importance of weather and early brood survival. Other workers, however, have found similar relationships between mortality of young grouse and unfavorable weather (Cartwright, 1944 Ritcey and Edwards, 1963), although Zwickel (1967) observed two young blue grouse broods in extremely inclement weather and found no chick losses. If deaths of spruce grouse chicks were brought on by bad weather, we had no data to determine whether the birds' innate susceptibility varied from time to time.

During the second month of life, losses of chicks are less severe than in the first month, assuming a decline from 5.7 eggs hatching (Table 20, p. 164). In 1969 an apparent increase occurred in brood size, but this can be explained by the small sample size and the fact that some of the broods counted in their second month were different broods and obviously larger ones than those counted in their first month. There was an indication that, on the whole, brood survival in the second month was inversely correlated with survival in the first month; that is, if a small number of chicks survived the first month, a larger proportion of the survivors would make it through the second month. An explanation might be that weak chicks get weeded out in the first month and the remaining brood members are more resistant to hazards encountered in the second month. The statistical correlation between first and second month survival was in the right direction (negative) but was not statistically significant ($r = -0.490$).

We attempted to correlate brood survival in the second month with various summer weather conditions, including

Table 21. Values used to correlate survival of spruce grouse chicks in the second month with weather conditions

A Year	B Percent survival in first month	C Reciprocal of Column B	D Average July–August temperature (°F)	E Proportion of possible sunshine in July–August	F C×D×E	G Percent survival in second month[a]
1965	61	1.64	62.8	.68	70.0	95
1966	91	1.10	67.0	.67	49.4	96
1967	88	1.14	64.1	.67	49.0	82
1968	56	1.79	65.2	.70	81.7	90
1969	53	1.88	68.0	.73	93.3	100

[a] Correlation of values in columns F and G yielded $r = 0.726$, not significant.

temperature, rainfall, and the amount of sunshine. Warm temperatures might produce better feeding and growth conditions for the young, and sunny weather might further increase the availability and visibility of insects for young grouse. The best correlation we could come up with was an index obtained by multiplying the average July–August temperature by the percentage of possible sunshine by the reciprocal of brood survival in the first month (Table 21). It seems to make sense if you think about it; warm temperatures could encourage health and growth, sunshine could bring out more insects to feed upon, and the toughened survivors of the first month could take advantage of these factors. The r value was 0.726, not significant.

From 1965 through 1968 it looked as though some density-dependent relationship influenced the percentage of successfully breeding females and the survival of their young (Table 19, p. 162). In the high-population years of 1965 and 1968 a lower proportion of females brought broods off the nest and a lower number in each brood survived, assuming equal egg clutch sizes each year. In the low-population years either a high proportion of hens brought off young and summer survival of the chicks was high, or both. It was almost as though they "tried harder" or were somehow physiologically more attuned to reproduction when the population was low and got careless when it was high. Some researchers (Chitty, 1967; Krebs et al., 1969) might explain this situation as being caused by genetic differences in behavior or viability of individuals between dense and sparse populations. Others (Calhoun, 1962) might explain it as a function of high population density producing stress and subsequent reduced maternal responsibility. We are not ready either to accept or to reject such explanations, especially since in 1969 the population, when at its lowest, had an extremely poor summer for production of chicks.

Perhaps the recent studies of Herzog and Boag (1977), which verify the defense of territories by female spruce grouse, offer the best explanation. In years of high populations the most aggressive and first-come females claim the best breeding habitat. The remaining hens are forced to accept second-rate accommodations and are therefore less successful in reproducing. Thus, what has been shown to occur among monogamous pairs of red grouse (Jenkins et al., 1967) apparently also occurs in the polygamous spruce grouse through territorial behavior of the hens. Herzog (1978) suggests that spruce trees, which are in limited supply in his Alberta study area and which provide nutritious food for incubating hens, may be prized requisites for a nesting territory. Although there was no shortage of spruces on the Yellow Dog Plains, other more subtle nesting or brood-rearing requirements may have been in short supply, with the unlucky females being unable to claim such furnishings during years of high female numbers. Therefore some of them may have had lower nesting and brood-rearing success. In 1969 the weather may have been so unfavorable that it caused widespread reproductive failure regardless of territorial possession, but this is only a guess.

In fall, the only mortality factor we obtained data on was the illegal kill by hunters. Johnston (1969) concluded that probably less than 10 percent of the fall spruce grouse population on the Yellow Dog Plains is shot. His observations were made in the fall of 1968, shortly after which a large population decline occurred. Hunting was not the cause. Further discussion of spruce grouse hunting will follow in Chapter 14.

Our winter observations are not adequate to assess directly specific mortality factors. Some workers, however, have identified weather conditions in winter as critical to spring populations. Edminister (in Bump et al., 1947) found that declines in ruffed grouse followed unfavorable winter snow conditions and low temperatures, and Formozov (1946) made a similar observation for hazel grouse. A lack of snow, or crusted snow coupled with cold temperatures, may prevent these birds from burrowing into the snow and thus cost them energy or increase their vulnerability to predators. A high metabolic cost to a female grouse, brought on by cold temperatures, food or cover shortages, or both, may be reflected in the quality of chicks she produces the following spring. Various workers have described such a possibility among several species of grouse (Choate, 1963; Dorney and Kabat, 1960; Gullion, 1970; Jenkins et al., 1963, 1967; Ritcey and Edwards, 1963; Siivonen, 1957).

We explored possible effects of snow conditions and low temperatures first on grouse survival and then on chick survival the following summer. Kueber (1973) analyzed weather conditions recorded at the Marquette County Airport about 30 miles from the study area, but at a similar elevation and a similar distance from Lake Superior, and attempted to correlate them with changes in spruce grouse populations.

A snow depth of 4 to 5 inches was considered suitable for snow roosting. Formozov (1946) notes that a minimum of 4 to 5 inches of snow is required for burrowing by black grouse, a larger bird than the spruce grouse, and Kueber assumed a similar requirement for spruce grouse. If subfreezing temperatures occurred and continued after a thaw, Kueber assumed that a crust was present and counted the number of days until an additional 4 inches of snow accumulated over the crust. While a crust was present, it was believed, cold nightly temperatures would place additional stress on birds which were unable to burrow. He found no relationship between survival of adults and the number of snow crust–cold night combinations. Among young birds, however, a pattern appeared in which survival of juvenile grouse decreased as the number of cold nights with crust increased.

Unfortunately our weather data were measured very indirectly. More direct observations should be made before we conclude that a snow crust coupled with cold temperatures does actually take a toll of young birds.

The effect of cold weather and snow crust could be interrelated with other mortality factors. Since spruce grouse males and possibly females exhibit territoriality which per-

sists throughout the winter, young birds may be expelled
from the best habitat and when weather conditions are adverse they may be more vulnerable to predation. Jenkins et
al. (1967) found that red grouse deprived of territories in
Scotland by territory-holders were more subject to parasitism and malnutrition, and particularly to predation, than
territorial birds.

We tried several approaches to correlating winter crust
and temperature conditions with brood survival the following summer but were unable to find a relationship. The
theory is that females subjected to stresses of bad weather
before the breeding season lay eggs from which hatch
chicks that do not survive as well as chicks from eggs laid
by females which have undergone little or no stress before
breeding. As noted earlier, a number of workers have described such effects among various species of grouse.

Survival and Mortality of Adults

By using only banded birds we were able to arrive at an
estimate of annual survival rates of birds over 1 year old.
The formula simply involved dividing the number of
banded birds over 1 year old that were known to be alive in
a particular year by the number of banded birds that were
known to be alive the preceding year. The term "known to
be alive" refers to birds that were seen either during that
year or in a succeeding year. This gives us a minimum survival rate, because we may have missed seeing some living
banded birds that had moved off the study area or that
were present but not noticed.

The proportion of birds missed was apparently not very
high, however. Of 23 banded adult females known to have
lived at least 3 years, 13 were seen every year, 6 were seen
2 of the 3 years, and 4 were seen only 1 of 3 years. The
probability of seeing a banded female in a particular year
was calculated as:

$$p = \frac{13 + (6 \times 2/3) + (4 \times 1/3)}{23} = 0.798.$$

Thus the probability of our seeing a banded adult female if she was alive in a particular year was about 80 percent,. or perhaps a little lower, since a few birds present might not have been seen at all in the 3 years. This would increase the size of the denominator by perhaps two birds and give a probability of about 0.74, or 74 percent.

For 23 banded adult males the values were:

$$p = \frac{15 + (7 \times 2/3) + (1 \times 1/3)}{23} = 0.869.$$

Males appear to be more consistently visible than females. Presumably we would see about 85 percent of the adult males present in a particular year.

Minimum survival rates are given in Table 22. An average of 50 percent of the males and about 45 percent of the females over a year old would survive into the following breeding season. These percentages fall about halfway be-

Table 22. Minimum survival rates of banded spruce grouse over 1 year old on the Yellow Dog Plains[a]

	1965–66	1966–67	1967–68	1968–69	All years
			Males		
2 years or older	—	.40 (10)	.53 (17)	.67 (9)	.53 (36)
Yearlings	—	.80 (5)	.00 (2)	.50 (4)	.55 (11)
Age unknown	.55 (20)	.59 (17)	.33 (3)	.21 (14)	.46 (54)
All males	.55 (20)	.56 (32)	.45 (22)	.41 (27)	.50 (101)
			Females		
2 years or older	—	.89 (9)	.46 (13)	.36 (11)	.55 (33)
Yearlings	—	0	.67 (3)	.33 (6)	.44 (9)
Age unknown	.31 (32)	.67 (9)	.50 (10)	.25 (8)	.39 (59)
All females	.31 (32)	.78 (18)	.50 (26)	.32 (25)	.45 (101)

[a]Minimum survival rate = BA_t/BA_{t-1}, where BA_t = number of banded birds known to be alive in year t and BA_{t-1} = number of banded birds known to be alive in the previous year. Sample size (in parentheses) includes birds known to be alive through sightings in subsequent years, but not necessarily seen on the study area during the year. Thus numbers of birds may differ from numbers presented in Table 16, which includes only birds seen on the study area in a given year.

tween the 68 to 77 percent survival reported for male Franklin's spruce grouse in Alberta (McLachlin, 1970) and the 31 to 38 percent survival of adult Alaskan spruce grouse (Ellison, 1974). Clutch sizes of Alaskan spruce grouse are larger than those of either Michigan or Alberta birds, and Michigan birds may produce larger clutches than Alberta birds (McCourt et al., 1973). There seems to be an inverse relationship between reproductive potential and survival among the different populations of spruce grouse. Such a balance of births and deaths apparently keeps the populations relatively stable. Spruce grouse only approximate the rule that more northern populations lay larger clutches of eggs. Lack (1954) argues that among birds in which the parents feed the young, clutch size has been genetically selected for depending upon available time for gathering food. That is, the long summer days in the north provide more time for parents to feed a larger brood. This hypothesis, however, does not consider birds such as grouse, in which the young forage for themselves.

Skutch (1967) suggests that the birth rate or clutch size may be an adaptive response to the death rate, with higher mortality rates in the north requiring larger clutch sizes and higher annual productivity for survival of the species. In temperate regions smaller clutch sizes may favor greater survival of adult birds by placing less severe physiological demands on females for egg laying. If this hypothesis is true, populations would be relatively stable in temperate regions and more widely fluctuating in far northern realms, where favorable conditions during certain years would result in bumper crops of birds, and unfavorable conditions bring on high mortality of both young and adults. Such appears to be the case.

Regardless of our theoretical explanations, the fact is that clutch sizes and the mortality rates of many bird species are broadly balanced so that most birds become neither a plague on their environment nor disappear entirely. This attests to the intricate but flexible web of relationships that exists among births and deaths in the community of life.

The survival rates of 45 to 50 percent for adult Michigan spruce grouse appear to be in the middle or high range for a variety of grouse species according to data summarized by Johnsgard (1973), with willow ptarmigan, prairie chickens, and sharp-tailed grouse having lower survival rates, ruffed grouse about the same, and blue grouse having higher survival rates.

Our data (Table 22) suggest that birds of unknown age had higher mortality (lower survival) than either known yearlings or known two-year-olds and older. These unknown-age birds were those which showed up on the study area in adult plumage. We were unable to tell whether they were yearlings or older birds. The chances are that many of them were yearlings recently immigrating or were wandering adults. The difference between survival rates of this group and those of known-age birds was not statistically significant.

Adult survival rates on the Yellow Dog Plains varied widely from year to year, but there was no consistent pattern correlating with breeding population levels. The highest survival rates for both males and females occurred between 1966 and 1967, but 1967 was a year of a low population. The lowest breeding population, that in 1969, was preceded by both a low adult survival rate and a low survival rate for chicks hatched in 1968.

If survival of adult spruce grouse from year to year averages about 50 percent, what recruitment of new birds is necessary to maintain a stable population? In the spring population, with 50 percent loss of adults there should be one new bird for every old bird present. This means that, if each hen lays six eggs and the adult sex ratio is 50:50, an average of one chick from those eggs must survive into the next breeding season in order to maintain the population. But not always half the adults survive, sometimes more than half survive and sometimes less. In some years not a single chick from those six eggs is around the following spring, but in other years more than one are. And so the population fluctuates from year to year.

We were unable to correlate variations in adult survival rates with any observed physical or biological elements in their environment. In a fairly small population such as that we were working with, random factors probably account for considerable variation in mortality. We have previously described disease and malnutrition as insignificant in regulating numbers of adult spruce grouse, and we could find no correleations with weather data.

Losses to predators would probably depend upon the number of encounters between spruce grouse and predators, which in turn depends upon the density of spruce grouse and the density and behavior of the predators. Predator density could be unrelated to spruce grouse density, but possibly related to density of hares or small mammals. Or a goshawk or two might more or less randomly spend a few months in the winter on the study area instead of somewhere else. The effect of this somewhat random chance could be measurable in numbers of spruce grouse surviving on the study area. I thought, however, that if increased predation were causing a decline in the number of spruce grouse, I might find more evidence of predation in years of population decline than in years of stability or increase. In 1967, a year followed by an increase of spruce grouse, we found remains of three preyed-upon birds but in 1965, a year followed by a decrease, we found only two remains. In 1966 we found five, in 1967, three, and in 1969, three. The sample sizes are very small but they show no striking relationship between observed predation rates and survival of adults.

Immigration and Emigration

We found a few young banded spruce grouse that moved from one end of our study area to the other, a distance of about 4 miles, and knew of one that traveled 8 miles entirely off the study area and off the Yellow Dog Plains. It is therefore reasonable to assume that many young birds emigrated off the area and were never seen again, even though they may have lived for a long time. But since some birds went, undoubtedly many others also came. It is hard to tell just how many entered and how many left the area, but we assume that immigration and emigration were about equal, allowing for random variation. We found that birds which disperse are nearly always first-year birds, which agrees with McCourt's (1969) findings. This made it diffi-   ؛ cult to calculate survival rates of birds of the year from band recoveries, since it was not possible to tell whether a bird had died or just moved away, and we had no good method of telling yearlings from older birds.

Since we have quite reliable data on annual survival rates of adults and yearlings, however, we can infer approximate survival rates of chicks (Table 23). For example the adult survival rate from 1967 to 1968 was 0.48 for 48 banded adults, meaning that 23 of 48 adults in 1967 were alive in the summer of 1968. The 1968 breeding population consisted of 53 birds. Since 23 of those were surviving adults, the other 30 were new birds, most of which were probably chicks from 1967. In 1967, 70 chicks were produced on the study area, indicating a survival rate of 30 out of 70 or 0.43. In 1968 we recovered 27 percent of the chicks banded

Table 23. Survival rates of spruce grouse chicks inferred from adult and yearling survival rates

	1966	1967	1968	1969
Number of adults in year $t-1$	58	45	48	53
Adult survival rate	.40	.64	.48	.36
Number of adults surviving in year t	23	29	23	19
Total population in year t	45	41	53	32
Number of yearlings in year t	22	12	30	13
Number of chicks produced in year $t-1$	82	75	75	75
Chick survival rate	.27	.16	.40	.17

in 1967, so 0.27 was a minimum survival rate. The difference between 0.27 and 0.43 is probably caused by immigration of young unbanded birds. This method assumes that most but not all of the recruits are yearlings. The adult mortality rate was calculated to include adults which did not always appear each year and therefore also allows for some of the recruits to be unbanded adults.

Summary of Population Ecology

In this chapter I have tried to describe some of the reasons for fluctuations in spruce grouse populations, but no conclusions are warranted from our observations. On the Yellow Dog Plains it appeared that cold weather in early summer caused losses of chicks and that a crust on the snow accompanied by cold temperatures might have made young birds more susceptible to predators. The number of predators present on the Yellow Dog Plains, probably influenced by factors other than spruce grouse populations, could be responsible for some increases or decreases in numbers of spruce grouse. Territorial behavior, or a modification of it, among females could affect nesting success and survival of chicks by forcing some birds into less favorable habitat. In a small population such as the one we studied, an imbalance between immigration and emigration of a relatively small number of birds could play a significant role in determining the size of a population.

Fortunately, the spruce grouse population on the Yellow Dog Plains is large enough and productive enough to be resilient. It recovers from the numerous adversities the birds encounter, and conversely it never seems to grow beyond some upper limit that seems to be set for it by elements beyond our present knowledge.

Chapter *14*

The Hunter and the Spruce Grouse

> When my father gave me the shotgun, he said I might
> hunt partridges with it, but that I might not shoot them
> from trees. I was old enough, he said, to learn
> wing-shooting.
>
> Aldo Leopold

Grouse-hunting near the more urban regions of our continent is, from what I read in magazines, a rather genteel
sport practiced with well-bred obedient dogs and expensive
shotguns. The quarry is usually the ruffed grouse or "par-
·tridge." Its startling, noisy, tree-dodging flight makes the
shooting of a legal bag limit of four or five birds in a day
an achievement realized by most urban hunters only once
or twice in a lifetime. The emphasis in eastern grouse-
hunting is on the sport—wondering at the superiority of
dogs to humans in reading odors, the unexpected flush of a
bird, and difficult wing-shooting. All this is accompanied by
the pleasant and encouraging rediscovery that concrete and
asphalt have not yet covered the entire world, and that
there is still some air fit for the human lung and solitude to
replenish the human spirit.

179

But as we get farther removed from the cities, the sport of bird-hunting gradually assumes a different character. It becomes less ritualized and more closely tied to our ancestral origins, which are associated with providing meat. Ruffed grouse are often hunted from automobiles or by stalking them without a dog, and they are often shot on the ground or in trees. I know of one old-time grouse hunter in Upper Michigan who, upon taking aim, takes his gun down from his shoulder if the bird flies before he can shoot. "No use wasting a shell," he grumbles, climbing back into his car. The clean air and brilliant autumn woods may be taken for granted (perhaps rightfully so) by the rural northwoods hunter. His success may frequently be measured by the number of "partridges" in the bag at the end of the day.

Some of us, myself included, have a tendency to disdain this sort of sportsman. We feel that the ruffed grouse is too noble a bird to be treated merely as a potential piece of meat for the table, and that its value lies primarily in its aesthetic sporting qualities, with its very palatable flesh of secondary importance. Still another group, the anti-hunters, condemns any hunting of wild animals, arguing that hunting should have been "civilized" out of us by now and that the proper relationship between man and grouse consists only of looking at one another. But as far as the effect on numbers in most grouse populations is concerned, there is probably little difference brought about by the road hunter, the sporting dog fancier, or the anti-hunter.

To many urban sportsmen and to nonhunters the spruce grouse, because of its unsuspecting nature, is not an appropriate game bird. Yet for the backwoods road hunter, whose recreational value system may be less distant from our primitive roots, a spruce grouse by the roadside is just as fitting a game bird as a ruffed grouse.

Arguments on the quality of the spruce grouse as game are not new. Bent (1932, p. 134) said: "The spruce grouse is not much esteemed as a game bird, as it lacks most of the qualities that appeal to the sportsman. Its haunts are usually too difficult to hunt in, it is too tame and stupid to make its pursuit interesting . . ."

David Backus of Land O' Lakes, Wisconsin, expressed a different point of view in a letter to me a few years ago: "Spruce grouse are probably most vulnerable to the random northern road hunter, who also, in my view, is responsible for the reputation of the bird as a fool. Spruce grouse can be pretty sporty if hunted in a gentlemanly manner, over pointing dogs. Those that flatly refuse to fly can always be left for another day."

Donald McKnight, an Alaskan biologist, wrote me about the spruce grouse in his state: "When and where they are heavily hunted they can provide good sport for the shotgunner. Generally, however, they are the basic 'fool hen' and can be taken easily with rifle or rock." McKnight also mentioned that in interior Alaska during years of high spruce grouse populations the Indians take many of them for food and refer to them as "chickens." Thus it seems that one man's sporting bird is another man's chicken.

According to Newfoundland biologist Jim Hancock, authorities there thought highly enough of the spruce grouse as a game bird to attempt to establish it on insular Newfoundland. In the spring of 1964, 134 spruce grouse from Labrador were released at Butter Pot Park and Gander Lakes. The birds have become established there and hunting them was made legal in 1975.

Regardless of differences of opinion over the sporting qualities of spruce grouse, they are shot legally in 6 of the 13 states in their range and in all Canadian provinces and territories except Nova Scotia and Prince Edward Island. Spruce grouse do not inhabit the latter province.

Tables 24 and 25 summarize information on hunting regulations and harvest figures which I gathered in a survey of states and provinces in the range of the spruce grouse. Estimating the total annual harvest of spruce grouse in North America is difficult because figures are not easily obtained. Six state and six provincial and territorial wildlife agencies provided some estimate of harvest. Since

1963 agencies have been apparently collecting more data on spruce grouse, for Lumsden and Weeden (1963) were able to obtain harvest estimates from only one state and three provinces.

In the United States the five states which made estimates of harvest and which permit harvest reported a yearly total of about 58,000 to 70,000 birds in the early 1970s. This excludes Alaska, which probably has the largest harvest of any of the states because of its large size and the amount of spruce grouse habitat. Since British Columbia estimates a harvest of 83,000 to 122,000 spruce grouse, a conservative guess for Alaska might be 50,000 to 60,000. By adding the Alaskan figures, we arrive at a conservative annual United States legal harvest of 108,000 to 130,000 spruce grouse.

In Canada no estimates were given for Northwest Territories, Quebec, Ontario, or Alberta. New Brunswick, adjacent to Quebec, estimates a kill of "up to 40,000" spruce grouse, and Manitoba, adjacent to Ontario, estimates 10,000 to 22,600 birds. Roughly figuring on the size of the provinces of Quebec and Ontario, numbers of hunters, and abundance of spruce grouse, an estimate of a harvest of perhaps 40,000 to 50,000 birds each in Quebec and Ontario might be in line. In Alberta the harvest is probably at least three to four times greater than the 1300 to 9000 birds

Table 24. Estimated annual harvest of spruce grouse in the United States, based upon information from state wildlife agencies[a]

State	Length of season in days (1975–76)	Estimated annual harvest, 1972–76
Minnesota	47	10,000–11,500
Montana	75–76	28,700–34,500
Wyoming	70–76	6,000–8,400
Idaho	71	4,200–5,400
Washington	92	9,200–11,000
Alaska	250	No estimate

[a]The following states in spruce grouse range do not permit hunting: Maine, New Hampshire, Vermont, New York, Michigan, Wisconsin, and Oregon. An illegal annual kill of 2,000 birds is estimated in Michigan, but no estimates are available from the other states.

taken in Saskatchewan, since Alberta has more spruce grouse range. Inasmuch as Montana, to the south, provides a harvest of about 30,000 birds per year and British Columbia, to the west, upwards of 80,000, an estimate of 10,000 to 15,000 for Alberta seems conservative. Using this guesswork, then, a total Canadian harvest of about 230,000 to 318,000 birds is arrived at. Adding this guess to the estimate for the United States harvest gives us a total annual harvest of 340,000 to 450,000 spruce grouse. Johnsgard (1973) estimated 440,000, using much the same approach as I have used.

This estimate of the total harvest places the spruce grouse in a surprising third place among the ten species of North American grouse in numbers harvested. The ruffed grouse is far and away the leading game species of grouse, with an annual kill of about 3,700,000 (Johnsgard, 1973). This species constitutes about 66.1 percent of the total number of grouse of all species taken each year. Following that is the sharp-tailed grouse, with about 455,000 birds taken each year, for 8.1 percent of the total. Close behind

Table 25. Estimated annual harvest of spruce grouse in Canada, based upon information from provincial and territorial wildlife agencies[a]

Province or territory	Length of season in days (1975–76)	Estimated annual harvest, 1972–74
Newfoundland	84	12,000–15,000[b]
New Brunswick	36	Up to 40,000
Quebec	122–250	No estimate
Ontario	92–111	No estimate
Manitoba	83–89	10,000–22,600
Saskatchewan	75	1300–9000
Northwest Territories	242	No estimate
Alberta	80	No estimate
British Columbia	up to 76[c]	83,000–122,000
Yukon Territory	153	4,600

[a]Novia Scotia does not permit hunting of spruce grouse. There are no spruce grouse on Prince Edward Island.

[b]Figures for 1976–77.

[c]Season length varies in different areas in British Columbia.

the sharp-tail is the spruce grouse, making up about 7.9 percent of the total number of grouse harvested in North America each year. Although the spruce grouse does not seem to be given much attention as a game bird either by hunters or by wildlife managers, its total contribution to the harvest is substantial, primarily because of its extensive range.

The other species of grouse and harvest estimates, according to Johnsgard (1973) are as follows: blue grouse, 370,000 (6.6 percent); ptarmigans (3 species) 300,000 (5.4 percent); sage grouse, 250,000 (4.5 percent); and prairie chickens (2 species) 85,000 (1.5 percent).

According to my survey of states and provinces road hunting accounted for 33 percent to 99 percent of hours spent in hunting grouse. A very small percentage of grouse hunters (0–20 percent) in various areas pursue the spruce grouse as a primary target. Most spruce grouse are shot by gunners who are primarily hunting ruffed grouse or blue grouse, or in many cases hunting whatever grouse happens along. In western states and provinces several respondents noted that big game hunters harvest many spruce grouse. In Idaho 69 percent of the forest grouse are estimated to be taken by big game hunters. I suppose if moose and elk are hard to find, a spruce grouse or two become tempting targets as well as providing a meal for the camp. Many western hunters use .22 rifles or sidearms to shoot spruce grouse, perhaps increasing the challenge somewhat. British Columbia has a novel 1-week bow and arrow grouse season, although it is on Vancouver Island, where the spruce grouse does not occur. In Newfoundland many spruce grouse are legally taken in snares set for snowshoe hares, according to biologist Jim Hancock.

Harvest figures summarized in Tables 24 and 25 are for the legal kill; but with a bird such as the spruce grouse many are undoubtedly taken out of season and by unlicensed hunters. A biologist from one western state estimates that the illegal kill is probably equal to the legal harvest, with backpackers and fisherman in summer and early fall taking rather large numbers of spruce grouse.

Many respondents commented that most hunters do not distinguish between species of grouse, and even in the one province and those states where spruce grouse are given legal protection, biologists question how effective that protection is.

In Michigan the spruce grouse has been protected since 1914. Because of this it was difficult for us to obtain much reliable information on how many birds are shot each year in Michigan, since hunters are understandably unwilling to submit incriminating evidence. In the fall of 1968, Johnston (1969) interviewed hunters on the Triple-A Road at the Yellow Dog Plains. This was an attempt to gather information on what kind of hunting pressure the spruce grouse on the Yellow Dog Plains were being subjected to and how many were being shot. We also wanted to know about the hunters' knowledge of spruce grouse. Johnston tried to emphasize that he was not a law enforcement officer, but Upper Michigan people are rightfully suspicious of strangers with clip boards, as our quaint ways and valuable resources seem to be constantly under study by people from the nether parts of the state. Whether Johnston got the truth or not is difficult to ascertain, but we felt that some information would probably be better than none at all.

Johnston interviewed 42 hunters on several weekends. Only 2 of the 42 hunters reported sighting spruce grouse in the 1968 season, for an average of only 2 sightings per 100 hunter hours. In good spruce grouse range in north-central Ontario hunters see 12 to 17 spruce grouse per 100 hours (Lumsden and Weeden, 1963). By comparison, ruffed grouse hunters in the Upper Peninsula of Michigan normally flush 40 to 250 ruffed grouse per 100 hours afield (Michigan Department of Natural Resources data).

None of the hunters interviewed admitted shooting a spruce grouse in the current season but one hunter reported that his acquaintances had shot four. Eight hunters confessed to shooting spruce grouse in previous years and all said they mistook them for ruffed grouse. Twenty-nine percent of the hunters said they could not identify the spruce grouse and several of those who claimed they could cited only the smaller size of the spruce grouse as the feature which distinguishes it from ruffed grouse. (There is overlap in autumn weights of the two species.)

The spruce grouse kill in 1968 from the Yellow Dog Plains reported by interviewed hunters was four birds. In addition we found two fresh empty shotgun shells about 20 yards from two piles of spruce grouse feathers, a rather suggestive situation. Two other banded birds were reported shot, one by an anonymous phone call, the other by a hunter who claimed he found it dead. From dates and locations we concluded that these were not the four birds reported by interviewed hunters.

Thus we know of a hunter take of eight spruce grouse from the Yellow Dog Plains in 1968. We estimated a fall population on the 25-square-mile area as about 200 to 250 birds. Even if the actual hunter kill was three or four times the eight birds that we knew about, the proportion of the Yellow Dog Plains population removed by hunting would have been less than 15 percent, a rate of removal not likely to have a serious influence on the population.

For many hunters of both the urban and the backwoods variety, the pleasant but quiet climax of a hunt comes when the game is served on the table. Palatability then becomes an important characteristic in estimating the quality of a game bird. What about the spruce grouse? Opinions vary. In contrast to the white breast meat of the ruffed grouse, that of the spruce grouse is dark. Many people prefer the white meat to the dark meat of a turkey, and likewise many prefer to eat ruffed grouse over spruce grouse. Here is a report from Bent (1932, p. 135):

> The spruce grouse is not highly regarded as a table bird, for its flesh is said to be unpalatable. This is probably so in winter, when it has been feeding on spruce and balsam leaves; its flesh is then dark and decidedly resinous in flavor. But during fall, when it feeds largely on berries, green herbiage, and insects, its flesh has a very different color and flavor. Brewster (1925) says that some young birds, shot in September, "proved delicious eating, their flesh being much sweeter and finer than that of any ruffed grouse. . . ."

David Backus of Wisconsin wrote me saying that it is a shame that illegally shot spruce grouse in that state are discarded as contraband, as "they are perfectly decent eating properly prepared."

In the fall of 1975 a friend gave me half of a female spruce grouse which he had mistakenly shot for a ruffed grouse. He tried his half, and said he didn't care much for its eating quality. I dipped mine in a mixture of salt and flour, browned it in a frying pan, covered it with water and simmered it for about half an hour. I thought it was excellent and preferred it to ruffed grouse.

My conclusion is that spruce grouse can be very good eating but there is individual variation of taste in both the eater and the eaten.

No one has asked me, but if anyone should, I would recommend opening the season on spruce grouse in the Upper Peninsula of Michigan during the September 15–November 13 ruffed grouse season. A one-bird daily limit and a two-bird season limit would allow people who mistakenly bring down a spruce grouse (females on the wing are easily misidentified, even by experienced hunters) to take the bird home and eat it, rather than toss it away. Thus an opportunity would be afforded to collect more accurate information on the status and abundance of this bird in Michigan through cooperative hunter sampling. The one-bird daily limit would discourage hunters from demolishing a flock, and the two-bird season limit would serve as a guideline for the conscientious hunter. I believe Michigan spruce grouse populations would be largely unaffected by permitting such limited hunting.

Chapter **15**

Some Thoughts About Spruce Grouse, Man, and Nature

Once after I had given a talk on spruce grouse to a group of high school science students a boy in the audience asked, "What is the ecological role of the spruce grouse?" It suddenly struck me that in 4 years of research I had never asked myself the large and important question that this high school kid had come up with in 45 minutes. He wanted to know how this bird fits into the ecosystem—the large and complex intermingling of living and nonliving elements which is the basis for life on the earth.

I probably did not answer him very satisfactorily, but since then I have thought much about his question. Of what value to the ecosystem is the spruce grouse? Of what value is any one species?

One way to approach answering the question is to ask what would happen if we removed that species, in this case the spruce grouse, from the system. I have tried to think of a plant or animal in the northwoods that would fare better without spruce grouse, but I have not been able to come up with any. Jack pines and spruces give up some of their needles to spruce grouse and without that loss their growth might be infinitesimally faster because of increased photosynthesis. Maybe some of the insect species that are eaten by spruce grouse chicks would enjoy larger populations, but spruce grouse take such an absurdly small proportion of insects that it is unlikely that insect numbers are really affected by spruce grouse. Blueberries and cranberries might produce better without spruce grouse depredating their leaves and flowers, but again the proportion eaten seems very minute; and of course their fruits are by their nature meant to be eaten so that their seeds may be dispersed after passing through the bird's digestive system. So spruce grouse probably help blueberries and cranberries more than they hurt them.

Spruce grouse may in a small way increase the rate of turnover of nutrients in their habitat and thereby increase the amount of life their surroundings can support. Conifer needles are broken down in their digestive tracts and returned to the soil either in the form of bird droppings, dead spruce grouse, the excretions of an animal that has eaten a spruce grouse, or the carcass of such an animal. Bird droppings in some favorite winter spruce grouse haunts are quite abundant—possibly enough to increase plant growth, although no one has measured such an effect, if any occurs.

The spruce grouse as a vegetarian concentrates and converts plant material into protein and fats of its body. The goshawk, great horned owl, red fox, and coyote are all somewhat better off for the presence of the spruce grouse, but probably none of those predators depends primarily on the spruce grouse as a source of protein.

Thus it seems that the role of the spruce grouse in the broad scheme of life is a minor one, and that the world could go on without it, just as life has gone on without the great auk, the passenger pigeon, and the heath hen. But we are all somewhat poorer for their loss, as we would be for the loss of the spruce grouse.

The spruce grouse serves as a minor source of food for man, It also serves as a source of aesthetic comfort and inspiration. Knowing that the "fool hen," a bird which has not yet learned the proper fear of man, can still exist quietly in the coniferous forests of North America provides some hope for us in the future. The sight of a male spruce grouse spreading its splendid glistening tail in a sunlit opening among the pines is likely to inspire in us a quality of thought that may temporarily at least transcend the Dow-Jones Index or the next presidential election, and cause us to wonder about our own role in the ecosystem.

The spruce grouse is not in danger of extinction; but in the southern parts of its range, where human economics may conflict with the best interests of spruce grouse, it may need our help. It will need protection from the multi-fronted attacks of man—from poisons and pesticides, from open-pit mines which turn woodlands into wastelands, from the invasions of thousands of cottages and motorboats, and from highways and all that they carry into the countryside. This bird will need large tracts of coniferous forests, and it may need occasional natural fires to encourage the jack pines, lodgepole pines, and spruces so vital to its existence in some parts of its range. The spruce grouse will need regulation of hunter harvest in line with a reproductive potential that is lower than that of most other grouse.

But in our zeal for controlling all processes on the earth we must resist the temptation to overmanage. The spruce grouse is a bird of wild places and we need to keep such places wild. We know that these birds can be reared quite easily under artificial circumstances, but a spruce grouse in an aviary, or even in a manmade forest where trees are planted and wildfires are snuffed out by synthetic chemicals and bulldozers, is only a living imitation of a real spruce grouse. A spruce grouse can be truly whole only when it is part of a population of spruce grouse which in turn is part of the community of life—the community which includes the fox and the owl, the pines, the spruces, the north wind, and the winter snow.

Reference Matter

Appendix

Where and How to See a Spruce Grouse in Upper Michigan

I am somewhat torn about writing this section. The prospect of hundreds of birdwatchers trampling over the reindeer moss frightens me, but I suppose everyone won't arrive at once; and unless we encourage people to become interested in wildlife and translate their interest into political support, our remaining wild lands and wildlife habitat may be forever devastated in the currently prevailing materialistic fervor for economic growth. Accordingly, I am encouraging readers to seek out a spruce grouse or two in their own domain, and spend a quiet morning sharing the pine-scented air with a bird that will not mind your visit if you behave yourself and leave after a short stay.

In the eastern Upper Peninsula the area along Highway M–28 near Seney harbors good populations of spruce grouse. There are some spruce grouse on the Seney National Wildlife Refuge but not in the areas normally traversed on the guided tours. Between 10 and 20 miles west of Seney look for dry ground, jack pines and spruces on the north side of the highway, and a place to cross the drainage ditch that parallels it. You can park right off the highway and walk into the woods. Bring insect repellent and a compass. If you get lost, head south. You can't miss the highway, it goes straight east and west for 28 miles. Don't worry about poisonous snakes, as there aren't any. Stay on the sand ridges, especially along their lower edges where jack pines mix with spruces. Avoid the dense wet underbrush of tag alders and bog birch; there is no use tormenting yourself, and the birds don't frequent that stuff anyhow.

In the north-central part of the Upper Peninsula, the Baraga Plains south of L'Anse is a good spruce grouse area, but the one I know best is the Yellow Dog Plains. To get there you must drive through Marquette and take County Road 550 northwest almost to Big Bay. Turn left on County Road 510 and go 3 miles. Then turn right on the Triple-A Road and follow it for about 8 to 10 miles, uphill almost all the way. Watch for loaded pulpwood trucks. I recommend yielding; there is little room to pass.

When you come into the Yellow Dog Plains you'll know it. The vegetation changes from maples, hemlocks, and aspens to jack pines. The best areas for finding spruce grouse lie south of the Triple-A Road. Take a woods road or walk in off the Triple-A, and look especially in places where spruces are mixed with the jack pines. Again, bring a compass and insect repellent. If you get lost, go north to the Triple-A Road.

Wherever you look, I suggest a search pattern of two to four people moving along parallel to one another 40 to 50 feet apart. Walk at a comfortably slow pace and look for birds on the ground. Don't bother looking in the trees; birds in trees are difficult to spot, and it's hard on the neck. Don't expect the birds to flush, although they might. More often they stand still and let you walk past.

You may find a bird in 10 minutes, or it may take you 3 or 4 hours; but while you search you will find other rewards. In May thousands of trailing arbutus blossoms add their special fragrance to the air. In June pink lady-slipper orchids are plentiful and in places the fuchsia-colored blossoms of fringed polygala carpet the ground. White-throated sparrows, ruby-crowned kinglets, and Swainson's thrushes sing throughout the day. From mid-July through August bring a blueberry pail; in good years you may pick several quarts in a few hours. In September and October red blueberry leaves sprinkle the mat of gray reindeer moss and geese often pass overhead. The hunter can find ruffed grouse and woodcock in surrounding areas. From November through April, unless you are a winter camper, forget it. The spruce grouse are in the trees and hard to locate, and it is very cold and far from the plowed road.

If you try once or twice without success, call me up in Marquette. I'll try to help you find a spruce grouse.

References Cited

Alder, H. E. 1935. Determining the sex of day-old chicks, Nebraska Experimental Station Circular 51. 81 pp.

Aldrich, J. W. 1963. Geographic orientation of American Tetraonidae. Journal of Wildlife Management 27(4): 529–545.

American Ornithologists' Union. 1931. Check-list of North American birds. 4th Ed. American Ornithologists' Union, Lancaster, Pa. xix + 526 pp.

American Ornithologists' Union. 1957. Check-list of North American birds. 5th Ed. The Lord Baltimore Press, Baltimore, Md. 691 pp.

American Ornithologists' Union. 1973. Thirty-second supplement to the American Ornithologists' Union Check-list of North American birds. Auk 90(2): 411–419.

American Ornithologists' Union. 1976. Thirty-third supplement to the American Ornithologists' Union Check-list of North American birds. Auk 93(4): 875–879.

Ammann, G. A. 1963. Status of spruce grouse in Michigan. Journal of Wildlife Management 27(4): 591–593.

Barrows, W. B. 1912. Michigan bird life. Michigan Agricultural College, East Lansing. xiv + 882 pp.

Beer, J. 1943. Food habitats of the blue grouse. Journal of Wildlife Management 7(1): 32–44.

Bendell, J. F. 1955. Disease as a control of a population of blue grouse, *Dendragapus obscurus fuliginosus* (Ridgway). Canadian Journal of Zoology 33(3): 195–223.

Bendell, J. F. 1972. Population dynamics and ecology of the Tetraonidae. Proceedings of the Fifteenth International Ornithological Congress, pp. 81–89. E. J. Brill, The Hague, Netherlands.

Bendell, J. F., and P. W. Elliott. 1967. Behaviour and the regulation of numbers in blue grouse. Canadian Wildlife Service Report Series No. 4. 76 pp.

197

Bennett, G. F. 1970. Development of trypanosomes of the *T. avium* complex in the invertebrate host. Canadian Journal of Zoology 48(5): 945–957.

Bent, A. C. 1932. Life histories of North American gallinaceous birds. Smithsonian Institution. United States National Museum Bulletin 112, Washington, D.C. 490 pp.

Boag, D. A. 1965. Indicators of sex, age, and breeding phenology in blue grouse. Journal of Wildlife Management 29(1): 103–108.

Boag, D. A. 1966. Population attributes of blue grouse in southwestern Alberta. Canadian Journal of Zoology 44(5): 799–814.

Boag, D. A. 1972. Effect of radio packages on behavior of captive red grouse. Journal of Wildlife Management 36(2): 511–518.

Boag, D. A., and J. W. Kiceniuk. 1968. Protein and caloric content of lodge pole pine needles. Forestry Chronicle 44(4): 28–31. (French abstract).

Boag, D. A., A. Watson, and R. Parr. 1973. Radio-marking versus backtabbing red grouse. Journal of Wildlife Management 37(3): 410–412.

Brinkmann, A. 1950. Microfilariae from ruffed grouse (*Bonasa umbellus* (L.)) in Ontario, Canada. Universitetet i Bergen Årbok. Naturvitenskapelig rekke Nr. 3. 1–12.

Bump. G., R. W. Darrow, F. C. Edminister, and W. F. Crissey, 1947. The ruffed grouse: life history, propagation, management. New York State Conservation Department Publication, Albany. xxxvi + 915 pp.

Calder, W. A. 1968. Respiratory and heart rates of birds at rest. Condor 70(4): 358–365.

Calhoun, J. B. 1962. Population density and social pathology. Scientific American 206(2): 1399–1408.

Cartwright, B. W. 1944. The crash decline in sharptail grouse and Hungarian partridge in western Canada and the role of the predator. Transactions of the North American Wildlife Conference 9: 324–330.

Chitty, D. 1967. The natural selection of self-regulatory behavior in animal populations. Proceedings of the Ecological Society of Australia 2: 51–78.

Choate, T. S. 1963. Habitat and population dynamics of white-tailed ptarmigan in Montana. Journal of Wildlife Management 27(4): 684–699.

Clarke, C. H. D. 1935. Blood parasites of ruffed grouse (*Bonasa umbellus*) and spruce grouse (*Canachites canadensis*), with description of *Leucocytozoon bonasae* n. sp. Canadian Journal of Research 12: 640–650.

Cottam, G., and J. T. Curtis. 1956. The use of distance measures in phytosociological sampling. Ecology 37(3): 451–460.

Coues, E. 1903. Key to North American birds. Vol. 2. Dana Estes and Co., Boston. 1152 pp.

Crichton, V. 1963. Autumn and winter foods of the spruce grouse in central Ontario. Journal of Wildlife Management 27(4): 597.

Crow, E. L., F. A. Davis, and M. W. Maxfield. 1960. Statistics manual. Dover, New York. xvii + 288 pp.

Dasmann, R. F. 1964. Wildlife biology. Wiley, New York. 231 pp.

Dorney, R. S. 1963. Sex and age structure of Wisconsin ruffed grouse populations. Journal of Wildlife Management 27(4): 599–603.

Dorney, R. S., and C. Kabat. 1960. Relation of weather, parasitic disease and hunting to Wisconsin ruffed grouse populations. Wisconsin Conservation Department Technical Bulletin 20, Madison. 64 pp.

Dorney, R. S., and A. C. Todd. 1959. Spring incidence of ruffed grouse blood parasites. Journal of Parasitology 46(6): 687–694.

Edminster, F. C. 1947. The ruffed grouse, its life story, ecology and management. Macmillan, New York. xvii+ 385 pp.

Ellison, L. N. 1966. Seasonal foods and chemical analysis of winter diet of Alaskan spruce grouse. Journal of Wildlife Management 30(4): 729–735.

Ellison, L. N. 1967. Spring movements and behavior of territorial and nonterritorial male Alaskan spruce grouse. Paper presented at meeting of Northwest Section of the Wildlife Society. Mimeo. 13 pp.

Ellison, L. N. 1968a. Sexing and aging Alaskan spruce grouse by plumage. Journal of Wildlife Management 32(1): 12–16.

Ellison, L. N. 1968b. Movements and behavior of Alaskan spruce grouse during the breeding season. Paper presented at meeting of California-Nevada Section of the Wildlife Society. Mimeo. 11 pp.

Ellison, L. N. 1971. Territoriality in Alaskan spruce grouse. Auk 88(3): 652–664.

Ellison, L. N. 1972. Role of winter food in regulating numbers of Alaskan spruce grouse. Ph.D. Thesis. University of California, Berkeley. 101 pp.

Ellison, L. N. 1973. Seasonal social organization and movements of spruce grouse. Condor 75(4): 375–385.

Ellison, L. N. 1974. Population characteristics of Alaskan spruce grouse. Journal of Wildlife Management 38(3): 383–395.

Erickson, A. B., P. R. Highby, and C. E. Carlson. 1949. Ruffed grouse populations in Minnesota in relation to blood and intestinal parasitism. Journal of Wildlife Management 13(2): 188–194.

Emerick, R. H. 1968. Behavioral responses of spruce grouse (*Canachites canadensis*) hens and broods to predators. Unpublished report. Department of Biology, Northern Michigan University, Marquette. 14 pp.

Eng, R. L., and G. W. Gullion. 1962. The predation of goshawks upon ruffed grouse on the Cloquet Forest Research Center, Minnesota. Wilson Bulletin 74: 227–242.

Fallis, A. M. 1965. Protozoan life cycles. American Zoologist 5(1): 85–94.

Fallis, A. M., and G. F. Bennett. 1958. Transmission of *Leucocytozoon bonasae* Clarke to ruffed grouse (*Bonasa umbellus L.*) by the black flies *Simulium latipes* Mg. and *Simulium aureum* Fries. Canadian Journal of Zoology 36(4): 533–539.

Fallis, A. M., and G. F. Bennett, 1960. Description of *Haemoproteus canachites* n. sp. (*Sporozoa: Haemoproteidae*) and sporogony in *Culicoides* (Diptera: Ceratopogonidae). Canadian Journal of Zoology 38: 455–464.

Farner, D. S. 1960. Digestion and the digestive system. *In* Biology and comparative physiology of birds, ed. A. J. Marshall, Vol. 1, pp. 411–467. Academic Press, New York.

Fenna, L., and D. A. Boag. 1974. Adaptive significance of the caeca in Japanese quail and spruce grouse (*Galliformes*). Canadian Journal of Zoology 52: 1577–1584.

Forbush, E. H. 1927. Birds of Massachusetts and other New England states. Massachusetts Department of Agriculture, Boston. xix + 461 pp.

Formozov, A. N. 1946. Snow cover as an integral factor of the environment and its importance in the ecology of mammals and birds. (Trans. by W. Prychodko and W. O. Pruitt). Occasional Paper No. 1. Boreal Institute, University of Alberta, Edmonton. 176 + xiv pp.

Fowle, C. D. 1946. The blood parasites of the blue grouse. Science 103 (2685): 708–709.

Garnham, P. C. C. 1966. Malaria parasites and other Haemosporidia. Blackwell, Oxford. 1114 pp.

Grange, W. B. 1948. Wisconsin grouse problems. Wisconsin Conservation Department Publication 328. Madison. 318 pp.

Gruson, E. S. 1972. Words for birds. Quadrangle Books, New York. xiv + 305 pp.

Grzimek, B. 1972. Grzimek's animal life encyclopedia. Vol. 7. Birds I. Van Nostrand Reinhold, New York. 579 pp.

Gullion, G. W. 1970. Factors influencing ruffed grouse populations. Transactions of the North American Wildlife and Natural Resources Conference. 35: 93–105.

Gurchinoff, S., and W. L. Robinson. 1972. Chemical characteristics of jack pine needles selected by feeding spruce grouse. Journal of Wildlife Management 36(1): 80–87.

Hachisuka, M. 1928. Variations among birds (chiefly game birds). Ornithological Society of Japan, Supplementary Publication 12. x + 85 pp.

Hamerstrom, F., and F. Hamerstrom. 1963. The symposium in review. Journal of Wildlife Management. 27(4): 869–887.

Hamerstrom, F., and F. Hamerstrom. 1964. Grouse. In A new dictionary of birds, ed. A. L. Thomson, pp. 343–345. McGraw-Hill, New York.

Harju, H. J. 1969. Acoustical communication of the spruce grouse. M.A. Thesis, Northern Michigan University, Marquette. xiii + 108 pp.

Harju, H. J. 1971. Spruce grouse copulation. Condor 73(3): 380–381.

Harris, V. T. 1952. An experimental study of habitat selection by prairie and forest races of the deer mouse, Peromyscus maniculatus. Contributions from the Laboratory of Vertebrate Biology of the University of Michigan. 56: 1–53.

Hartley, P. H. T. 1950. An experimental analysis of interspecific recognition. In Physiological mechanisms in animal behavior, Symposia of Society for Experimental Biology. pp. 313–336. Academic Press, New York.

Herman, C. M. 1963a. The occurrence of protozoan blood parasites in Anatidae. Transactions of the International Union of Game Biologists. 6: 341–349.

Herman, C. M. 1963b. Disease and infection of the Tetraonidae. Journal of Wildlife Management. 25(2): 209–210.

Herzog, P. W. 1978. Food selection by female spruce grouse during incubation. Journal of Wildlife Management. 42(3): 632–636.

Herzog, P. W., and D. A. Boag. 1977. Seasonal changes in aggressive behavior of female spruce grouse. Canadian Journal of Zoology 55: 1734–1739.

Herzog, P. W., and D. A. Boag. 1978. Dispersion and mobility in a local population of spruce grouse. Journal of Wildlife Management 42(4): 853–865.

Hjorth, I. 1970. Reproductive behavior of Tetraonidae with special references to males. Viltrevy, Swedish Wildlife 7(4): 181–596.

Hoffman, R. S. 1961. The quality of the winter food of blue grouse. Journal of Wildlife Management 25(2): 209–210.

Höst, P. 1942. Effect of light on moults and sequences of plumage in the willow ptarmigan. Auk 59(3): 388–403.

Jenkins, D., A. Watson, and G. R. Miller. 1963. Population studies on red grouse, *Lagopus lagopus scoticus* (Lath.) in northeast Scotland. Journal of Animal Ecology 32(3): 317–376.

Jenkins, D., A. Watson, and G. R. Miller. 1967. Population fluctuations in the red grouse *Lagopus lagopus scoticus*. Journal of Animal Ecology 36(1): 97–122.

Johnsgard, P. A. 1973. Grouse and quails of North America. Univ. of Nebraska Press, Lincoln. xx + 553 pp.

Johnston, R. E. 1969. A survey of hunters in spruce grouse habitat in Michigan. The Jack Pine Warbler 47(4): 111–114.

Jollie, M. 1955. A hybrid between the spruce grouse and the blue grouse. Condor 57(4): 213–215.

Jones, T. L., and W. L. Robinson. 1969. Blood parasites of Michigan spruce grouse, *Canachites canadensis*. Journal of Parasitology 55(3): 492.

Jonkel, C. J., and K. R. Greer. 1963. Fall food habits of spruce grouse in northwestern Montana. Journal of Wildlife Management 27(4): 593–596.

Keith, L. B. 1963. Wildlife's ten-year cycle. Univ. of Wisconsin Press, Madison. xvi + 201 pp.

Keppie, D. M. 1975. Clutch size of the spruce grouse, *Canachites canadensis franklinii*, in southwest Alberta. Condor 77(1): 91–92.

Keppie, D. M. 1977. Snow cover and the use of trees by spruce grouse in autumn. Condor 79(3): 382–384.

Keppie, D. M., and P. W. Herzog. 1978. Nest site characteristics and nest success of spruce grouse. Journal of Wildlife Management 42(3): 628–632.

King, D. G. 1973. Feeding habits of the blue grouse in the subalpine. Syesis 6: 121–125.

Klopfer, P. H. 1963. Behavioral aspects of habitat selection: the role of early experience. Wilson Bulletin 75(1): 15–22.

Krebs, C. J., B. L. Keller, and R. H. Tamarin. 1969. *Microtus* population biology; demographic changes in fluctuating populations of *M. ochrogaster* and *M. pennsylvanicus* in southern Indiana. Ecology 50(4): 587–607.

Kueber, R. J. 1973. The influence of winter weather conditions on the survivorship of *Canachites canadensis* in northern Michigan. M.A. Thesis. Northern Michigan University, Marquette, 46 + ix pp.

Lack, D. 1943. The life of the robin. H. F. and G. Witherby, London. 200 pp.

Lack, D. 1954. The natural regulation of animal numbers. Clarendon Press, Oxford. 343 pp.

Lack, D. 1966. Population studies of birds. Clarendon Press, Oxford. 341 pp.

Lance, A. N., and A. Watson. 1977. Further tests of radio-marking on red grouse. Journal of Wildlife Management 41(3): 579–582.

Leider, M. J. 1969. Physiological and ecological responses of spruce grouse (*Canachites canadensis*) to blood parasitism in northern Michigan. M.A. Thesis. Northern Michigan University, Marquette. 50 pp.

Leopold, A. 1933. Game management. Scribner's, New York. xxi + 481 pp.

Leopold, A. S. 1953. Intestinal morphology of gallinaceous birds in relation to food habits. Journal of Wildlife Management 17(2): 197–203.

Levine, N. D. 1961. Protozoan parasites of domestic animals and of man. Burgess, Minneapolis. 412 pp.

Lewis, J. B., J. D. McGowan, and T. S. Baskett. 1968. Evaluating ruffed grouse reintroduction in Missouri. Journal of Wildlife Management 32(1): 17–28.

Lindroth, H., and L. Lindgren. 1950. On the significance for forestry of the capercaillie, *Tetrao urogallus* L., feeding on pine-needles, etc. Suomen Riista 5: 60–81. (In Finnish, English summary).

Lumsden, H. G. 1961. Displays of the spruce grouse *Canachites canadensis* (Aves: Tetraonidae). Canadian Field Naturalist 75(3): 152–160.

Lumsden, H. G. 1969. A hybrid grouse, *Lagopus* × *Canachites* from Northern Ontario. Canadian Field Naturalist 83(1): 23–30.

Lumsden, H. G., and R. B. Weeden. 1963. Notes on the harvest of spruce grouse. Journal of Wildlife Management 27(4): 587–590.

MacDonald, S. D. 1968. The courtship and territorial behavior of Franklin's race of the spruce grouse. Living Bird 7: 5–25.

MacDonald, S. D. 1970. The breeding behavior of the rock ptarmigan. Living Bird 9: 195–238.

Madgwick, H. A. I. 1964. Variations in the chemical composition of red pine (*Pinus resinosa* Ait.) leaves: a comparison of well grown and poorly grown trees. Forestry 37(1): 87–94.

Manning, A. 1967. An introduction to animal behavior. Addison-Wesley, Reading, Mass. 208 pp.

Marshall, W. H., and J. J. Kupa. 1963. Development of radio telemetry techniques for ruffed grouse studies. Transactions of the North American Wildlife and Natural Resources Conference 28: 443–456.

Masui, K., and J. Hashimoto. 1933. Sexing baby chicks. Journal Printing Co., Vancouver, B.C. 91 pp.

McBee, R. H., and G. C. West. 1969. Cecal fermentation in the willow ptarmigan. Condor 71(1): 54–58.

McCourt, K. H. 1969. Dispersion and dispersal of female and juvenile Franklin's grouse in southwestern Alberta. M.S. Thesis. University of Alberta, Edmonton. 137 pp.

McCourt, K. H., D. A. Boag, and D. M. Keppie. 1973. Female spruce grouse activities during laying and incubation. Auk 90(3): 619–623.

McCourt, K. H., and D. M. Keppie. 1975. Age determination of juvenile spruce grouse. Journal of Wildlife Management 39(4): 790–794.

McLachlin, R. A. 1970. The spring and summer dispersion of male Franklin's grouse in lodgepole pine forest in southwestern Alberta. M.S. Thesis. University of Alberta, Edmonton. 153 pp.

Miller, H. E. 1967. Spruce grouse study, Seney Nuonal Wildlife Refuge. Unpublished Report, Seney National Wildlife Refuge, Germfask, Mich. 8 pp.

Moss R., and J. A. Parkinson. 1971. The digestion of heather (*Calluna vulgaris*) by red grouse (*Lagopus lagopus scoticus*). British Journal of Nutrition 27(2): 285–298.

National Research Council. 1966. Nutrient requirements for domestic animals. No. 1. Nutrient requirements for poultry. 5th Rev. Ed. Publ. 1345. Washington, D.C. 28 pp.

Noble, G. K. 1939. The role of dominance in the social life of birds. Auk 56(3): 263–273.

Owen, R. B., Jr. 1969. Heart rate, a measure of metabolism in blue-winged teal. Comparative Biochemical Physiology 31(3): 431–436.

Payne, R. B. 1972. Mechanisms and control of molt. *In* D. S. Farner and J. R. King, eds., Avian biology, Vol. 2, pp. 103–155. Academic Press, New York.

Pendergast, B. A. 1969. Nutrition of spruce grouse in the Swan Hills, Alberta. M.S. Thesis, University of Alberta, Edmonton. 73 pp.

Pendergast, B. A., and D. A. Boag. 1970. Seasonal changes in diet of spruce grouse in central Alberta. Journal of Wildlife Management 34(3): 605–611.

Pendergast, B. A., and D. A. Boag. 1971a. Maintenance and breeding of spruce grouse in captivity. Journal of Wildlife Management 35(1): 177–179.

Pendergast, B. A., and D. A. Boag. 1971b. Nutritional aspects of the diet of spruce grouse in central Alberta. Condor 73(4): 437–443.

Pendergast, B. A., and D. A. Boag. 1973. Seasonal changes in the internal anatomy of spruce grouse in Alberta. Auk 90(2): 307–317.

Prawdzik, T. R. 1963. Ruffed Grouse escaping a Cooper's hawk. Journal of Wildlife Management 27(4): 639–642.

Pulliainen, E., L. Paloheimo, and L. Syrjala. 1968. Digestibility of blueberry stems (*Vaccinium myrtillus*) and cowberries (*Vaccinium vitis-idaea*) in the willow grouse (*Lagopus lagopus*). Annales Academiae Scientiarum Fennicae A.IV 126: 1–15.

Rand, A. L. 1947. Clutch size in the spruce grouse and theoretical considerations of some factors affecting clutch size. Canadian Field-Naturalist 61(4): 127–130.

Rand, A. L. 1948. Variation in the spruce grouse in Canada. Auk 65(1): 33–40.

Redfield, J. A. 1975. Comparative demography of increasing and stable populations of blue grouse (*Dendragapus obscurus*). Canadian Journal of Zoology 53(1): 1–11.

Ridgway, R., and H. Friedmann. 1946. The birds of North and Middle America. Part X. Smithsonian Institution. United States National Museum Bulletin 50. Washington, D.C. 484 pp.

Ritcey, R. W., and R. Y. Edwards. 1963. Grouse abundance and June temperatures in Wells Gray Park, British Columbia. Journal of Wildlife Management 27(4): 604–606.

Roberts, T. S. 1936. The birds of Minnesota. Univ. of Minnesota Press, Minneapolis. xxvi + 718 pp.

Robinson, W. L. 1969. Habitat selection by spruce grouse in northern Michigan. Journal of Wildlife Management 33(1): 113–120.

Robinson, W. L., and D. E. Maxwell, 1968. Ecological study of the spruce grouse on the Yellow Dog Plains. Jack Pine Warbler 46(3): 75–83.

Rue, L. L. III. 1973. Game Birds of North America. Popular Science Publishing Co., New York. 490 pp.

Rusch, D. H., and L. B. Keith. 1971. Seasonal and annual trends in numbers of Alberta ruffed grouse. Journal of Wildlife Management 35(4): 803–822.

Rusch, D. H., E. C. Meslow, P. D. Doerr, and L. B. Keith. 1972. Response of great horned owl populations to changing prey densities. Journal of Wildlife Management 36(2): 282–296.

Sadler, K. C. 1961. Grit selectivity by the female pheasant during egg production. Journal of Wildlife Management 25(3): 339–341.

Short, L. L., Jr. 1967. A review of the genera of grouse. American Museum Novitates No. 2289. American Museum of Natural History, New York. 33 pp.

Siivonen, L. 1957. The problem of the short-term fluctuations in numbers of tetraonids in Europe. Finnish Game Foundation, Game Reserve Paper 19. 44 pp.

Skutch, A. F. 1967. Adaptive limitation of the reproductive rate of birds. Ibis 109(4): 479–599.

Stabler, R. M., N. J. Kitzmiller, L. N. Ellison, and P. A. Holt. 1967. Hematozoa from the Alaskan spruce grouse, *Canachites canadensis*. Journal of Parasitology 53(2): 233–234.

Stoneberg, R. P. 1967. A preliminary study of the breeding biology of the spruce grouse in northwestern Montana. M.S. Thesis. University of Montana, Missoula. 82 pp.

Sullivan, R. E. 1968. White blood cell counts in relation to the incidence of Haemoproteus in the spruce grouse. Unpublished report. Department of Biology, Northern Michigan University, Marquette. 18 pp.

Suomalainen, H., and E. Arhimo. 1945. On the microbial decomposition of cellulose by gallinaceous birds (family Tetraonidae). Ornis Fennica 22(1): 21–23.

Svoboda, F. J., and G. W. Gullion. 1972. Preferential use of aspen by ruffed grouse in northern Minnesota. Journal of Wildlife Management 36(4): 1166–1180.

Taber, R. D. 1969. Criteria of age and sex. *In* Wildlife management techniques, ed. R. H. Giles. pp. 325–401. 3rd Ed. The Wildlife Society, Washington, D.C.

Taverner, P. A. 1931. A new hybrid grouse *Lagopus lagopus* (Linnaeus) × *Canachites canadensis* (Linnaeus). National Museum of Canada Annual Report 1930: 89–91.

Thompson, W. C., and L. M. Black. 1935. The problem of distinguishing the sex of day-old chicks. New Jersey Agricultural Experiment Station Circular 358. 20 pp.

Tinbergen, N. 1939. Why do birds behave as they do? Bird Lore 41(1): 23–30.

Treichler, R., R. W. Stow, and A. L. Nelson. 1946. Nutrient content of some winter foods of ruffed grouse. Journal of Wildlife Management 10(1): 12–17.

Tufts, R. W. 1961. The birds of Nova Scotia. Nova Scotia Museum, Halifax. 481 pp.

Uttal, L. J. 1939. Subspecies of the spruce grouse. Auk 56(4): 460–464.

Voitkevich, A. A. 1966. The feathers and plumage of birds. Sedgwick and Jackson, London. 335 pp.

Watson, A., and R. Moss. 1970. Dominance, spacing behaviour and aggression in relation to population limitation in vertebrates. *In* Animal populations in relation to their food resources, ed. A. Watson. pp. 167–220. Blackwell, Oxford.

Weeden, R. B., and J. B. Theberge. 1972. The dynamics of a fluctuating population of rock ptarmigan in Alaska. Proceedings of the Fifteenth International Ornithological Congress, pp. 90–106. E. J. Brill, The Hague, Netherlands.

Weir, D. G. 1973. Status and habits of *Megapodius pritchardii*. Wilson Bulletin, 85(1): 79–82.

Wells, C. G., and L. J. Metz. 1963. Variation in nutrient content of loblolly pine needles with season, age, soil, and position on the crown. Proceedings of the Soil Science Society of America 27(1): 90–93.

Welty, J. C. 1975. The life of birds. 2nd Ed. Saunders, Philadelphia. xv + 623 pp.

White, D. P. 1954. Variation in the nitrogen, phosphorus, and potassium contents of pine needles with season, crown position, and sample treatment. Proceedings of the Soil Science Society of America 18(3): 326–330.

Wynne-Edwards, V. C. 1962. Animal dispersion in relation to social behavior. Hafner, New York. xi + 653 pp.

Yamashina, M. Y. 1939. Note sur le Tétras Falcipenne de Sibirie. L'Oiseau et Revue Francaise d'Ornithologie, n.s. 9: 3–9.

Zwickel, F. C. 1966. Winter food habits of capercaillie in northeast Scotland. British Birds 59(8): 325–336.

Zwickel, F. C. 1967. Some observations of weather and brood behavior in blue grouse. Journal of Wildlife Management 31(3): 563–568.

Zwickel, F. C., and J. F. Bendell. 1967a. A snare for capturing blue grouse. Journal of Wildlife Management 31(1): 202–204.

Zwickel, F. C., and J. F. Bendell. 1967b. Early mortality and the regulation of numbers of blue grouse. Canadian Journal of Zoology 45(5): 817–851.

Zwickel, F. C., and J. F. Bendell. 1972a. Observations on food habits of incubating female blue grouse. Condor 74(4): 493–494.

Zwickel, F. C., and J. F. Bendell. 1972b. Blue grouse, habitat, and populations. Proceedings of the Fifteenth International Ornithological Congress, pp. 150–169. E. J. Brill, The Hague, Netherlands.

Zwickel, F. C., D. A. Boag, and J. H. Brigham. 1974. The autumn diet of spruce grouse: a regional comparison. Condor 76(2): 212–214.

Zwickel, F. C., and J. H. Brigham. 1970. Autumn sex and age ratios of spruce grouse in north-central Washington. Journal of Wildlife Management 34(1): 218–219.

Zwickel, F. C., and A. N. Lance. 1966. Determining the age of young blue grouse. Journal of Wildlife Management 30(4): 712–717.

Zwickel, F. C., and C. F. Martinsen. 1967. Determining age and sex of Franklin spruce grouse by tails alone. Journal of Wildlife Management 31(4): 760–763.

Index

Latin names of plants are from H. A. Gleason and A. Cronquist, *Manual of Vascular Plants of Northeastern United States and Adjacent Canada.* Van Nostrand, Princeton, N. J., 1969 and from C. L. Hitchcock, A. Cronquist, M. Ownbey, and J. W. Thompson, *Vascular Plants of the Pacific Northwest.* University of Washington Press, Seattle, 1969.

Latin names of birds are from American Ornithologists' Union, *Checklist of North American Birds,* 5th Edition, Lord Baltimore Press, Baltimore, 1957, and from the 1973 and 1976 supplements; from B. Grzimek, *Grzimek's Animal Life Encyclopedia. Birds.* Van Nostrand-Reinhold, N. Y., 1972; and from A. L. Thompson, ed., *A New Dictionary of Birds.* McGraw-Hill, N. Y., 1964.

Latin names of mammals are from E. R. Hall and K. R. Kelson, *The Mammals of North America.* Vols. 1 and 2. Ronald Press, New York, 1959.

Names of families and orders of insects are from common usage.

Age, determination of: chicks, 118–19; full-grown birds, 120–21, 157

Age ratios: in spruce grouse population, 157–60

Alaskan spruce grouse *(Canachites canadensis atratus):* description, 8–10; habitat of, 48; wariness of, 60; snow roosting, 61; wandering nonterritorial birds, 67; territory size of males, 69; territory claimed by yearling males, 70; mutual avoidance of breeding females, 86; incubating females, 88; clutch size, 91–92, 164, 173; renesting of, 99; discreetness of broods in, 102; fall flocks, 111; age determination of, 121, 157; weight of, 129–30; strains of captivity on, 132; consumption of needles by, 132–34; population density of, 155; sex ratio of, 157; proportion of females with broods, 161–62; brood size of, 164; food not limiting factor of, 165; hunting of, 181; harvest of, 182

Alberta: Franklin's grouse habitat in, 49; spruce grouse not roosting in snow, 61; wandering nonterritorial spruce grouse, 67; size of male spruce grouse territory, 69; aggressiveness and territory of female spruce grouse, 86–88, 169; incubating spruce grouse feeding on new spruce needles, 88; clutch size of Franklin's grouse in, 91, 173; weight of spruce grouse in, 129–30; predation on ruffed grouse in, 150;

209

Alberta, *cont.*
studies of spruce grouse in, 154; population density of spruce grouse in, 155; proportion of female spruce grouse with broods, 161; food not limiting spruce grouse numbers, 165; spruce prized in spruce grouse territories, 169; estimated harvest of spruce grouse in, 182–83
Alder (*Alnus* spp.), 48
Alder, tag (*Alnus rugosa*), 19, 20
Anderson, Leon, 34
Ants (*Hymenoptera: Formicidae*), 39, 55
Aphids (*Homoptera: Aphidae*), 55
Ash, black (*Fraxinus nigra*), 46
Aspen (*Populus* spp.), 19, 58
Aspen, small-toothed or quaking, (*Populus tremuloides*), 49, 57
Atlantic Ocean, 5–6
Audubon, John J., 90–91
Auk, great (*Pinguinis impennis*), 190
Autumn: on Yellow Dog Plains, 41–42; diet of spruce grouse in, 53–56; critical time of survival of young spruce grouse, 164–65

Backus, David: report on spruce grouse in Wisconsin, 47; comment on sporting quality of spruce grouse, 181; comment on palatability of spruce grouse, 187
Banding: general, 5; chicks, 28–29; adults, 29; number banded in study, 29; band too tight removed, 76; returns of banded young, 112, 158; age at which banded, 115; found on preyed upon spruce grouse, 148; recovery of adults, 157; used to estimate survival of adults, 171–72
Bear, black (*Ursus americanus*), 39
Bearberry (*Arctostaphylos uva-ursi*), 47, 49, 54
Behavior: general, 59–62; tameness, 59–61, 79–80; response to predators, 60–61; burrowing into snow, 61–62; of adult males, 63–80; of immature and yearling males, 67; wandering by nonter-

ritorial males, 67; of females and broods, 81–112; response of female to recorded female calls, 82, 86–88; aggressiveness of females, 82–86; of female with brood, 100–105; antagonism of female to strange chick, 103, 104–5; related to physiology of spruce grouse, 125, 128; possible effect of disease upon, 140. *See also* Display; Fighting; Mating
Bilberry (*Vaccinium membranaceum*), 54, 56, 133
Birch (*Betula* spp.), 46, 48
Birch, white (*Betula papyrifera*), 57
Birds: species found on Yellow Dog Plains, 23
Black fly (Diptera: Simuliidae): on Yellow Dog Plains, 39; eaten by chicks, 55; biting researchers, 94; vector of *Leucocytozoon*, 140; parasitized by trypanosomes, 141
Black grouse (*Lyrurus tetrix*): revised to *Tetrao tetrix*, 15; taxonomy, 15–17; snow roosting, 61; digestion of woody materials, 134
Blood cells: infected by parasites, 137–46; white cell count of spruce grouse related to parasites, 146
Blood parasites: of spruce grouse, 137–46; unimportant in mortality of grouse, 165. *See also* Haemoproteus; Leucocytozoon; Microfilariae; Trypanosoma
Blueberry (*Vaccinium* spp.): on Yellow Dog Plains, 36; in spruce grouse habitat, Alaska, 48; leaves and fruit eaten by spruce grouse, 53–54, 190; prescribed in habitat, 56; spruce grouse eating fruits out of hand, 60; leaves in and near spruce grouse nests, 89, 90; leaves and buds eaten by newly hatched chicks, 99; leaves eaten by incubating female, 98; in spring snow, 147
Blueberry, low sweet (*Vaccinium angustifolium*), 50, 53
Blue grouse (*Dendragapus obscurus*):

similarities to spruce grouse, 11; hybridization with spruce grouse, 14; taxonomy, 15–17; males respond to female spruce grouse call, 82; early feeding by, 99; brooding by female, 102; effect of weather on survival of broods, 102; tolerance of chicks for one another, 102; return of banded young, 112; molt of chicks, 120; molt of adults, 121; *Haemoproteus* in, 141; *Leucocytozoon* in, 142, 144; population studies of, 154; brood patch and laying, 160–61; broodless females, 161; brood size and population, 163; survival rate, 174; annual harvest of, 184

Blue jay *(Cyanocitta cristata)*, 23

Bonasa sewertzowi. See Hazel grouse, black-breasted

Bonasa umbellus. See Ruffed grouse

Bracken. *See* Fern, bracken

Breathing rate: of spruce grouse, 125–28; possible effect of blood parasites on, 140, 142–44; of ruffed grouse, 126–28

British Columbia: blue grouse population studies in, 154; harvest of spruce grouse in, 182, 183; bow and arrow grouse season, 184

Brood patch: as indicator of laying, 160

Brood: kind of data recorded, 27; tended by mother, 40; using same cover as adults, 52; young avoiding bog, 52; numbers in, 91, 162–63; scattering and reassembling, 101; home range size of, 103; combined broods, 104–5; responses of, to predators, 105–7; break-up and dispersal, 109–12; proportion of females with, 161–62; size and population dynamics, 163

Broodless females: spruce grouse, associating with one another, 86; movement of, 103; blue grouse, 161; cause of, 161

Buffalo berry *(Shepherdia canadensis)*, 48

Calcium: in young spruce needles, 88, 134

Calls:
—of females: for feeding, 81; aggressive, 81–82, 86–87; alarm, 83, 100; assembly, 83; warning, 83–84; assembly, imitated by human, 84
—of males: challenge or "squeak," 72, 85; threat, 72–73; in territorial defense, 80
—tape-recorded: to attract spruce grouse, 60; to stimulate males, 76–79; response of males to, 78–79

Canada: range of spruce grouse, 6; harvest of spruce grouse in, 182–83

Canada spruce grouse *(Canachites canadensis canace)*, 7

Capercaillie *(Tetrao urogallus):* taxonomy, 15–17; eating needles, 131; digestion of woody material, 134

Capercaillie, black-billed *(Tetrao parvirostris)*, 15–17

Capture: in mist net, 5, 27, 60; by noose, 28; chicks, 28–29; female, 59; Franklin's grouse, 60

Cedar, white. *See* White cedar

Centrocercus urophasianus. See Sage grouse

Chickadee, black-capped *(Parus atricapillus)*, 23, 106

Chickadee, boreal *(Parus hudsonicus)*, 23, 106

Chicks: capture of, 28–29; feeding, 40, 55; survival, 40, 164–71, 176–77; eating from human hand while captive, 55, 60; response to female alarm and assembly call, 84; adoption of, 91, 104–5; maximum number found in young brood, 91; early feeding, 99; orphans observed, 99; leaving nest, 100; tolerance for one another, 103; responses of, to predators, 105–7; dispersal of orphans, 107–9; survival of orphans, 107–8; description of

Chicks, *cont.*
newly hatched, 113; early feeding
of, 113; growth of, 113–15;
weight of, 113–15; sex determination of, 116; flying of, 116–17;
physiology of, 126–28; infections
by blood parasites, 143–45; survival of blood parasite infection,
144–45; production of, in population, 161
Chokecherry *(Prunus virginiana):* on
Yellow Dog Plains, 21
Climate: on Yellow Dog Plains, 22
Cloaca, of spruce grouse: temperature of, 126
Clutch size: of spruce grouse,
90–92; in renests, 99; of adults
and yearlings compared, 160; related to survival rates, 173
Comb: female described, 3; male
described, 4; use in display, 38,
71, 80, 84; as attack releaser,
75–76; of chicks, 116
Cooper's hawk. *See* Hawk, Cooper's
Copulation: with stuffed female,
78; described, 84–85
Courtship: hybridization, 12–14; of
Franklin's grouse, 9. *See also*
Copulation; Display
Cover requirements: spruce grouse,
51; of spruce and ruffed grouse
compared, 57. *See also* Habitat
Cowwheat *(Melampyrum lineare),* 53
Coyote *(Canis latrans):* predator on
spruce grouse, 149–50; benefits
from spruce grouse, 190
Cranberry *(Vaccinium* spp.), 190
Cranberry, mountain *(Vaccinium
Vitis-idaea),* 48, 54, 55, 56
Crow *(Corvus brachyrhynchos),* 113
Crowberry *(Empetrum nigrum),* 54
Cycles: of abundance of grouse,
153–54; of spruce grouse on
study area, 156

Deciduous forest: edge of range of
spruce grouse, 6
Deer fly (Diptera: Tabanidae), 55,
60, 141
Delongchamp, Robert: coauthor,
113–23

Dendragapus falcipennis. *See* Siberian
spruce grouse
Dendragapus obscurus. See Blue
grouse
Density-dependent population control, 168–69
Deserts: southern edge of range of
spruce grouse, 6
Devil's club *(Oplopanax horridum),* 48
Diet: of spruce grouse, 131–35. *See
also* Food
Digestion: calories, 132; cellulose,
134; protein, 134
Digestive tract: adapted for winter
diet, 44; larger in winter, 130,
135; function in digestion of
woody material, 134
Diseases, 137–46
Dispersal: of orphan chicks, 107–9;
of young birds, 109–12; distances
of, 110–12
Display:
—of male spruce grouse: 36–39,
65–67; in summer, 40; habitat in
Minnesota, 47; Alaska, 48;
drumming flight, 36, 38, 48, 79,
85; hormonal influence on, 70;
weather influence on, 70, 78; descriptions of, 70–74; interpretation of, 71; in response to stuffed
female and tape-recorded calls,
78–79; in defense of territory,
80; precopulatory, 84–85
—of female spruce grouse: distraction, 100–101
Dog: killing spruce grouse with
transmitter, 32; spruce grouse response to, 60; difficulty scenting
spruce grouse on nest, 96
Droppings: clocker, 96; possible
role in nutrient cycling, 190
Drumming:
—of spruce grouse: loudness of, 73;
standing, 73; flight, 73–74, 77–78;
in response to female call, 82
—of Franklin's grouse: standing,
73; flight, 74
—of ruffed grouse: loudness of, 73
Ducks: *Leucocytozoon* in, 141, 142
Dwarf dogwood *(Cornus canadensis),*
90

Ecological role of spruce grouse, 189–91
Eggs: spruce grouse, left uncovered in female's absence, 89; covered by Franklin's grouse, 89; color of, 93; weight and dimension of, 93; shells left in nest, 100; affecting weight of female, 130; eaten by predators, 148–49; fertility of, 160; production of, and population ecology, 160–61. *See also* Clutch size; Hatching; Incubation; Laying
Emigration, 155, 158, 175–76, 177
Energy requirements, 132
Extinction, 191

Falcipennis falcipennis. See Siberian spruce grouse
Fern, bracken *(Pteridium aquilinum),* 50–51, 52, 147
Fiber: content of needles fed upon by grouse, 133–34
Fighting: attack by male Franklin's grouse on stuffed male, 75; described, 75; among male spruce grouse, 75–80; among females, 88, 102
Fir *(Abies* spp.), 45–46
Fir, balsam *(Abies balsamea),* 19, 47
Fir, subalpine *(Abies lasiocarpa),* 48
Fire: on Yellow Dog Plains, 20, 22; providing spruce grouse habitat, 64, 191
Flicker, yellow-shafted *(Colaptes auratus),* 92
Flight: age at attainment, 116–17
Flocks: in autumn, 42, 110–11; in winter, 44, 52
Food:
—of spruce grouse: Alberta, 53; Montana, 53; Ontario, 53; Yellow Dog Plains, 53; habitat related, 53–56; winter diet of needles, 53–56, 131; Alaska, 54; analysis of, 132–35; in not limiting populations, 165
—of ruffed grouse: in winter, 57–58
Fossil grouse, 11–12
Fox, red *(Vulpes fulva):* predator on

spruce grouse nest, 90, 148, 160; on spruce grouse, 149; benefits from spruce grouse, 190
Franklin's spruce grouse *(Canachites canadensis franklinii):* race, 8–10; separate species, 9; wing clap in flight, 9, 74; in Montana, 48; in Alberta, 49; drumming while standing, 73; male attacking stuffed male, 75; male display unaffected by snow, 78; aggressiveness of females, 86, 87; territoriality of females, 87–88; mutual avoidance of females, 88; female covers eggs with litter, 89; simple nest of, 89; clutch size of, 91; laying rate of, 92; incubation period, 95; leaving nest while incubating, 96; renesting by, 99; distance of dispersal, 112; determining age of chicks, 118; molting of adults, 122–23; proportion of females with broods, 161–62
Fungi: eaten by spruce grouse, 53–54

Geese: *Leucocytozoon* in, 141, 142
Goshawk *(Accipiter gentilis):* predator of spruce grouse, 44, 147–52; response of spruce grouse chicks to mounted goshawk, 105–6; predator of ruffed grouse, 150–51; benefits from spruce grouse, 190
Grass: seeds eaten by spruce grouse, 53
Grasshopper (Orthoptera: Acrididae), 54
Gray jay *(Perisoreus canadensis),* 23
Great Lakes area: range of spruce grouse, 6
Grit: eaten by red grouse, 55; minerals in, 55, 133; in diet of spruce grouse, 55–56; gravel roads as source of, 56
Grouse family: taxonomy of, 14–17; comparison with pheasant family, 16; investigations of disease in, 139; investigations of population ecology of, 153–54
Growth, 113–15

Haas, George, 34
Habitat: requirements of spruce grouse, 45–58; prescription for, 56; role of, in population dynamics, 154–55
—selection: of chipping sparrow, 50–51; of prairie deer mouse, 51; of spruce grouse, 51; possible effect of blood parasites on, in spruce grouse, 140, 144
Hackmatack. *See* Tamarack
Hancock, James, 181, 184
Haemoproteus canachites: life cycle of, 138–39; description of, 140; infection of spruce grouse, 141–45; survival rate of infected spruce grouse, 144–45
Harju, Harold: coauthor, 63–80; mentioned, 39
Hatching: observed, 94, 96–99; movement of chicks before, 96; duration from pipped eggs to, 96–99; dates of, on study area, 99–100
Hawk, Cooper's *(Accipiter cooperii)*, 61
Hawk, red-tailed *(Buteo jamaicensis)*, 150
Hawks: preying on territorial male spruce grouse, 68
Hazel grouse, black-breasted *(Tetrastes severtzowi):* revised to *Bonasa sewertzowi,* 15; taxonomy, 15–17
Hazel grouse *(Tetrastes bonasia):* revised to *Bonasa bonasia,* 15; taxonomy, 15–17; snow roosting, 61; age of flying, 117; digestion of woody material, 134; winter weather and population declines of, 169
Head jerk: as part of display, 72, 74, 84
Heart: spruce grouse, rate, 125–28; ruffed grouse, rate, 126–28; possible effect of blood parasites on, 140, 142–44
Heath hen *(Tympanuchus cupido cupido),* 190
Hemlock *(Tsuga canadensis),* 19, 45
Herman, Margaret, 53, 70

Hormones: in courting male, 70; in chicks, 116
Horsetail *(Equisetum* spp.), 54, 55
Huckleberry *(Vaccinium* spp.), 48
Hudson Bay, 5, 13
Hudsonian spruce grouse *(Canachites canadensis canadensis):* 7, 9
Hunters: illegal shooting of spruce grouse, 40–41, 66; in Upper Michigan, 40–41; attitude about shooting spruce grouse, 59; shooting territorial male, 66, 68; effect on spruce grouse population, 169; types of grouse hunters, 179–80; reporting spruce grouse seen or shot, 185–86; identification of spruce grouse by, 185–86. *See also* Hunting
Hunting: effect on population on Yellow Dog Plains, 169; of ruffed grouse, 179–80; of spruce grouse, general, 179–87; road hunting, 180, 184; qualities of spruce grouse as game bird, 180–81; in Alaska, 181; in Newfoundland, 181; total annual harvest estimated, 181–84; illegal kill of spruce grouse, 184–85; on Yellow Dog Plains, 185–186; recommended in Upper Peninsula of Michigan, 187; regulations aligned with low reproductive rate, 191. *See also* Hunters
Hybrids and hybridization of grouse, 12–14

Idaho: range of spruce grouse, 6; site of blue grouse × spruce grouse hybridization, 14; harvest of spruce grouse in, 182; hunting of spruce grouse by big game hunters, 184
Immigration: of spruce grouse, 155, 158, 175–76, 177
Imprinting: of spruce grouse voice, 83
Incubation: effect on aggressive response, 82; behavior of female, 93–99; response to chain saw,

93–94; length of period, 95–96; feeding near nest, 96; leaving nest during, 96; effect of weather on, 96–99
Insect repellent, 39
Insects: as spruce grouse food, 39, 53–55, 190; importance in diet of chicks, 55–56. *See also* individual species

Jack pine. *See* Pine, jack
Junco, dark eyed *(Junco hyemalis)*, 106

Kestrel *(Falco sparverius)*, 107

Labrador tea *(Ledum groenlandicum)*, 23, 47
Lady-slipper, pink *(Chimaphilo umbellata)*, 22
Lagopus lagopus. See Ptarmigan, willow
Lagopus leucurus. See Ptarmigan, white-tailed
Legopus mutus. See Ptarmigan, rock
Lake Superior, 19
Larch, American. *See* Tamarack
Larch, western *(Larix occidentalis)*, 48, 54
Laying: determinate or indeterminate, 92; rate, 92; proportion of females, 160–61
Leopold, Aldo, 179
Leucocytozoon: description of, 140–41; survival rates of infected spruce grouse, 141–45; infection of spruce grouse, 142–45
Lichen, 54
Logging: on Yellow Dog Plains, 42, 64
Longevity, 135–36
Lynx *(Lynx canadensis)*, 150
Lyrurus tetrix. See Black grouse

McGowan, Jerry, 60
McKnight, Donald, 181
Maine: spruce grouse habitat in, 45–46; hunting of spruce grouse illegal in, 182
Mallard *(Anas platyrhynchos):* imprinting of mother's voice on, 83

Malnutrition: in red grouse, 171
Manitoba: spruce grouse habitat in, 48; estimate of spruce grouse harvest in, 182–83
Maple *(Acer* spp.), 19
Maple, red *(Acer rubrum):* on Yellow Dog Plains, 36; in ruffed grouse habitat, 57; buds eaten by ruffed grouse, 58
Maple, sugar *(Acer saccharum)*, 57
Markusen Electronics, 30–31
Mating: behavior of male, 36–39, 84–85; of spruce grouse, 36–38; behavior of female, 38–39, 84–85; with stuffed female, 66. *See also* Copulation; Display
Megapod, Malau *(Megapodius pritchardii)*, 117
Michigan: spruce grouse habitat in, 46–47; spruce grouse populations in, 153, 155; illegal kill estimated in, 182, 185; spruce grouse hunting illegal in, 182; hunting for spruce grouse recommended in Upper Peninsula, 187
Michigan Technological University, 59–60
Microfilariae: description of, 141; infection of spruce grouse, 142–43
Minerals, 133–34
Minnesota: spruce grouse habitat in, 47; studies of ruffed grouse in, 154; spruce grouse harvest in, 182
Mist net: as capture method, 5, 27, 60
Molt: of males, 40, 121–22; of spruce grouse, 40; of chicks, 117–20; of adults, 120–23; of females, 121–22
Montana: Franklin's grouse habitat in, 48; distance from summer to winter range, 70; population densities of spruce grouse in, 155; spruce grouse harvest in, 182
Moose *(Alces alces)*, 23
Mortality: of chicks, 164–71; blood parasites not important, 165; summer weather and, 166–68;

Morality, *cont.*
hunting not important on Yellow Dog Plains, 169
Mosquito (Diptera: Culicidae): on Yellow Dog Plains, 39; biting researchers, 94; parasitized by *trypanosoma*, 141
Moss *(Musci)*, 54
Mountain ash *(Sorbus americana)*, 53
Mountain lover *(Pachistima myrsinites)*, 49
Mouse, prairie deer *(Peromyscus maniculatus bairdii)*, 51
Mussehl, Thomas, 60
Movement of broods from nest site, 87

National Science Foundation, 94
Needles: eaten by spruce grouse, 44; winter, 52–56, 131–35; new spruce fed on by incubating female spruce grouse, 88; found in spruce grouse nests, 89; eaten by blue grouse, 131; eaten by capercaillie, 131; caloric content of, 132; selection of, by spruce grouse, 133–34; influence on flavor of spruce grouse, 186
Nesting: little preparation of site, 89; location of, relative to females in early spring, 87. *See also* Nests
Nests: abandonment of, 81, 160–61; description of, 89; material not carried by female, 89; in territory of male, 90; difficulty of finding, 94; predation on, 148–49, 160–61. *See also* Nesting
New Brunswick: spruce grouse food habits in, 54; not roosting in snow, 61; estimated spruce grouse harvest in, 182–83
New Hampshire, 182
New York, 182
Newfoundland: spruce grouse established on island of, 181; estimated harvest of spruce grouse in, 183; snaring grouse legal in, 184
Noose: as capture method, 28, 39, 60
Northern Michigan University, 5

No-see-um (Diptera: Ceratopogonidae): as parasite vector, 137–39
Northwest Territories, 182–83
Nova Scotia: clutch size of spruce grouse in, 91; spruce grouse hunting illegal in, 183
Nutrients, 190
Nutrition. *See* Food

Oak *(Quercus rubra)*, 36
Okhotsian grouse. *See* Spiny-winged grouse
Ontario: spruce grouse habitat in, 46–47; winter food of spruce grouse in, 53; male spruce grouse displays in, 84; life cycle of *Haemoproteus canachites*, 139; estimated harvest of spruce grouse in, 182–83
Oregon, 5, 182
Owl, barred *(Strix varia):* spruce grouse response to, 61; possible predator of spruce grouse, 150
Owl, great horned *(Bubo virginianus):* predator of spruce grouse and ruffed grouse, 150; benefits from spruce grouse, 190
Owl, short-eared *(Asio flammeus)*, 105–6
Owl, snowy *(Nyctea scandiaca)*, 106–7
Owls: general, 68, 106
Oxytrope *(Oxytropis sp.)*, 54

Pacific Ocean, 5
Palatability: of spruce grouse compared with ruffed grouse, 186–87
Parasitism, 171. *See also* Blood parasites
Partridge, 6. *See also* Ruffed grouse
Passenger pigeon *(Ectopistes migratorius)*, 190
Pecking: as part of display, 37, 72; in fighting, 75, 79
Pedioecetes phasianellus. See Sharp-tailed grouse
Peterson, Charles, 91
Pheasant *(Phasianus colchicus)*, 55

Pheasant family: comparison with grouse family, 16

Physiology: causing reproductive isolation, 12; of spruce grouse, 125–36

Pigeon *(Columba livia)*: Haemoproteus in, 142

Pine, jack *(Pinus Banksiana):* on Yellow Dog Plains, 19–22; limb used in display by spruce grouse, 36, 68; in Michigan, 46, 50; in Ontario, 46; mixed with spruces, 46–47; in Minnesota, 47; in Manitoba, 48; mature stands not favored, 51; winter cover, 52; winter food, 53–56; prescribed in habitat, 56; response to fire, 64; nest cover, 89–90; needles, 131–35, 190; analysis of needles of, 132–34; needed in habitat, 191

Pine, lodgepole *(Pinus contorta):* in Montana, 48; in Alberta, 49; needles of, eaten by Franklin's grouse, 54; prescribed in habitat, 56; quantity of needles eaten by spruce grouse, 131–32; mineral content of, 133; important in spruce grouse habitat, 191

Pine, ponderosa, *(Pinus ponderosa),* 53

Pine, red *(Pinus resinosa):* logged, 20; comparison with jack pine, 21; in Michigan, 47

Pine, Scotch *(Pinus sylvestris),* 131

Pine, white *(Pinus strobus):* logged, 20; comparison with jack pine, 21; in Michigan, 47; nest cover, 89

Pipsissewa *(Chimaphila umbellata),* 47

Plumage: of female spruce grouse, 3–4; of male spruce grouse, 4–5; of races of spruce grouse, 7–10; of hybrid spruce grouse × willow ptarmigan, 13; of hybrid spruce grouse × blue grouse, 14; development of, in spruce grouse chicks, 117–20. *See also* Molt

Poplar. *See* Aspen

Poplar, balsam *(Populus balsamifera),* 49

Population characteristics, 156–60

Population ecology, 153–87

Population regulation, 146. *See also* Population ecology

Poultry, 133

Prairie chicken, greater *(Tympanuchus cupido):* hybridization with sharp-tail, 11; taxonomy, 15–17; longevity, 136; survival rates, 174; annual harvest of, 184

Prairie chicken, lesser *(Tympanuchus pallidicinctus),* 15, 184

Predation: on nests, attraction of male displaying, 90; on second nest, 99; response of broods to predators, 105–7; of spruce grouse, 147–52, 175; as limiting factor on grouse, 165; combined with winter weather, 170–71

Preening, 85

Protein: importance in diet, 132; content of needles, 132–33; conversion of plant material into protein and fats of spruce grouse, 190

Ptarmigan, rock *(Lagopus mutus),* 15, 90

Ptarmigan, white-tailed *(Lagopus leucurus):* taxonomy, 15–17; tameness, 59; return of banded young, 112; longevity, 136

Ptarmigan, willow *(Lagopus lagopus):* hybridization with spruce grouse, 13–14; taxonomy, 15, 17; clutch size, 91; induced laying of, 91; digestion of woody material, 134; survival rates, 174

Ptarmigans: annual harvest of, 184

Puffing up display, 71–72

Pulpwood cutting: on Yellow Dog Plains, 22, 27; response of incubating grouse to, 93–94

Quail, Japanese *(Coturnix coturnix japonica),* 135

Quebec: estimate of spruce grouse harvest in, 182–83

Raccoon *(Procyon lotor),* 23

Races: *Canachites canadensis canace,* 7, 9; *C. c. candadensis,* 7, 9; *C. c. osgoodi,* 7, 9; *C. c. atratus,* 8, 10;

Races, *cont.*
  C. c. *franklinii*, 8, 9; C. c.
  torridus, 8, 9
Radio telemetry. *See* Transmitter,
  radio
Rain: effect on incubating female,
  97–99; effect on young chicks,
  102, 166–67
Range, geographic: 5–6
Raspberry *(Rubus* spp.), 46
Rectrices. *See* Tail
Red crossbill *(Loxia curvirostra)*, 23
Red grouse *(Lagopus lagopus
  scoticus):* behavior and radio
  packages, 33–34; eating quartz
  grit, 55; territory and survival,
  64, 171; digestion of lignin, 135;
  longevity, 136; studies of population regulation in, 154, 169
Red maple. *See* Maple, red
Red pine. *See* Pine, red
Reindeer moss (lichen) *(Cladonia*
  spp.), 36, 47, 50
Renesting, 99
Robin *(Turdus migratorius)*, 36, 113
Robin, European *(Erithaca rubecula)*,
  76
Ruffed grouse *(Bonasa umbellus):*
  drumming, 6, 38; taxonomy, 15,
  17; hunted near Yellow Dog
  Plains, 41–42; mistaken for
  spruce grouse, 42; habitat compared with that of spruce grouse,
  46, 57–58; abundance, in Michigan, 57; feeding in winter, 57; on
  Yellow Dog Plains, 57; response
  to Cooper's hawk, 61; clutch size
  compared to spruce grouse, 93;
  incubation behavior compared to
  spruce grouse, 93; female leaving
  scattered brood, 101; molt of
  chicks compared to spruce
  grouse, 120; physiology of, compared to spruce grouse, 126–28;
  longevity of, 136; *Haemoproteus*
  in, 141; *Leucocytozoon* in, 142;
  predation on, as major mortality
  factor, 148, 150; nests preyed
  upon by red squirrel, 149; studies
  of population, 154; breeding
  densities of, 155; winter weather

and mortality of, 169; survival
  rates, 174; hunting of, 179–80;
  annual harvest of, 183; palatability compared with spruce grouse,
  186, 187

Sage grouse *(Centrocercus
  urophasianus):* taxonomy, 15, 17;
  similar mating posture to spruce
  grouse, 85; longevity, 136; annual harvest of, 184
Salts, de-icing: applied to roads attract spruce grouse, 56
Sandhill crane *(Grus canadensis)*, 21
Scotland, 154
Sedge *(Carex* spp.), 54, 55
Seney Refuge, 47
Serviceberry *(Amelanchier* spp.), 21,
  58
Sex: determination of, in spruce
  grouse chicks, 115–16
Sex ratio, 156–57
Sharp-tailed grouse *(Pedioecetes
  phasianellus):* hybridization with
  prairie chicken, 12; taxonomy,
  14, 17; revision to *Tympanuchus
  phasianellus*, 15; on the Yellow
  Dog Plains, 21; longevity, 136;
  survival rates, 174; annual harvest of, 183
Siberian spruce grouse *(Falcipennis
  falcipennis):* described, 10;
  taxonomy, 10, 15; reclassification
  to *Dendragapus falcipennis*, 11, 15
Skunk *(Mephitis mephitis)*, 23
Snow: accumulation on Yellow Dog
  Plains, 22–23, 43–44; crust affecting spruce grouse burrowing,
  44, 62, 170; affecting survival,
  62, 170–71; possible effect on
  male displays, 78–79; in spring
  on Yellow Dog Plains, 147
Snowberry *(Symphoricarpos rivularis)*,
  49, 54
Snow burrowing, 61. *See also* Snow
  roosting
Snowmobiles, 42–43
Snow roosting: of spruce grouse, 7,
  44, 61; roosts described, 61–62;
  of black grouse, 61, 170; affected
  by crust, 44, 62

Snowshoe hare *(Lepus americanus)*, 150, 184

Sparrow, chipping *(Spizella passerina)*, 50–51

Sparrow, white throated *(Zonotrichia albicollis)*, 106

Sphagnum moss *(Sphagnum* spp.), 20, 45, 52

Spiny-winged grouse. *See* Siberian spruce grouse

Spring: on Yellow Dog Plains, 35–39; diet of spruce grouse, 54

Springer, Jon, 57

Spruce *(Picea* spp.): surrounding study area, 19–20; on Yellow Dog Plains, 22, 50; in Maine, 45; in Michigan, 46; mixed with jack pines, 46–47; in Minnesota, 47; in Wisconsin, 47; in Alaska, 48; mature stands not favored, 51; needles eaten by spruce grouse, 53–56, 190; prescribed in habitat, 56; nest cover, 89; needles as food in Alberta, 169; needed in spruce grouse habitat, 191. *See also* individual species

Spruce, black *(Picea mariana):* on uplands of Yellow Dog Plains, 23; in Michigan, 46, 50; in Ontario, 46; in Minnesota, 47; in Wisconsin, 47; winter cover, 52; low branches as winter roost cover, 62

Spruce, Engelmann *(Picea engelmanni)*, 48, 54

Spruce, red *(Picea rubens)*, 46

Spruce, white *(Picea glauca):* in Maine, 46; in Michigan, 46; in Minnesota, 47; in Alberta, 49; analysis of minerals in needles, 133

Squirrel, gray *(Sciurus carlinensis)*, 23

Squirrel, red *(Tamiasciurus hudsonicus):* as nest predator, 149, 160

Starflower *(Trientalis borealis)*, 90

Subspecies of spruce grouse. *See* Races

Sullivan, Robert, 94

Summer: on Yellow Dog Plains, 39–41; diet of spruce grouse in, 54–56

Sunne, Craig: coauthor, 113–23

Survival: of chicks, 164–71, 176–77; of adults, 171–75

Tail: male and female described, 4; swishing, 4, 72; use in display, 4, 38, 71–74; of Franklin's race, 8–9; of female, position in copulation, 85; molt of rectrices, 122–23

Tamarack *(Larix laricina):* in bogs near Yellow Dog Plains, 20; in Maine, 45, 46; in Michigan, 46–47; in Minnesota, 47; needles eaten by spruce grouse, 53

Tameness. *See* Behavior

Tape recorder: attacked by spruce grouse male, 75–76. *See also* Calls, tape-recorded

Taxonomy of grouse, 7–17

Temperature: of spruce grouse, 125–28; of ruffed grouse, 126–28; possible effect of blood parasites on, in spruce grouse, 140

Territory: general theory, 63, 69, 86; of monogamous birds, 64, 169; of polygamous birds, 64; adaptation for reducing predation, 150

—of female: speculated, 38, 85, 87; defended by aggressiveness, 81–82, 86; mutual avoidance, 86–87, 102; selective advantage of, 88–89; importance of, in population regulation, 168–69

—of male: display, 38; summer, 40–41; autumn, 42; habitat in Alaska, 48; general requirements of, 63, 68; not controlling reproduction, 64; succession of seven owners, 65–67; age of owners, 67; length of tenure by individuals, 67; claimed for life, 67–68; size of, on Yellow Dog Plains, 68–69; size compared with Alberta and Alaska, 69; natural features as boundaries of, 69; seasonal movements from, 70; yearlings in Alaska, 70; behavior with

Territory, of male, *cont.*
female on, 74; dispute without fighting, 76–77; dispute among three males, 77–78
Tetrao parvirostris. See Capercaillie, black-billed
Tetrao tetrix. See Black grouse
Tetrao urogallus. See Capercaillie
Tetrastes severtzowi. See Hazel grouse, black-breasted
Thimbleberry *(Rubus parviflorus),* 49
Trailing arbutus *(Epigaea repens),* 22, 50, 90
Transmitter, radio: on ruffed grouse, 30; manufacturer, 30–31; fitting of, 31, 32; weight of, 31; range of, 31–32; effect on spruce grouse behavior, 32–34; effect on spruce grouse weight, 32–33; effect on spruce grouse survival, 33; for locating nests, 34; for locating broods, 35; disappearance with bird, 65; used to verify renesting in Alaska, 99; on dispersing young, 109
Trypanosoma, 141
Tundra, 5, 13
Turkey *(Meleagris gallopavo),* 186
Tympanuchus cupido. See Prairie chicken, greater
Tympanuchus pallidicinctus. See Prairie chicken, lesser
Tympanuchus phasianellus. See Sharp-tailed grouse

University of Alberta, 87
University of Montana, 60
University of Wisconsin, 154

Valdez spruce grouse *(Canachites canadensis atratus),* 8–10
Vegetation of Yellow Dog Plains, 19, 27
Verch, Richard, 4, 5
Vermont, 182
Vocalizations. *See* Calls

Waisanen, Calvin, 21, 25
Wandering: of juvenile and yearling males, 67, 70; of adults, 70. *See also* Dispersal

Washington: range of spruce grouse, 5; food habits of spruce grouse in, 54–55; age determination of spruce grouse in, 157; sex ratios of spruce grouse in, 157; harvest of spruce grouse in, 182
Weasel *(Mustela* sp.), 149–50
Weather: effect on incubating female spruce grouse, 97–99; effect on brooding of young by mother spruce grouse, 101; effect on young spruce grouse, 102, 165; temperature and chick survival, 166–68, 169; effect on ruffed grouse survival, 169; winter effect on females and egg viability, 169–70
Weight: of spruce grouse chicks, 113–15; adults, 128–31; annual cycle of, 129; and geographical differences, 129–30; reasons for variation, 130; effect of motherhood on, 131
White cedar *(Thuja occidentalis),* 45, 47
White mandarin *(Streptopus amplexifolius),* 54
White pine. *See* Pine, white
White-winged crossbill *(Loxia leucoptera),* 23
Willow *(Salix* spp.), 49, 58
Winter: on Yellow Dog Plains, 42–44; diet of spruce grouse in, 52
Wintergreen *(Gaultheria procumbens),* 47
Wisconsin: spruce grouse habitat in, 47; spruce grouse hunting illegal in, 182; illegally shot spruce grouse discarded in, 187
Wood duck *(Aix sponsa),* 83
Wyoming: blue grouse respond to spruce grouse call, 82; spruce grouse harvest in, 182

Yearlings, spruce grouse: territory, 70
—female: mating, 38; responding to aggressive call, 87–88; nesting home range of, 88; clutch size of,

160; brood size of, 162–63; survival of, 174
—male: behavior in summer, 40–41; wandering, 67–70; survival of, 174
Yellow Dog Plains: spruce grouse found on, 3, 5; appearance from air, 19; geology, 19–20; logging on, 20–22; derivation of name, 23–24; hunters on, 41–42, 185–86; spruce grouse habitat compared with Wisconsin, 47; analysis of habitat on, 49–53
Yellow Dog River, 20

DESIGNED BY GARY G. GORE
COMPOSED BY CREATIVE COMPOSITION, INC.
ALBUQUERQUE, NEW MEXICO
MANUFACTURED BY NORTH CENTRAL PUBLISHING CO.,
ST. PAUL, MINNESOTA
TEXT AND DISPLAY LINES ARE SET IN BASKERVILLE

ⓌⒿ

Library of Congress Cataloging in Publication Data
Robinson, William Laughlin, 1933–
Fool hen.
Bibliography: p.
Includes index.
1. Spruce grouse.
2. Birds—Michigan—Yellow Dog Plains.
I. Title.
QL96.G285R62   598'.616   79–3962
ISBN 0–299–07960–0